LAYERS AND LEVELS
OF REPRESENTATION IN
LANGUAGE THEORY
A FUNCTIONAL VIEW

Edited by

Jan Nuyts
Belgian National Fund for Scientific Research
University of Antwerp

A. Machtelt Bolkestein
University of Amsterdam

Co Vet
University of Groningen

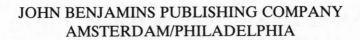

JOHN BENJAMINS PUBLISHING COMPANY
AMSTERDAM/PHILADELPHIA

1990

Library of Congress Cataloging-in-Publication Data

Layers and levels of representation in language theory : a functional view / edited by Jan Nuyts, A. Machtelt Bolkestein, Co Vet.
    p.   cm. -- (Pragmatics & beyond, ISSN 0922-842X ; new ser. 13)
Includes bibliographical references and index.
1. Hierarchy (Linguistics) 2. Functionalism (Linguistics) I. Nuyts, Jan. II. Bolkestein, A. Machtelt. III. Vet, Co. IV. Series.
P128.H53L38   1990
415 -- dc20   90-33948
ISBN 90 272 5023 5 (Eur.)/1-55619-279-7 (US) (alk. paper)

Contents

List of Contributors

A. Machtelt Bolkestein
Dept. of Classical Languages
University of Amsterdam
Oude Turfmarkt 129
NL-1012 GC Amsterdam
THE NETHERLANDS

Simon C. Dik
Institute for General Linguistics
University of Amsterdam
Spuistr. 210
NL-1012 VT Amsterdam
THE NETHERLANDS

Peter Harder
Dept. of English
University of Copenhagen
Njalsgade 80
DK-2300 Copenhagen S
DENMARK

Kees Hengeveld
Dept. of Spanish
University of Amsterdam
Spuistr. 134
NL-1012 VB Amsterdam
THE NETHERLANDS

Cees Hesp
Vechtstr. 55-III
NL-1078 RJ Amsterdam
THE NETHERLANDS

Erland Hjelmquist
Dept. of Psychology
University of Göteborg
POB 14158
S-400 20 Göteborg
SWEDEN

Jan Nuyts
Dept. of Germanic Languages
Universitaire Instelling Antwerpen
Universiteitsplein 1
B-2610 Wilrijk
BELGIUM

Jan Rijkhoff
Institute for General Linguistics
University of Amsterdam
Spuistr. 210
NL-1012 VT Amsterdam
THE NETHERLANDS

viii

Robert D. Van Valin, Jr.
Dept. of Linguistics
University of California
Davis, CA 95616
USA

Elseline Vester
Dept. of Latin
Free University
POB 7161
NL-1007 MC Amsterdam
THE NETHERLANDS

Co Vet
Dept. of Romance Languages
University of Groningen
Oude Kijk in 't Jatstr. 26
POB 716
NL-9700 AS Groningen
THE NETHERLANDS

Preface

This volume is an indirect result of the 3rd International Conference on Functional Grammar held at the Free University in Amsterdam in June 1988. Part of the articles included are revised and expanded versions of papers presented there, and part of them are inspired by discussions at that conference. Their common ground is that they all focus on the question of the nature of the structures which should be assumed to underlie utterances in order to do justice to the full array of phenomena exhibited in natural language, albeit in two different but not unrelated respects.

The majority of papers take as their point of departure a recent proposal for a certain type of basic representations in the grammar advanced within the theoretical framework of Functional Grammar (FG) by Kees Hengeveld (1989) and Simon Dik (1989), and examine its value from different angles. This proposal involves an expansion of the representations accepted in FG so far, so as to enable this theory to handle certain properties of natural languages which relate to their interpersonal function, i.e. to the language system as a means of communication between a speaker and a hearer in a particular situation and context, rather than to their descriptive or representational function. This includes matters such as aspect, tense, modality, and illocutionary force, i.e. elements which tend to be neglected in the majority of more formally oriented theories of grammar. The main theoretical claim is that the structure underlying utterances may fruitfully be described as consisting of several hierarchically ordered layers which each represent a distinct type of entity and exhibit distinct properties.

Some papers are concerned with the question whether the type of underlying representation currently accepted in FG (including the layered structure) is sufficiently abstract to count as the deepest level of representation underlying language use, and thus to count as the format in which human conceptual knowledge is stored. In a number of recent articles Simon Dik has made suggestions for a general conception of the human cognitive apparatus (with FG being a model of (part of) the linguistic component), and these do include the claim that the underlying predications in FG are suitable as a general representational format for this cognitive apparatus. This proposal implies that conceptual knowledge would be represented in a verbal format (content words being the basic building blocks of FG predications), and it is particularly this aspect of the theory which is being reviewed here.

The volume starts with a number of papers dealing with the first aspect of the topic. The first paper, *The hierarchical structure of utterances* by Hengeveld, is not only an introduction to but also a synthesis of some of the papers following it. Hengeveld presents the basic characteristics of the layered structure assumed to underlie utterances, and discusses some phenomena motivating this assumption. In the next three papers some central aspects of the layered structure are investigated in more detail and further developed. In *The hierarchical structure of the clause and the typology of adverbial satellites* Dik, Hengeveld, Vester, and Vet examine the relevance of the layered structure for a description of the function, behavior and distribution of non-obligatory sentence constituents such as various classes of adjunct and disjunct adverbials. In *Sentential complements in Functional Grammar* Bolkestein investigates whether the distinction between the layers is relevant for a subclassification of sentential complements and their governing expressions. And in *Semantic relations in non-verbal predication* Hengeveld illustrates how the layered structure contributes to a typology of non-verbal predications across languages.

The following two papers concern modality and tense. Vet's *Asymmetries in the use of tense and modality* discusses the implications for the layered structure of cases where the use of a tense form has a modalizing or illocutionary force modifying effect, leading to a proposal for a somewhat different representation of the underlying structure. Harder's paper on *Tense, semantics and layered syntax* considers the relation between semantics and syntax and the position of the layered model with respect to these modules, concluding that it should be viewed as a content syntax. He defends an instructional view of linguistic meaning, illustrating this by means of a discussion of the English tense operators.

In *Toward a unified analysis of terms and predications* Rijkhoff argues that it is possible to distinguish similar levels of structure for utterances as a whole and within nominal phrases: in both domains the notions of quality, quantity, and locality are claimed to play a crucial role. Van Valin's *Layered syntax in Role and Reference Grammar* contrasts the layered structure proposed in FG with the Role and Reference Grammar approach to layering (which has partly inspired the FG proposal for layering), and shows how the two models differ in the amount of emphasis given to semantics and syntax.

The next two papers handle both the topic of layering and the topic of the nature of the basic cognitive representations. In *On the semantics of conditionals* Dik proposes a (mainly semantically based) typology of conditional utterances,

and he shows on the one hand how a layered structure may contribute to the
analysis of the different types of conditional clauses distinguished, and on the
other hand how they can be described in the framework of his suggestions for
a more encompassing conception of the human cognitive apparatus. Nuyts'
Linguistic representation and conceptual knowledge representation argues against
Dik's proposal to represent human conceptual knowledge in terms of FG
predications on linguistic and language psychological grounds (both experimental and theoretical), and makes suggestions for an alternative representational
format. The latter includes considerations of how something like the layered
structure could be integrated at the conceptual level of representation.

The last papers, Hesp's *The Functional Grammar computational natural
language user and psychological adequacy* and Hjelmquist's *Context and language*
also argue against the suggestion that conceptual knowledge would be verbal,
mainly on the basis of an extensive review of experimental data gathered in
language psychology over the last decades. Hjelmquist also offers some more
general comments from a language psychologist's point of view.

Finally, some words of gratitude are in order here. We are very grateful to
the Institute for Functional Research of Language and Language Use (IFOTT)
of the University of Amsterdam for the material and personal help (the latter
especially in the person of Inge Genee) provided in preparing the manuscript.
We are also grateful to those who helped bridging the communication gap of
one ocean and one continent by electronic mail (a system which does not always
prove to be efficient) while one editor was in California and both others were
in the low countries. The ordering of the names of the editors may be a
potential source of despair to bibliographers, but it is intentional, Jan Nuyts
being the invaluable final 'post' editor who has made this book look the way it
does. It probably does not belong to the traditional habits of this text type for
the editors to thank each other for the pleasant cooperation, but we do it
anyway.

Amsterdam   Machtelt Bolkestein
Groningen   Co Vet
Antwerp   Jan Nuyts

December 1989

References

Dik, S.C.
   1989   *The theory of functional grammar, pt.1: The structure of the clause*. Dordrecht: Foris.

Hengeveld, K.
   1989   "Layers and operators in functional grammar". *Journal of Linguistics* 25: 127-157.

The Hierarchical Structure of Utterances

Kees Hengeveld
University of Amsterdam

0. Introduction[1]

It is probably fair to say, using Halliday's (1970, 1985) tripartite classification of communicative functions, that most work in Functional Grammar (FG) (see Dik 1978, 1989) has been devoted to phenomena which are best considered as pertaining to the *ideational* and *textual* functions of language, rather than to phenomena pertaining to the *interpersonal* function of language. Correspondingly, the highest level of analysis has long been the predication, designating a State of Affairs (SoA), containing constituents which can be assigned syntactic and pragmatic functions.[2]

In the study of the interpersonal function of language, the focus of attention is not on the predication, embodying the ideational function of language, nor on the syntactic and pragmatic functions of the constituents of the predication, embodying the textual function of language, but it is on the utterance containing the predication. Apart from a description of a SoA, an utterance contains elements providing the addressee with information concerning the speaker's intentions in producing the utterance and his attitude towards the information he is presenting within the utterance. These elements embody the interpersonal function of language, which can be conceived of as a three-place relation between a speaker, an addressee and the content of the utterance produced by the speaker. This three-place relation is translated into a three-place predicate when it is reported:

(1)   John said to me that Peter is ill
      say (John) (me) (Peter is ill)

From a meta-communicative point of view, every utterance is an instantiation of such a three-place relation, even if it is not a reported one. The nature of the relation is indicated by the illocutionary force indicating devices selected by the speaker (such as word order, intonation and sentence mood), which in (2) are represented by the abstract predicate DECL (declarative):

(2)   Peter is ill
      DECL (speaker) (addressee) (Peter is ill)

The use of abstract performative predicates to account for basic illocutions of sentences, as illustrated here, has become known, since Ross (1970), as the *performative hypothesis*. Many objections have been raised against Ross' analysis, some of which will be discussed later in this paper.

Ross embedded what in FG terms would probably be called the predication under the abstract performative predicate. If we take the predication as the unit embodying the ideational function of language, i.e. as a description of a SoA and the participants involved therein, this is not entirely correct. From an interpersonal point of view, what is governed by the abstract performative predicate is the propositional content of the speech act, not the description of a SoA as such. Unlike SoAs, propositional contents can be asserted, known, denied or questioned, i.e. "they are entities of the kind that may function as the objects of such so-called propositional attitudes as belief, expectation and judgement" (Lyons 1977: 445). These properties of propositional contents show that (i) they have to be separated from the illocutionary forces they may be subjected to and (ii) they have to be separated from the SoAs they describe.

The latter conclusion makes it necessary to study a predication from both an interpersonal and an ideational perspective. From an interpersonal perspective, a predication constitutes the *propositional content* of a speech act. From an ideational perspective, a predication constitutes the description of a *SoA*.

Other labels have been proposed to capture approximately the same distinction: Vendler (1967) uses the terms 'fact' and 'event', Barwise and Perry (1983) 'attitude' and 'situation' and Aronszajn (1988) 'thought' and 'circumstance'. To distinguish between the linguistic correlates of what all these pairs of terms describe I use the terms *proposition* and *predication*, respectively. Thus I will use *proposition* for the linguistic unit that refers to a propositional content and *predication* for the linguistic unit that refers to a SoA.

1. The representation of utterances

In Hengeveld (1988, 1989) I propose to represent utterances by means of a multi-layered hierarchical clause model, which captures the different levels of analysis discussed above. The present paper is meant to give a brief description of the layout of this model and to discuss some of its implications. For a more elaborate account the reader is referred to the papers mentioned earlier.

The general format of the model is given in figure 1.

$$(E_I: [ILL (S) (A) (X_I: [\quad\quad\quad] (X_I))] (E_I))$$

$$(e_I: [pred_\beta (x_I: pred_N (x_I)) .. (x_n)] (e_I))$$

Figure 1: **The representation of utterances**

The structure in figure 1 as a whole gives a representation of the speech act (E_I). Within this speech act a propositional content (X_I) is processed. This propositional content contains a description of a SoA (e_I). This SoA involves several individuals $(x_I) ... (x_n)$.

The highest level of this structure is called, following Halliday (1970, 1985), the *interpersonal level*. It is structured on the basis of an abstract illocutionary frame (ILL), which has the speaker S, the addressee A and the propositional content X_I as its arguments. The lowest level is called the *representational level*, following Bühler (1934), rather than *ideational level*, which would be in line with Halliday's terminology. This level is structured on the basis of a predicate frame, which has one or more individuals[3] $(x_I) ... (x_n)$ as its arguments.

One of the most important features of this structure, which is partly inspired by Foley and Van Valin (1984) (see also Van Valin this vol.), is that layers of lower complexity are fully contained within layers of higher complexity. For instance, every proposition contains a predication, i.e. every propositional content contains a description of a SoA. In this respect the layered approach differs from the approach followed by e.g. Vendler (1967) and Aronszajn (1988).

2. Layers, variables and frames

2.1. Layers and variables

Within the hierarchical structure presented in figure 1 four layers, each provided with its own variable, can be distinguished. All variables are followed by restrictors of decreasing complexity, which contain the main information on their respective layers.[4] The four layers are listed in (3):

(3)   **General format of layers**

clause: $(E_1: [\text{ILL (S) (A)} (X_1: \text{etc. } (X_1))] (E_1))$

proposition: $(X_1: [(e_1: \text{etc. } (e_1))] (X_1))$

predication: $(e_1: [\text{pred}_\beta (x_1)^n] (e_1))^5$

term: $(x_1: \text{pred}_N (x_1))$

An informal illustration of the four layers may serve to give a first approximation of the differences between them:

(4)   **Illustration of layers**

clause: $(E_1: \text{'Did John go?'} (E_1))$

proposition: $(X_1: \text{John went } (X_1))$

predication: $(e_1: \text{John's going } (e_1))$

term: $(x_1: \text{John } (x_1))$

In (4) the yes/no-question E_i (*Did John go?*) contains the questioned proposition X_i ('John went'), within which reference is made to the SoA e_i ('John's going'), which involves a single participant x_i ('John'). Thus, layers of lower complexity are fully contained within layers of higher complexity, as is shown in figure 2.

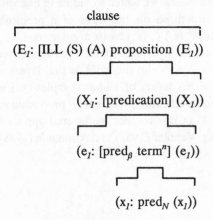

clause

$(E_1: [\text{ILL (S) (A)} \text{ proposition } (E_1))$

$(X_1: [\text{predication}] (X_1))$

$(e_1: [\text{pred}_\beta \text{ term}^n] (e_1))$

$(x_1: \text{pred}_N (x_1))$

Figure 2: **Nesting of layers**

The format of each layer, a variable followed by a restrictor, is that proposed for terms in Dik (1978) and for predications in Vet (1986). Each layer is provided with its own variable, because each can serve as an antecedent for anaphoric reference, as is shown in Hengeveld (this vol.). A second reason to provide each layer with its own variable is that the nature of the difference between the four layers can be understood in terms of the kinds of entity they designate, as is represented in figure 3.

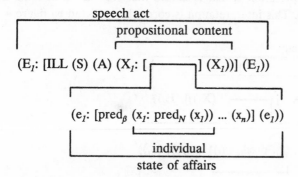

Figure 3: **Designation of layers**

Each of the four layers designates an entity of a different order (cf. Lyons 1977: 442-447). An *individual* is a first order entity. It can be located in space and can be evaluated in terms of its existence. A *SoA* is a second order entity. It can be located in space and time and can be evaluated in terms of its reality. A *propositional content* is a third order entity. It can be located in space nor time and can be evaluated in terms of its truth. A *speech act* is a fourth order entity. It locates itself in space and time and can be evaluated in terms of its felicity. The ways in which the different layers can be evaluated are summarized in figure 4 below.

The fact that existence, reality, truth and felicity can be said to be relevant with respect to different portions of the layered structure of the utterance has far-reaching consequences. The most important one in the present context is that it solves one of the major semantic problems which have been raised against the performative hypothesis and which has become known as the 'performadox' (Boër and Lycan 1980; see also Levinson 1983: 257). The problem centers around the truth-conditional interpretation of the (abstract or explicit) performative predicate and its optional modifications, such as illocutionary adverbs. Figure 4 offers a straightforward solution to this problem: The (abstract) illocutionary predicate is outside the domain within which the question of truth is relevant. Only the proposition is evaluated in terms of its truth.[6] This can be demonstrated by means of the following sentences:

(5)   A: I state to you that John is ill
       B: That's not true

Here the normal interpretation is that B denies that John is ill, not that he denies that A states so. This interpretation is correctly predicted by figure 4.

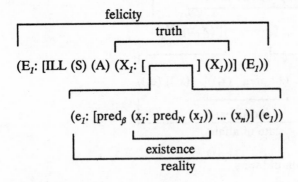

Figure 4: **Evaluation of layers**

2.2. Frames

Apart from the four layers discussed above, there are two types of frame, which are given in (6):

(6)   **Frames**
         illocutionary frame   ILL (S) (A) (X_1)
         predicate frame pred_β (x_1) ... (x_n)

In the same way that the predicate frame provides a blueprint for the representational level, the illocutionary frame[7] provides a blueprint for the interpersonal level. The analysis of basic illocutions in terms of illocutionary frames stresses the relational nature of speech acts, but also accounts for several aspects of their form. Many of these are listed in Ross (1970).

One of the reasons to assume that every sentence is governed by an abstract performative predicate is that this predicate[8] can be modified by adverbs, as is illustrated in (7):

(7) Frankly, I don't like you
(cf. I state to you frankly that I don't like you)

One of the reasons to assume that speaker and addressee are present at the same abstract level is that they may serve as antecedents for reflexives (Ross 1970) and may govern agreement relations, as is illustrated in the following Spanish examples:

(8) *Est-oy*　　　　　　 *content-o/a*
COP-PRES.1SG happy-MASC/FEM
"I (male/female speaker) am happy"

(9) *¿Est-ás*　　　　　 *content-o/a*?
COP-PRES.1SG happy-MASC/FEM
"Are you (male/female addressee) happy?"

Some of the illocutionary frames to be distinguished are listed in (10):

(10) **Illocutionary frames**
　　　declarative　　　　　　DECL　(S) (A) (X_I)
　　　interrogative (Q-word)　INT　　(S) (A) (X_I)
　　　interrogative (Y/N)　　INT　　(S) (A) (Indet X_I)
　　　imperative　　　　　　IMP　　(S) (A) $(e_I$: [+control] $(e_I))$

As the last example illustrates, not all illocutionary frames have a proposition as their third argument. An imperative frame specifies a relation between a speaker S, an addressee A and the controlled SoA e_I to be realized by A. The truth value of the third argument is irrelevant in the case of imperatives and this is reflected in the absence of a propositional level, but it is relevant in the case of declaratives, Q-word interrogatives and yes/no interrogatives (in the latter only in the sense that the truth value is indeterminate (Indet) and has to be specified by the addressee).

The abstract illocutionary predicates may be replaced[9] by *performatively used* speech act verbs, which often have a more specific value than the abstract predicates. *Reportatively used* speech act verbs are part of the propositional content, have a truth-conditional interpretation and are themselves governed by an abstract illocutionary predicate. Thus there are three different possibilities: (i) abstract performative predicate, (ii) explicit performative verb and (iii) reportative speech act verb.[10] These possibilities may be represented as follows:

(11) (E$_i$: [DECL (S) (A) (X$_i$: [John is ill] (X$_i$))] (E$_i$))
      "John is ill"

(12) (E$_i$: [say$_V$ (S) (A) (X$_i$: [John is ill] (X$_i$))] (E$_i$))
      "I say to you that John is ill"

(13) (E$_i$: [DECL (S) (A) (X$_i$: [Mary said to me (X$_j$: [John is ill] (X$_j$))] (X$_i$))]
      (E$_i$))
      "Mary said to me that John is ill"

Note that in (12) the speech act verb is not part of the propositional content X$_i$
of the main clause, but replaces the abstract performative predicate, whereas
in (13) the speech act verb is part of the propositional content X$_i$ of the main
clause and itself governs the reported propositional content X$_j$.

3. Operators and satellites

One of the main goals of the hierarchical model of the utterance presented in
2. is to account for the scope relations between several types of grammatical
and lexical modification. For each layer, there are particular categories of
operator and satellite which serve to provide additional grammatical and lexical
information on their respective layers, the main content of which is provided by
the kernel structures which function as their first restrictors. For a simple
example, consider the following sentence:

(14) I saw him yesterday

In (14) both the past tense form of the verb and the adverb *yesterday* locate the
SoA 'my seeing him' on the time axis. The grammatical and the lexical strategy
have approximately the same function and both modify the same layer, the
predication, which designates the SoA for which a temporal setting is specified.
   For a second example, consider the following sentences:

(15) John must be ill

(16) Surely John is ill

In (15) the modal auxiliary *must* indicates that the speaker commits himself to the truth of the propositional content 'John is ill', in (16) the modal adverb *allegedly* serves to indicate this. The grammatical and the lexical strategy have approximately the same function and both operate on the same layer, the proposition, which represents the propositional content to the truth of which the speaker commits himself.

The grammatical and lexical means that modify the different layers are represented within the model of the utterance by means of operators and satellites, respectively, which will be discussed separately below. The representation of (14) given in (17) illustrates the format (taken from Vet 1986) that will be used to represent them. In this case the level of representation is the predication with its grammatical and lexical modifications[11]:

(17) operator   kernel structure   satellite
(Past e_i: [see$_V$ (I) (him)] (e_i): yesterday$_{Adv}$ (e_i))

3.1. Operators

Each layer within the utterance has its own categories of operators. Disregarding term operators (Ω), the categories listed in figure 5 may be distinguished.

$(E_1$: [π_4ILL (S) (A) ($\pi_3 X_1$: [   ] (X_1))] (E_1))

$(\pi_2 e_1$: [$\pi_1$pred$_\beta$ (Ωx_1: pred$_N$ (x_1)) .. (x_n)] (e_1))

π_1:	predicate operators	π_3:	proposition operators
π_2:	predication operators	π_4:	illocution operators

Figure 5: **Operators**

Predicate operators (π_1) capture the grammatical means which specify additional properties of the set of SoAs designated by a bare predication. These additional properties may concern the internal temporal constituency (Comrie 1976) of the SoA (qualificational aspect), its internal spatial constituency (directionals, cf. Foley and Van Valin 1984) and the presence or absence of the property or relation expressed by the predicate (predicate negation).

Predication operators (π_2) capture the grammatical means which locate the

SoAs designated by a predication in a real or imaginary world and thus restrict the set of potential referents of the predication to the external situation(s) the speaker has in mind. This restricting function may concern the time of occurrence of the SoA (tense), the frequency of occurrence of the SoA (quantificational aspect) and the actuality of occurrence of the SoA (objective mood (realis-irrealis), polarity).

Proposition operators (π_3) capture the grammatical means through which the speaker specifies his attitude towards the (truth of the) propositional content he puts forward for consideration. The speaker may do so by specifying the source of the propositional content (evidential mood) or by specifying his personal assessment of the propositional content (subjective mood).

Illocution operators (π_4) capture the grammatical means through which the speaker modifies the force of the basic illocution of his utterance so as to make it fit his communicative strategy. The speaker may do so by mitigating the force of the speech act (mitigating mode) or by reinforcing it (reinforcing mode). The basic functions of the four types of operator may be summarized as follows:

(18) **Overview of operators**
- π_1: additional properties of the SoA
- π_2: setting of the SoA
- π_3: validity of the propositional content
- π_4: communicative strategy of the speaker

For some illustrations of these functions consider (19) (from Hidatsa (Siouan), Matthews 1965) and (20) (from Quechua (Andean), Cole 1982):

(19) *Wíra i ápáari ki   stao   wareac*
     tree it grow   INGR REMPAST QUOT
     "They say the tree began to grow a long time ago"

π_1: The predicate *ápáari* is followed by the ingressive morpheme *ki*, which specifies a particular property of the SoA by focusing on a particular phase in its development.

π_2: The remote past morpheme *stao* provides a setting for the (ingressive) SoA by locating it on the time axis.

π_3: By means of the quotative morpheme *wareac* the speaker attributes the propositional content of the speech act (within which reference is made to remote past ingressive SoA) to a third party.

(20) *Pay-ka*   *shamu-nga-m-ári*
     he-TOP   come-FUT3-FIRSTHAND-REINF
     "He will come!"

π_2: The predicate *shamu* is followed by the future tense morpheme *-nga*, which specifies the setting of the SoA.

π_3: Through the evidential mood morpheme *-m* the speaker indicates he has first-hand evidence for the propositional content of the speech act (within which reference is made to a future SoA).

π_4: Through the addition of the reinforcing mode morpheme *-ári* the speaker imposes his declarative speech act (within which a proposition for which the speaker has first-hand evidence is processed) more strongly upon the addressee.

The order of the morphemes with respect to the predicate in these examples reflects the ordering of operators within the model of the utterance and thus reflects the scope relations between the categories tense, mood and aspect expressed by these operators. This is hypothesized to be universally the case in Hengeveld (1989), in line with Foley and Van Valin (1984), Bybee (1985) and Lehmann (1988). Note, however, that the hypothesis holds for (sub)sets of operators sharing the same expression format, e.g. prefixes, suffixes, clitics or auxiliaries, only. Thus Dik (1989: 324) notes that the hypothesis should be interpreted in such a way that if operators are expressed on both sides of the predicate, both the set preceding and that following the predicate must conform to the hypothesized ordering. Below the general pattern in (21) some possible orderings of operators are given to illustrate this:

(21)

	π_4	π_3	π_2	π_1	$pred_\beta$	π_1	π_2	π_3	π_4
a	+					+	+	+	
b	+	+				+	+		
c	+	+	+			+			
d	+		+			+		+	

etc.

The following example (from Ngiyambaa (Pama-Nyungan), Donaldson 1980) is an illustration of such a mixed ordering of operators:

(22) *Minja-ŋinda=wa:=ndu-bula:*   *buma-la-ŋila-nha*
     what-for=EXCLAM=you-two   hit-each.other-CONT-PRES
     "What have you got to keep on fighting over?"

In Ngiyambaa predicate and predication operators are expressed by means of suffixes on the predicate. Examples are the continuative aspect suffix -ŋila (π_1) and the present tense suffix -nha (π_2). Most proposition and illocution operators are expressed by means of clitics on the first word in the sentence. An example is the exclamative clitic wa: (π_4) in (22), which has a reinforcing function. The ordering of the operators in (22) is represented in (23):

(23) π_4 π_3 π_2 π_1 pred$_\beta$ π_1 π_2 π_3 π_4
        +   +   +

3.2. Satellites

Just as every layer may be modified by operators, so may it be further extended by satellites (see Dik et al. this vol.), as is indicated in figure 6, in which the model of the utterance is completed.[12]

$(E_1: [\pi_4 ILL:\sigma_4 (S) (A) (\pi_3 X_1: [\;\rule{2cm}{0.4pt}\;] (X_1): \sigma_3 (X_1))] (E_1): \sigma_5 (E_1))$

$\pi_2 e_1: [\pi_1 pred_\beta:\sigma_1 (\Omega x_1: pred_N (x_1)) ... (x_n)] (e_1): \sigma_2 (e_1)$

layers and frames		operators		satellites	
x_1:	term	Ω:	term operators		
pred:	predicate frame	π_1:	predicate operators	σ_1:	predicate satellites
e_1:	predication	π_2:	predication operators	σ_2:	predication satellites
X_1:	proposition	π_3:	proposition operators	σ_3:	proposition satellites
ILL:	illocution frame	π_4:	illocution operators	σ_4:	illocution satellites
E_1:	clause			σ_5:	clause satellites

Figure 6: **Layers, frames, operators, satellites**

The functions of these satellites are comparable to those of the corresponding operators. Thus *predicate satellites* (σ_1) specify additional properties of the SoA (e.g. Manner, Direction), *predication satellites* (σ_2) specify the spatial, temporal and cognitive setting of the SoA (e.g. Location, Time, Reason), *proposition satellites* (σ_3) are concerned with the validity of the propositional content (e.g. Attitude, Condition) and *illocution satellites* (σ_4) have to do with the speaker's communicative strategy (e.g. Manner (of speech act)). Finally, in order to account for textual relations, there is a class of *clause satellites* $(\sigma_5)^{13}$, which has no grammatical equivalent. Satellites of this class capture the lexical means through which the speaker locates his utterance within the context of the discourse and thus restricts the set of potential perlocutions of this utterance.

In summary, the basic functions of the five types of satellite may be formulated as follows:

(24) **Overview of satellites**
  σ_1:   additional properties of the SoA
  σ_2:   setting of the SoA
  σ_3:   validity of the propositional content
  σ_4:   communicative strategy of the speaker
  σ_5:   setting of the utterance

The following example illustrates these functions:

(25) Honestly, you certainly danced beautifully yesterday, if I may say so

This sentence can be analyzed in the following way:

(25) a.   you   danced **beautifully**
  b.   you   danced beautifully **yesterday**
  c.   you **certainly**   danced beautifully yesterday
  d. **Honestly,** you certainly   danced beautifully yesterday
  e. Honestly, you certainly   danced beautifully yesterday,
                                       if I may say so

σ_1: The Manner satellite *beautifully* specifies an additional property of the SoA.
σ_2: The Time satellite *yesterday* specifies the setting of the SoA.
σ_3: Through the Attitudinal satellite *certainly* the speaker expresses his commitment with respect to the propositional content.
σ_4: Through the Manner satellite *honestly* the speaker reinforces the basic illocution of the utterance.
σ_5: Through the Condition satellite *if I may say so* the speaker contemplates the felicity of the speech act within the actual communicative setting.

In principle all five satellite types may be expressed through adverbs, although a sentence which contains five adverbs, like the following, is quite strange:

(26) Finally (σ_5), you honestly (σ_4) certainly (σ_3) danced beautifully (σ_1) recently (σ_2)

Note that, as in the case of operators, the order in which the satellites appear reflects their position with respect to the predicate within the underlying structure of the utterance. The respective orderings of the satellites in (25) and (26) are represented in (27):

(27) σ_5 σ_4 σ_3 σ_2 σ_1 pred$_\beta$ σ_1 σ_2 σ_3 σ_4 σ_5

            +   +   +   +   +

       +   +   +   +   +

4. Subordination

So far I have mainly been concerned with simple utterances, i.e. utterances in which arguments and satellites refer to first order entities (x). In order to be able to analyze complex utterances arguments and satellites referring to higher order entities have to be accounted for.

4.1. Complements

The layers in the hierarchical model of the utterance given in figure 1 may not only be modified by operators and satellites, but may also be turned into arguments of higher predicates. Consider the following examples:

(28) Hopefully you will pass the exam

(29) I hope you will pass the exam

In both sentences the proposition 'you will pass the exam' is characterized as being a fulfillable wish of the speaker. In (28) this is achieved by providing it with the modal adverb *hopefully*, in (29) by turning it into the complement of the verb *hope*, as is represented in (30)-(31), respectively:

(30) (X_i: [you will pass the exam] (X_i): hopefully$_{Adv}$ (X_i))

(31) hope$_V$ (S)$_{Exp}$ (X_i: [you will pass the exam] (X_i))$_{Go}$

Just as a proposition may be turned into the argument of a higher predicate, so may all other layers be governed by a higher predicate. For instance, utterance predicates[14] used for direct speech reports have a fourth order argument, the quoted speech act; believe predicates have a third order argument, the believed propositional content; immediate perception predicates have a second order argument, the witnessed SoA. Predicates with first order arguments only, such as *give* and *read* conclude the scale. The arguments of these predicates are of decreasing internal complexity, as is shown in (32):

(32) say_V $(x_1)_{Ag}$ $(E_1: \text{clause } (E_1))_{Go}$
$\text{believe}_V(x_1)_{Exp}$ $(X_1: \text{proposition } (X_1))_{Go}$
see_V $(x_1)_{Exp}$ $(e_1: \text{predication } (e_1))_{Go}$
read_V $(x_1)_{Ag}$ $(x_1: \text{pred}_N (x_1))_{Go}$

This approach to complementation makes it possible to account for many differences in the form and behaviour of complements. With respect to differences in the form of complements, compare the following Fijian (Austronesian, Dixon 1988) examples:

(33) *Au aa tu'u-ni Eroni vei Nana Maa*
1SG PAST tell-TR Eroni REC Nana Maa
"I told Nana Maa about Eroni"

(34) *E aa tu'u-na vei au a o-na la'o mai*
3SG PAST tell-TR REC 1SG ART CL-3SG go here
a Koovana.levu
ART Governor-General
"He told me about the Governor-General's coming here"

(35) *E aa tu'u-na vei au ni na la'o mai*
3SG PAST tell-TR REC 1SG COMP FUT go here
a Koovana.levu ni saubogi
ART Governor-General LOC tomorrow
"He told me that the Governor-General will come here tomorrow"

(36) *E   tu'u-na sara   o   Raavouvou.ni.Boumaa:*
3SG tell-TR MODIF ART Raavouvou.of.Boumaa
"Qawa i   yai   a   oo-taru   bu'a!"
light   LOC here ART CL-1INCL fire
"The Raavouvou of Boumaa told him: "Let our fire be lighted here""

The Fijian verb *tu'una* "tell (about)" can take four different types of Goal argument. The Goal argument in (33) designates a first order entity, the person told about. It takes the form of a noun phrase. The Goal argument in (34) designates a second order entity, the event told about. It takes the form of a nominalization, introduced by the article *a*. The Goal argument in (35) designates a third order entity, the transmitted propositional content. It takes the form of a finite construction introduced by the complementizer *ni*. The Goal argument in (36) designates a fourth order argument, the reported speech act. It takes the form of a full clause. Note that in the first two cases the translation "tell about" is appropriate, whereas in the last two cases the translation "tell" is appropriate. In Fijian the same verb is used in all four constructions.

Thus Fijian *tu'una* "tell (about)" occurs in the following configurations, each with a different Goal argument, each realized in a different form:

(37) $\text{tu'una}_V \ (x_1)_{Ag} (x_2)_{Go} \quad (x_3)_{Rec}$ (cf. (33))
    $\text{tu'una}_V \ (x_1)_{Ag} (e_1)_{Go} \quad (x_2)_{Rec}$ (cf. (34))
    $\text{tu'una}_V \ (x_1)_{Ag} (X_1)_{Go} \quad (x_2)_{Rec}$ (cf. (35))
    $\text{tu'una}_V \ (x_1)_{Ag} (E_1)_{Go} \quad (x_2)_{Rec}$ (cf. (36))

With respect to the differences in the behaviour of complements the layered approach allows for an explanation of many restrictions on the expressibility of satellites and operators within complements (cf. Bolkestein 1989, this vol.). For instance, a predicational complement cannot contain operators or satellites expressing propositional attitudes. The following sentence is ungrammatical if the adverb *certainly*, a proposition satellite, is interpreted as modifying the complement, a predication:

(38) *I saw him certainly leave

This ungrammaticality follows from the absence of a propositional level in predicational complements, as is indicated in the representation in (32).

The classification of argument types can be further refined by taking into account the role of operators. A distinction can be made between a layer + the

full set of operators corresponding to that layer on the one hand and a layer +
a restricted set of operators on the other hand. A restriction on the set of
operators that can be expressed within the complement of a certain predicate
will in general take the form of the obligatory application of a single operator.
An illustration of the latter point is:

(39) I want him to leave *yesterday/today/tomorrow

(40) It is possible that he left yesterday/leaves today/will leave tomorrow

Both the complement of *want* and the complement of *possible* are predications.
They refer to 'wanted' and 'possible' events. 'Wanted events' are necessarily
subsequent to the 'wanting event'. Arguments of the verb *want* therefore have
only one possible temporal interpretation: they refer to events which may occur
subsequently to the event referred to in their matrix clause. This *subsequence*
is signalled by the infinitival form of the complement. 'Possible events', on the
other hand, are not tied in any way to the 'being possible event'. Arguments of
the adjective *possible* can refer to events which occurred anterior to, simultaneous with, or subsequent to the event referred to in their matrix clause.

The distinction between complements in which there is a free choice of
operators and complements in which the choice of operators is restricted by the
predicate leads to a large number of different complement types. Some
examples are listed in (41):

(41) compl.

compl.	predicate-class	example
E_1	utterance (direct sp.)	$say_V (x_1)_{Ag} (E_1)_{Go}$
$\pi_3 X_1$	propositional attitude	$believe_V (x_1)_{Exp} (\pi_3 X_1)_{Go}$
$CertX_1$	knowledge (semi-fact.)	$realize_V (x_1)_{Exp} (CertX_1)_{Go}$
$\pi_2 e_1$	commentative	$possible_A (\pi_2 e_1)_\emptyset$
$Subs\ e_1$	desiderative	$want_V (x_1)_{Exp} (Subs\ e_1)_{Go}$

In this way many properties of particular groups of complement-taking
predicates can be handled. For instance, the semi-factive character of knowledge
predicates can be accounted for by means of a 'frozen' propositional operator
'Cert(ainty)' (cf. Hengeveld 1988).

4.2. Satellites

Satellites can not only be classified according to the layer they modify (3.2), but also according to their internal structure. Most of the types of subordinate construction recognized in 4.1 appear to be relevant in the case of satellites too (cf. Dik et al. this vol.). Consider the following series of examples:

(42) We did some exercises because we had to play a match

(43) Before going to the match I prepared dinner

(44) I have bought this car in Amsterdam

(45) John types expertly

The Reason satellite in (42) designates a third order entity (the propositional content 'we have to play a match'), the Time satellite in (43) designates a second order entity (the SoA 'my going to the match'), the Location satellite in (44) designates a first order entity (the individual 'Amsterdam'). Finally, some satellites, such as the Manner satellite *expertly* in (45), have the internal complexity of a mere predicate, designating a property or relation. These satellite types are of decreasing internal complexity, as is shown in (46):

(46) $(X_1: \text{proposition } (X_1))_{Reason}$
$(e_1: \text{predication } (e_1))_{Time}$
$(x_1: \text{pred}_N (x_1))_{Location}$
$(\text{pred}_{Adv})_{Manner}$

As in the case of complements, this approach makes it possible to account for many formal differences between satellites and allows for an explanation of restrictions on the expressibility of satellites and operators within satellites. For instance, propositional attitudes may be expressed within propositional satellites, whereas this is impossible in predicational satellites:

(47) We did some exercises, because we probably had to play a match/because we might have to play a match

(48) *Before probably going to the match I prepared dinner

The classification of satellites, too, can be refined by distinguishing between satellites in which there is a free choice of operators and satellites in which the choice of operators is predetermined by the preposition or conjunction introducing the satellite, which in turn is triggered by its semantic function. Compare for instance the following sentences:

(49) I am wearing my boots in case it has rained/rains/will rain

(50) I am wearing my boots in order to keep/*have kept my feet dry

Both the satellite in (49) and that in (50) designate SoAs: in (49) the satellite designates the potential circumstance of the SoA described in the main clause, in (50) the satellite designates the SoA that the SoA described in the main clause should lead to. The latter is necessarily subsequent to the SoA described in the main clause, whereas the former is not.

Some examples of satellite types that can be accounted for following the approach illustrated here are given in (51):

(51) satell. semantic function   example

π_3X_1 Reason   because
CertX$_1$ Concession (semi-fact.)   though
π_2e_1 Potential circumstance   in case
Subs e$_1$ Purpose   in order to

Note that the semi-factive nature of some conjunctions, such as *though* in one of its uses (as opposed to *even if*), can be accounted for by means of the same procedure that was applied in the case of semi-factive complements.

5. Conclusion

In this paper I have tried to give a brief description of a hierarchically structured model for the representation of utterances, within which two levels and several layers are claimed to be relevant. Each layer consists of a variable restricted by a kernel structure (2.1). Each level is structured on the basis of a frame (2.2). Each layer may be modified by operators (3.1) and satellites (3.2). The layers contained within the model of the utterance constitute a typology of complement constructions (4.1) and adverbial constructions (4.2).

Notes

1.   I would like to thank Simon Dik, Hotze Mulder, Jan Rijkhoff and the editors of this
      volume, in particular Machtelt Bolkestein, for their comments on an earlier version of this
      paper.

2.   A notable exception to this tendency are proposals concerning the representation of illocu-
      tion in FG (de Jong 1981, Moutaouakil 1986). These proposals, however, still considered
      the predication to be the highest unit of analysis, though adding an illocutionary operator
      to it.

3.   For subordinate constructions see below.

4.   Layers of even higher and lower complexity than the ones discussed here are proposed by
      van den Hauwe (1988) and Rijkhoff (this vol.) respectively.

5.   The ^{n} in this formula indicates that a predication may contain more than one term.

6.   Note, however, that those adverbials modifying the speech act which can themselves be
      considered propositions can be evaluated in terms of their truth, irrespective of the truth
      of the main clause, as in:

      (a)   A: Watch out, because there is a bull in the field!
             B: That's not true!

      Here it is the reason adverbial which is claimed not to be true, not the main clause, which,
      being an imperative sentence, cannot be assigned a truth value at all. For the treatment of
      adverbials, see below.

7.   For a different view on the representation of illocution in FG see de Jong (1981),
      Moutaouakil (1986), Dik (1989, this vol.), Vet (this vol.). For a general discussion of the
      problems involved see Risselada (1988).

8.   The performative predicate shows up in adverbial expressions like *metaphorically speaking*,
      to tell you the truth, etc.

9.   This is a partial departure, inspired by Risselada (1988), and Vet (this vol.) from Hengeveld
      (1988).

10.   The situation is further complicated by the fact that speech act verbs in the first person
      present tense may be used in a reportative, i.e. self-descriptive sense, and by the fact that
      some verbs of saying may refer to *pronouncing* rather than to *executing* an illocutionary act
      (Lyons 1977: 740).

11.   See Dik (1989) for a different view on the representation of satellites.

12.   The representation of satellites given here cannot be fully motivated. It is in fact only valid for restrictive satellites. I refrain from giving the representation needed for handling non-restrictive satellites. See Hannay and Vester (1987), Hengeveld (1989), Bolkestein (1989) and Dik et al. (this vol.) for discussion.

13.   In Dik et al. (this vol.) illocution satellites (σ_4) and clause satellites (σ_5) are subsumed under the heading *illocution satellites*.

14.   The labels for the different classes of complement-taking predicates used here are taken from Noonan (1985).

References

Aronszajn, M.
    1988   "Thought and circumstance". *Journal of Semantics* 6: 271-307.

Barwise, J. and J.Perry
    1983   *Situations and attitudes*. Cambridge: MIT-Press.

Boër, S.G. and W.G.Lycan
    1980   "A performadox in truth-conditional semantics". *Linguistics and Philosophy* 4/1: 71-100.

Bolkestein, A.M.
    1989   "Latin sentential complements from a functional grammar perspective". *Cahiers de l'Institut de Linguistique de Louvain* 15: 41-52.

Bühler, K.
    1934   *Sprachtheorie*. Jena: Fischer.

Bybee, J.L.
    1985   *Morphology: A study of the relation between meaning and form*. Amsterdam: Benjamins.

Cole, P.
    1982   *Imbabura Quechua*. Amsterdam: North Holland.

Comrie, B.
    1976   *Aspect*. Cambridge: Cambridge UP.

Dik, S.C.
    1978   *Functional grammar*. Amsterdam: North Holland. (3rd printing: 1981, Dordrecht: Foris.)
    1989   *The theory of functional grammar, pt.1: The structure of the clause*. Dordrecht: Foris.

Dixon, R.M.W.
    1988. *A grammar of Boumaa Fijian*. Chicago: University of Chicago Press.

Donaldson, T.
 1980 *Ngiyambaa*. Cambridge: Cambridge UP.

Foley, W.A. and R.D.Van Valin
 1984 *Functional syntax and universal grammar*. Cambridge: Cambridge UP.

Halliday, M.A.K.
 1970 "Functional diversity in language, as seen from a consideration of modality and mood in English". *Foundations of Language* 6: 322-361.
 1985 *An introduction to functional grammar*. London: Edward Arnold.

Hannay, M. and E.Vester
 1987 "Non-restrictive relatives and the representation of complex sentences". In J.van der Auwera and L.Goossens (eds.), *Ins and outs of the predication*. Dordrecht: Foris, 39-52.

Hauwe, J.van den
 1988 "Extra-clausal constituents in functional grammar". Paper presented at the 3rd International Conference on Functional Grammar, Amsterdam, june 1988.

Hengeveld, K.
 1988 "Illocution, mood and modality in a functional grammar of Spanish". *Journal of Semantics* 6: 227-269.
 1989 "Layers and operators". *Journal of Linguistics* 25: 127-157.

Jong, J.de
 1981 "On the treatment of focus phenomena in functional grammar". In T.Hoekstra, H.van der Hulst and M.Moortgat (eds.), *Perspectives on functional grammar*. Dordrecht: Foris, 89-115.

Lehmann, C.
 1988 "Towards a typology of clause linkage". In J.Haiman and S.A.Thompson (eds.), *Clause combining in grammar and discourse*. Amsterdam: Benjamins, 181-225.

Levinson, S.C.
 1983 *Pragmatics*. Cambridge: Cambridge UP.

Lyons, J.
 1977 *Semantics*. Cambridge: Cambridge UP.

Matthews, G.H.
 1965 *Hidatsa Syntax*. The Hague: Mouton.

Moutaouakil, A.
 1986 *Towards an adequate representation of illocutionary force in FG*. Working Papers in Functional Grammar 10.

Noonan, M.
1985 "Complementation". In T.Shopen (ed.), *Language typology and syntactic description, vol.2.* Cambridge: Cambridge UP, 42-140.

Risselada, R.
1988 "Some problems concerning illocution in functional grammar". Paper presented at the 3rd International Conference on Functional Grammar, Amsterdam, june 1988.

Ross, J.R.
1970 "On declarative sentences". In R.A.Jacobs and P.S.Rosenbaum (eds.), *Readings in English transformational grammar.* Waltham: Ginn, 222-272.

Vendler, Z.
1967 *Linguistics in philosophy.* Ithaca: Cornell UP.

Vet, C.
1986 *A pragmatic approach to tense in functional grammar.* Working Papers in Functional Grammar 16.

The Hierarchical Structure of the Clause and the Typology of Adverbial Satellites

Simon C. Dik
University of Amsterdam

Kees Hengeveld
University of Amsterdam

Elseline Vester
Free University at Amsterdam

Co Vet
University of Groningen

0. Introduction[1]

Natural language sentences not only allow one to refer to States of Affairs (SoA) in the world or in some possible world, they also provide subsidiary information of a rather heterogeneous nature: information on additional properties of the SoAs themselves, on the speaker's attitude towards the content of the speech act, on the type of speech act the speaker wants to realize, etc. In Functional Grammar (FG) a sentence is represented as a layered structure. The highest layer is that of the clause, representing the speech act; the next one that of the proposition, representing the content of the speech act; the layer below this is that of the predication. The predication constitutes the representational part of the sentence: it refers to some SoA in the world or in some possible world.

The representation of the clause as a hierarchically structured unit consisting of several layers of increasing complexity offers the possibility to reanalyse the position of satellites in FG. This paper deals with the way in which satellites can provide information with respect to these different layers. It is argued that satellites can be subdivided into distinct types which contribute to the specification of a particular layer, and that when this is done a number of differences in the behaviour of these groups of satellites can be accounted for in a straightforward way. 1. gives a brief description of the status of satellites within a layered structure of the clause. 2. is devoted to the typology of satellites in terms of the different layers at which they apply. Some formal and behavioural correlates of the typology arrived at are given in 3. 4. demonstrates the relevance of some other parameters in the typology of satellites: the internal complexity of satellites and the restrictive/non-restrictive opposition.

1. The status of satellites

In FG adverbial constituents are generally referred to as *satellites*. Satellites differ from arguments in the fact that they are optional. Here they will be considered as optional additions to a specific layer in the hierarchical structure of the clause.

In order to appreciate the status of satellites first consider the following alternative expression types:

(1) **It is rumoured that** John is ill

(2) John **would** be ill

(3) **Allegedly** John is ill

A speaker who wishes to make clear to an addressee that he has obtained the propositional content which he is transmitting from a third party may use different strategies: he may turn this propositional content into the argument of a higher predicate which indicates the non-firsthand status of the content presented, as in (1); he may indicate this status of the proposition through the use of a special verbal mood, as in (2); or he may add this information to the proposition through the addition of a satellite, as in (3). The first and the last method represent *lexical* strategies for conveying the required extra information, the second a *grammatical* strategy. All three strategies can be seen as means to give expression to a single semantic category, known as 'quotative', 'reportative' or 'hearsay', although in general the lexical strategies present more specific information than the grammatical strategy, which necessarily has more general applicability.

We consider satellites to be optional lexical means conveying additional information on one of the layers in the hierarchical clause model. *Optional* since they can be left out without affecting the grammaticality of the sentence. *Lexical* in opposition to *grammatical* categories such as tense, mood, and aspect. *Conveying additional information*, since the main information pertaining to a particular layer is carried by the kernel structure to which the satellite is added.

2. Satellite typology

2.1. General outline

Just as a satellite may provide additional information relevant to the propositional layer, as in (3), it may provide additional information relevant to any of the other layers distinguished within the model of the clause, which is given here for the sake of convenience:[2]

(4)   clause

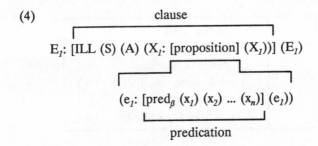

$$E_1: [\text{ILL (S) (A)} (X_1: [\text{proposition}] (X_1))] (E_1)$$

$$(e_1: [\text{pred}_\beta (x_1) (x_2) \dots (x_n)] (e_1))$$

predication

A (nuclear) predication refers to a set of possible SoAs (or to an event type). For example, the predication 'hit (John) (Bill)' can potentially be used to refer to any situation in which John is in a hitting relation with respect to Bill. Within the predication itself we can distinguish three layers:[3]
(i) the nuclear predication, which defines the event type referred to (cf. Barwise and Perry 1983);
(ii) the core predication, which defines a subcategory of the event type defined by the nuclear predication;
(iii) the extended predication, which contains a position for the tense operator and, optionally, expressions which specify the (temporal, spatial and/or cognitive) setting of the SoA.[4]
The variable e_1 symbolizes the SoA described in the nuclear predication; the variable X_1 represents the propositional content of the utterance. The responsibility for the truth of a proposition is assumed by the speaker (S) vis-à-vis the addressee (A) by means of an illocutionary act (E_1).

The lower level in (4) can thus be seen as constituting the *representational level* of the utterance: this level deals with the description of a SoA obtaining in some real or imaginary world to which the speaker wants to refer. The upper level in (4) can be seen as representing the *interpersonal level*: this level deals with the way in which the speaker presents the information concerning the situation referred to to the addressee.

This layered structure of the clause offers several units to which satellites can be attached. In the following table these units are listed together with their corresponding satellite type. The names given to these satellites refer to the 'hosting' part of the utterance; for ease of reference abbreviations (σ_1, σ_2, etc.) are provided. The four types of satellite correspond to four types of operators (π_1, π_2, π_3, π_4), which capture the corresponding grammatical distinctions relevant to the different levels.

(5) **Satellites (terminology)**

hosting layer	satellite type	
predicate	predicate satellites	(σ_1)
predication	predication satellites	(σ_2)
proposition	proposition satellites	(σ_3)
illocution	illocutionary satellites	(σ_4)

Given the functions of the different layers, these four types of satellite may be defined as in (6), taken from Hengeveld (1989):[5]

(6) **A definition of satellites**
   (i)   **Predicate satellites** capture the lexical means which specify additional properties of the set of SoAs designated by a nuclear predication.
   (ii)   **Predication satellites** capture the lexical means which locate the SoAs designated by a predication in a real or imaginary world and thus restrict the set of potential referents of the predication to the external situation(s) the speaker has in mind.
   (iii)   **Proposition satellites** capture the lexical means through which the speaker specifies his attitude towards the proposition he puts forward for consideration.
   (iv)   **Illocutionary satellites** capture the lexical means through which the speaker modifies the force of the basic illocution of a linguistic expression so as to make it fit his communicative strategy.

As a first illustration, consider the following series of examples:

(7)   Mary danced **beautifully** (σ_1)

(8)   Mary danced beautifully **yesterday** (σ_2)

(9)   Mary **probably** (σ_3) danced beautifully yesterday

✓(10) **Frankly,** (σ_4) Mary probably danced beautifully yesterday

In (7) the adverb *beautifully* specifies an additional property of Mary's dancing.
The addition of the adverb gives us a more specific picture of the type of
dancing in which Mary is involved. In (8) the adverb *yesterday* does not give a
more specific picture of Mary's dancing, but rather gives additional information
about the *occurrence* or setting of the dancing event. In (9) the adverb *probably*
indicates the speaker's attitude towards the information he is presenting. In (10)
the adverb *frankly* comments on the performance of the speech act.

Thus these four different satellites give optional further information
pertaining to additional features of the SoA (σ_1), the location of the SoA (σ_2),
the speaker's attitude towards or evaluation of the propositional content (σ_3),
and the character of the speech act (σ_4).

The classification proposed here is similar to the classification of adverbial
constructions proposed in Quirk et al. (1985), elaborating on Greenbaum
(1969):

(11) **The classification of adverbial constructions**

Quirk et al. (1985)	corresponding satellite type
adjuncts: - predication - sentence	representational level: - predicate satellites - predication satellites
disjuncts: - attitudinal - style	interpersonal level: - proposition satellites - illocutionary satellites

Many of the relevant differences in the behaviour of the different satellite types
were already noted by Greenbaum (1969), Bartsch (1972), Platt and Platt
(1972), Quirk et al. (1972), Allerton and Cruttenden (1974), and Quirk et al.

(1985). We hope to demonstrate in 3. that these differences can be accounted for within the model used here. But first we will try to arrive at a more detailed classification of the several satellite types.[6]

2.2. Predicate satellites

Predicate satellites (σ_1) represent the lexical means through which additional features of the SoA as defined in the nuclear predication can be specified. The general criterion for σ_1 status is whether the SoA as specified by the nuclear predication is somehow different with the satellite than it is without. The following subtypes can be distinguished.

(i) Additional participants:

- *Beneficiary* (Ben) is the person or institution for whose benefit (sometimes: against whose interest) the SoA is effected:

    (12) a.   John bought some flowers **for Mary**
          b.   The police set a trap **for John** (= against John)

- *Company* (Com) specifies an entity together with whom the SoA is effected:

    (13) a.   John went to Paris **with Mary**
          b.   The roof came down **with the walls**

- *Instrument* (Instr) specifies the tool with which some Action is carried out or a Position maintained. It thus requires a [+control] SoA in the nuclear predication.

    (14) John cut the meat **with a knife**

- *Inner Cause* (IC) specifies the entity presented as causing a process.

    (15) He died **of pneumonia**

(ii) Means and manner:

- *Manner* satellites indicate the way in which an Action is carried out, a Position is maintained, or in which a Process goes about:

    (16) a.   John drove the car **recklessly**

    b.   John **quietly** stayed in his hotel

    c.   The tree fell down **silently**

A further refinement of Manner satellites is required into Controller-oriented, Goal-oriented, and SoA-oriented ones:

(17) a.   John answered **eagerly**
            (John was eager in answering: Controller-oriented)
      b.   John writes **illegibly**
            (what he writes is illegible: Goal-oriented)
      c.   Annette dances **beautifully**
            (her dancing is beautiful: SoA-oriented)

- *Speed* satellites indicate the amount of Action/Process run through per unit of time; they require [+dyn] SoAs:

(18) John answered the question **quickly**
       (did the answering in a short time)

- *Quality* satellites designate the role/function/authority by virtue of which an Action is carried out, or a Position maintained; they require [+con] SoAs:

(19) a.   John accompanied Mary **as her lawyer**
      b.   John stayed in the country **as an exile**

This characterization of Quality is not intended to account for all predicative adjuncts. In most cases the predicative adjunct describes a circumstance in which rather than a function by virtue of which the action of the nuclear SoA is carried out.

(iii) Spatial orientation:

Source, *Path*, and *Direction* designate the point of origin, the orientation, and the terminal point of a movement:

(20) John drove **from Amsterdam** (Source) **to Rotterdam** (Direction) **along the highway** (Path)

The following table summarizes what was said here about *predicate satellites*:

(21) The classification of predicate satellites

semantic domain	satellite function
additional participants	Beneficiary, Company, Instrument, Inner Cause
manner and means	Manner, Speed, Quality
spatial orientation	Source, Path, Direction

2.3. Predication satellites

Predication satellites (σ_2) represent the lexical means through which the SoA designated by the nuclear predication can be located with respect to spatial, temporal, and cognitive dimensions. They specify the setting within which an SoA occurs. The following subtypes can be distinguished.
(i) Spatial setting:
A *Location* (Loc) satellite designates the place where a certain SoA took place:

(22) John met Peter **on the platform**

Spatial setting should be distinguished from *spatial orientation* (see Quirk et al. 1985 for these examples):

(23) She kissed her mother **on the cheek** (σ_1)

(24) She kissed her mother **on the platform** (σ_2)

In (23) the satellite specifies the spatial orientation of the action, and can therefore be considered a predicate satellite. In (24) the satellite specifies the spatial setting of the SoA, and can therefore be considered a predication satellite. For some behavioural differences between the two satellite types see 3. Note here that (24), but not (23), can receive a paraphrase stressing its event-locating character:

(25) *Her kissing her mother took place on the cheek

(26) Her kissing her mother took place on the platform

Note also that both satellites can appear in the same sentence:[7]

(27) She kissed her mother **on the cheek on the platform**

(ii) Temporal setting:
- A *Time* (Time) satellite specifies the time at which (from which, until which)
a certain SoA took place:

(28) a.   John met Peter **at five o'clock**
      b.   John walked in the park **from after lunch until three o'clock**

- A *Duration* (Dur) satellite specifies the time during which a certain SoA took
place:

(29) John walked in the park **for three hours**

- A *Frequency* (Freq) satellite specifies the number of times a certain SoA took
place:

(30) John met Peter **repeatedly**

(iii) Setting relative to other SoAs:
- A *Circumstance* (Circ) satellite specifies an SoA which occurs simultaneously
with the SoA referred to in the main predication:

(31) Mary was smoking a cigarette, **while John was washing the car**

(32) **No more matters arising,** the meeting was closed

- A *Cause* (Cause) satellite specifies an SoA the occurrence of which instigates
the occurrence of the SoA referred to in the main predication:

(33) **The tree fell down because of the heavy rainfall**

A Cause (σ_2) satellite should be distinguished from an Inner Cause (σ_1)

satellite:

    (34) He died **of hunger** (Inner Cause)

    (35) He died **because he had no money to buy food** (Cause)

In (34) the satellite specifies the force instigating the process of dying, in (35) the satellite specifies the event causing the event described in the main clause. Only (35) can receive a paraphrase stressing its event-locating character:

    (36) *His dying took place of hunger

    (37) His dying took place because he had no money to buy food

Both satellite types can cooccur in one sentence:

    (38) He died of hunger because he had no money to buy food

The difference between the two satellite types is furthermore reflected in the different expressions for their semantic functions, *of* vs. *because (of)*.
- A *Condition* (Cond) satellite specifies an SoA on the occurrence of which the occurrence of another SoA depends:

    (39) He'll take his umbrella in case of rain
          (His taking his umbrella will take place in case of rain)

(iv) Cognitive setting:
- *Purpose* satellites provide a motivation for the occurrence of a (necessarily [+control]) SoA^1 by specifying a future SoA^2 that the controller wishes to achieve through SoA^1. For example:

    (40) John ran to the station **in order to catch the train**

Note that the purpose is necessarily ascribed to the controller: it was John who wanted to catch the train, and therefore he ran to the station.
- *Reason* satellites provide a motivation for why an SoA (again, necessarily [+control]) took place in terms of a causal ground ascribed to the controller.[8] Such a Reason may consist in a close paraphrase of a Purpose:

(41) John ran to the station **because he wanted to catch the train**

The difference with (40) is, that the Reason satellite in (41) describes John's
wish to achieve the future SoA rather than that future SoA as such. The Reason
may also consist in some preceding SoA:

(42) John ran to the station **because he had been late the day before**

The following table summarizes what was said here about *predication
satellites*:

(43) **The classification of predication satellites**

semantic domain	satellite function
spatial setting temporal setting setting relative to other SoAs cognitive setting	Location Time, Frequency, Duration Cause, Circumstance, Condition Reason, Purpose

2.4. Proposition satellites

Proposition satellites (σ_3) deal with those lexical means through which the
speaker evaluates (part of) the propositional content he presents in a speech
act.
- An *Attitudinal* (Att) satellite specifies the speaker's attitude towards (part of)
the propositional content, and corresponds to Greenbaum's *attitudinal disjunct*
(see also Bartsch 1972; Bellert 1977). Depending on the part of the proposition
they bear on, this group of satellites can be further classified into (a) content-
oriented, (b) event-oriented, and (c) participant-oriented Attitudinal satellites:
(a) Content (X) oriented attitudes. Within this category we find satellites
expressing both subjective and evidential modalities (or propositional attitudes),
such as:

(44) a. **In my opinion,** we should do it (subjective epistemic)
     b. **Hopefully,** you will succeed (subjective volitional)

    c.   **In my experience,** such questions are seldom solved (experiential)
    d.   **Apparently,** John has failed (inferential)
    e.   **Allegedly,** John was guilty of perjury (quotative)

(b) Event (e) oriented attitudes. The attitudinal disjunct can also have bearing on the event to which reference is made within the propositional content, as in:

    (45) **Fortunately,** we found him immediately

Through the adverb it is not expressed that the propositional content is fortunate, but rather that it is fortunate that the finding-event took place.
(c) Participant (x) oriented attitudes. A third subsection of the clause that the attitudinal disjunct can have a bearing on is one of the participants in the event to which reference is made within the propositional content processed in the speech act, as in:

    (46) **Wisely,** John didn't answer the question

This sentence can be paraphrased as *It was wise of John not to answer the question.*
Note that in English the same adverb *wisely* can be used as a Manner satellite (σ_1) and as an Attitudinal satellite (σ_3). The differences between these can be read off from the placement of the adverb and the intonation pattern with which the construction is provided:

    (47) a.   **Wisely,** John answered the question
           b.   John, **wisely,** answered the question
           c.   John answered the question, **wisely**

    (48) a.   ??**Wisely** John answered the question
           b.   ?John **wisely** answered the question
           c.   John answered the question **wisely**

Although these differences are not absolute, the Manner satellite clearly prefers a non-initial position, whereas the Attitudinal satellite has a preference for initial position. Furthermore, the Manner satellite is intonationally integrated into the predication, whereas the Attitudinal satellite is usually marked off from the rest by prosodic inflections which suggest that it is less integrated with the rest. This corresponds, in iconic fashion, to the different roles these satellites play in the fabric of the clause. In German and Dutch we find formal differences between the adverbs, corresponding to their roles as σ_1 or σ_3 satellites:[9]

(49) a. *Klugerweise beantwortete Hans die Frage*
         wisely   answered   John the question
         "Wisely, John answered the question" (= (47))
     b. *Hans beantwortete die Frage klug*
         John answered   the question wisely
         "John answered the question wisely" (= (48))

(50) a. *Wijselijk beantwoordde Jan de vraag*
         wisely   answered   John the question
         "Wisely, John answered the question" (= (47))
     b. *Jan beantwoordde de vraag wijs*
         John answered   the question wisely
         "John answered the question wisely" (= (48))

- A *Source* (So) satellite specifies a third party presented as being responsible for the information contained in the propositional content:

(51) **According to John** there's a bull in the field

- An *Evidence* (Evid) satellite specifies an SoA the occurrence of which provides the evidence on which the propositional content is based:

(52) **Given his absence of the last few days,** he has probably gone to Rome after all

- A *Motivation* (Mot) satellite specifies a fact which supports the fact designated by the propositional content of the speech act:[10]

(53) John's at Sue's house, **because his car's outside**

The following table summarizes what was said here about *proposition satellites*:

(54) **The classification of proposition satellites**

semantic domain	satellite function
propositional attitude validity of proposition	Attitude Source Evidence Motivation Condition

2.5. Illocutionary satellites

Illocutionary satellites (σ_4) represent the lexical means through which the illocutionary value of the clause can be specified or modified. The semantic functions of many of these satellites are the same as those of satellites at lower levels. The difference is, that illocutionary satellites are interpreted as modifying the speech act rather than the SoA to which reference is made within that speech act.
- *Manner* (Man) satellites at the level of the speech act indicate the way in which the speech act is carried out. They can be subdivided into three groups:
(a) Speaker-oriented:

(55) **Frankly,** I've had it

(b) Addressee-oriented:

(56) **Honestly,** did you tell him?

(c) Speech act-oriented:

(57) **Briefly,** it's no use

- A *Beneficiary* satellite at the illocutionary level specifies the person in whose interest the speech act is executed:

(58) **For your own sake,** stay away from him!

- A *Reason* satellite at this level provides a motivation for why the speech act is carried out:

(59) **Since you are interested,** John is a catholic

- A *Condition* satellite of level 4 specifies a condition on the felicity of the speech act (see Dik 1989; Harder 1989):

(60) John has left, **in case you haven't heard**

- A *Time* satellite specifies the position of the speech act in a series:

(61) **For the last time,** give it to me!

The following table summarizes these various distinctions in the domain of *illocutionary satellites*:

(62) **The classification of illocutionary satellites**

semantic domain	satellite function
additional participants manner of speech act communicative setting	Beneficiary (of speech act) Manner (of speech act) Time, Reason, Condition (of speech act)

3. Some formal and behavioural correlates

So far, the validity of the proposed classification has mainly been demonstrated by semantic arguments. In this section we intend to show that there are several formal and behavioural differences between the different satellite types proposed in 2. We start with giving the evidence for the distinction between satellites at the representational (σ_1, σ_2) and those at the interpersonal (σ_3, σ_4) level, and then proceed to discussing the differences between the satellites at each of these levels.

3.1. Representational (σ₁, σ₂) vs. interpersonal satellites (σ₃, σ₄)

There are a number of arguments that can be used to demonstrate that representational satellites belong to the extended predication: (i) they fall under the scope of pragmatic function assignment; (ii) they constitute one information unit with the core predication, (iii) they are under the scope of π_1 and π_2 operators, and (iv) they are typically conditioned by other properties pertaining to the representational level.

3.1.1. Pragmatic function assignment. The tests given by Quirk et al. (1985) to distinguish between adjuncts and disjuncts can be used to distinguish representational satellites from interpersonal satellites. Some of the relevant tests can be interpreted as giving an indication about Topic and Focus assignment. There is evidence that Topic and Focus assignment have the extended predication, i.e. the core predication with level 2 operators and satellites specified, as their domain. Assigning Focus to satellites of the interpersonal level is hardly possible, except in highly marked contexts:

(63)   ???John **probably** lost his wallet

(64)   ???**Briefly,** John lost his wallet

If this is correct, Focus on satellites may be taken as evidence that they form part of the extended predication and are therefore representational satellites. Two tests which give a clear indication of the Focus status of a constituent are: occurrence as an answer to a WH-question, as in (65), and occurrence in contrastive contexts such as constructions with alternative negation and interrogation, a Latin example of which is given in (66):

(65)   A: Why are you staying in tonight?
       B: Because my mother is ill.

(66)   *Id se sui*   *muniendi*   *non Galliae*
       it he himself.GEN.SG   protecting.GEN.SG.M   not Gaul.GEN.SG
       impugnandae   *causa*   *facere*
       attacking.GEN.SG.F for.the.sake.of   do
       "That he did it to protect himself, not to attack Gaul" (Caes.*Gal.*1,44,6)

The Purpose satellites *sui muniendi, non Galliae impugnandae causa* have

Contrastive Focus in (66).

A further test showing that representational satellites are part of the domain within which pragmatic functions are assigned is provided by Quirk et al. (1985), who show that all these satellites can be clefted.

3.1.2. Information unit. Representational satellites form one information unit together with the core predication.
(i) They fall under one unified intonation pattern.
(ii) They can be within the scope of a proform (Quirk et al. 1985; Rutherford 1970):

> (67) a. He'll take his umbrella in case it rains and so does Ann
> b. *He'll take his umbrella, in case you are wondering and so does Ann

In (67a) *so* in *so does Ann* refers to the extended predication, the σ_2 predication satellite Condition included. In (67b) it refers to the predication, not including the σ_4 illocutionary satellite Condition.
(iii) The whole unit, including the representational satellite, can be questioned with a yes/no question (Rutherford 1970; Bellert 1977):

> (68) Is John speaking loudly? Yes/no.

> (69) Does he take his umbrella in case it rains? Yes/no.

> (70) *Does he take his umbrella, in case you are wondering? Yes/no.

> (71) *Does India probably face famine?

Again the answer in (70) does not include the illocutionary satellite.

3.1.3. Scope of operators. Another indication of the level of a satellite is the scope of the operators. That is, σ_1 satellites fall under the scope of π_1 operators, and σ_2 and σ_1 satellites both fall under the scope of π_2 operators, that is the operators for negation, tense, and objective modality. Negation will be discussed separately in 3.4, here we give an example of scope phenomena concerning the tense operator.

A rule which illustrates the relevance of tense operator scope is the Latin *consecutio temporum*, which states that the tense in an argument or satellite clause is governed by the tense in the matrix sentence. This can be reinterpreted as a rule which states that finite clauses which fall under the scope of the tense operator have a tense form which is determined by that tense operator. The consequence of this reformulation is that only finite clauses which function as σ_1 and σ_2 satellites can be sensitive to the consecutio temporum rule. And indeed, the clauses which are presented as exceptions to the rule in Latin grammars, such as some consecutive and causal clauses, are interpersonal rather than representational satellites.

As an illustration may serve clauses introduced by *quoniam*. Bolkestein (fc.) shows that in Latin the kind of subordinator chosen for a causal clause gives an indication about the status of this clause: *quoniam*-clauses are σ_3 or σ_4 satellites, *quod*- and *quia*-clauses are σ_2 satellites.[11] Cf. also Greek *epei*-clauses (Rijksbaron 1976) and English *since* and *as* clauses (Quirk et al. 1985) which show a behaviour similar to *quoniam* clauses. The interpersonal level status of *quoniam*-clauses is indeed confirmed by Bolkestein's observation that especially in *quoniam*-clauses consecutio temporum is relatively often not observed.

3.1.4. Conditions on satellites. The occurrence of satellites may be conditioned by a variety of features of the clause structure. For representational satellites, these features typically pertain to the representational level. For example:

(72)	satellite	condition
σ_1	Instrument	[+control]
	Beneficiary	[+control]
	Manner	[+control] or [+dynamic]
	Speed	[+dynamic]
σ_2	Reason	[+control]
	Purpose	[+control]
	Duration	[-telic]
	Interval	[+telic]
	Time: yesterday	past
	tomorrow	future

On the other hand, satellites at the interpersonal level tend to be constrained by features pertaining to the interpersonal level. For example, as shown in example (71), a satellite such as *probably* cannot occur in the scope of interrogative illocution. At the same time, the constraints on these higher-level satellites seem to be much less specific than those on lower-level ones. We return to this point in 3.2.1.3 below.

3.2. Predicate (σ₁) vs. predication (σ₂) satellites

In the preceding section the two types of representational satellite, predicate and predication satellites, were taken together in order to compare their behaviour with that of satellites at the interpersonal level, propositional and illocutionary satellites. In this section we show that there are also several behavioural differences between predicate and predication satellites. These differences concern: (i) argument-like behaviour of predicate satellites (discussed in 3.2.1); (ii) ordering and position differences (3.2.2); (iii) paraphrase possibilities (3.2.3); (iv) behaviour under negation (separately discussed in 3.4).

3.2.1. Argument-like behaviour of predicate satellites. Given the intimate connection of predicate satellites with the predicate, we may expect predicate satellites to behave in a way similar to arguments in a number of respects. Evidence for such argument-like behaviour can be found in (i) Subject and Object assignment possibilities, (ii) the role of satellites in predicate formation, and (iii) semantic constraints on the occurrence of satellites.

3.2.1.1. Subject/Object assignment to predicate satellites. The FG approach to Subject and Object assignment holds that these functions can be assigned to terms (arguments or satellites) of the predication, and designate those entities which are taken as a primary or secondary point of departure for the presentation of the SoA designated by the predication.[12] It has further been assumed that both within and across languages the possibilities for Subj/Obj assignment decrease along the following Semantic Function Hierarchy (SFH):

(73) FirstArg > Go > Rec > Ben > Instr > Loc > Temp

Ben and Instr are clear examples of σ_1, with their own contribution to the definition of the SoA (see 2.2). They can therefore also act as points of departure for perspectivizing the SoA. But Loc and Temp at first sight present a problem for this theory: if these are examples of σ_2, they do not enter into the definition of the SoA as such, but rather serve to locate the SoA with respect to spatial and temporal dimensions. How could they then serve as point of departure for perspectivizing the SoA? Closer scrutiny of the relevant data has revealed, however, that it is especially the 'inner' semantic functions which can be assigned Subject function: those semantic functions, that is, which do indeed contribute to the definition of the SoA as such. These 'inner' semantic functions can therefore be interpreted as σ_1 rather than σ_2 satellites, and on that interpretation they do not provide counter-examples to the Subj/Obj assignment theory. Rather, this theory provides an additional criterion for distinguishing σ_1 and σ_2 satellites. Consider the following data.

The evidence for Subj assignment to Temp is very slight indeed. It is reported for two Philippine languages, Kalagan (Keenan 1972) and Cebuano (Bell 1983). Keenan gives no examples. Bell (ibid.: 146) gives the following example from Cebuano:[13]

(74) *Mogikan   ang   barko   sa alas sayis*
     ACT.leave SUBJ   ship   at clock six
     "The ship will leave at six o'clock"

(75) *Igikan   sa   barko   ang   alas sayis*
     INS.leave by   ship   SUBJ   clock six
     "Six o'clock will be left by the ship"

Bell adds, however, that constructions of type (75) are quite rare, except in relative constructions. In Cebuano (as in Kalagan) only Subjects can be relativized. Thus, the only way of expressing something like 'the time at which the ship will leave' is through embedding a construction of type (75). It may perhaps be assumed that it is this constraint on relativization which has occasioned Subj assignment to exceptionally go beyond its natural limits.

The evidence for Subj/Obj assignment to Loc is much more extensive. Thus, Subj assignment to Loc is reported for Maguindanao, Tagalog, Kapampangan, Kalagan, and Cebuano (all Philippine languages); for Malagasy (which also belongs to the Malayo-Polynesian languages); and Subj and Obj assignment to Loc is reported for Luganda, Chimwi:ni, Swahili, and Kinyarwanda (all Bantu languages). Note, however, that Loc does not necessarily have the status of a σ_2 satellite, which simply locates the whole SoA in some spatial domain. Locative terms can also have argument status and, depending on the way the notion 'locative' is used, they might also cover one or more of the 'inner' local or directional satellites which were assigned σ_1 status above. Could it be, then, that it is especially these 'inner' locatives which can be assigned Subj function? That there may be something to this idea can be seen even in English. Compare the following pair:

(76) a.   John was writing on the terrace
          = (a) "John inscribed something on the terrace"
          = (b) "John was writing something while being on the terrace"
    b.   The terrace was written on by John
          = only (a)

In the (a) interpretation of (76a), *the terrace* can be considered as an argument of the predicate *write on*, or at least as a σ_1 satellite closely associated with the predicate; in the (b) interpretation it is a σ_2 satellite. Only in the former case can Subj be assigned to it, witness the unambiguous character of (76b). Something similar is involved in the following pair (Quirk et al. 1972: 804):

(77) a.   This problem was very carefully gone into by the engineers
    b.   *The tunnel was very carefully gone into by the engineers

Again, it appears that Subj assignment is possible only when the term in question is close to being an argument of the nuclear predicate.

There are similar indications in this direction for the languages mentioned above. Thus, in her description of Kapampangan Mirikitani (1972) makes a distinction between 'terminus locative', defined as 'the case designating the place towards or from which an activity is directed' (= Source + Direction), and 'general locative', comparable to our σ_2 Locative satellite. It is the terminus locative, not the general locative, which may receive Subj function. For example, in the Kapampangan equivalents of:

(78) a.   I will go **to school** (terminus locative)
    b.   I will read **in school** (general locative)

it is only the terminus locative in (78a) which can be assigned Subj. Examples of predicates which take a terminus locative are 'write on something', 'cook in something', and 'go, walk to some place'.

Though we have not been able to check this for all the Philippine languages mentioned above, it is probable that the situation in these languages is similar. For example, Bell (1983: 209) notes that Loc in Cebuano includes Source and Direction, and the only example she gives of a Loc to which Subj is assigned is again 'cook something in a pot', where the Loc term is obviously closely associated with the predicate. As for the Bantu languages, many of the examples in which Subj or Obj is assigned to Loc again concern 'inner' Locatives which either have the status of arguments of the predicate, or of σ_1 satellites. Gary and Keenan (1977: 114) provide a direct parallel to (76) in Kinyarwanda. Compare:

(79) a. *Yohani y-a-andits-e*   *ku   meza   n-ikaramu*
         John   he-PAST-write-ASP   on   table   with-pen
         "John wrote on the table with the pen"

     b. *Yohani y-a-andits-e-ho*   *ameza   n-ikaramu*
         John   he-PAST-write-ASP-on   table   with-pen
         "John wrote-on the table with the pen"

(79a) has the same ambiguity as (76a); but (79b) can only be interpreted as saying that John inscribed something on the table with the pen. Many of the examples from Kinyarwanda given in Gary and Keenan (1977), Dryer (1983), and Perlmutter and Postal (1983) likewise concern 'inner' Locatives, as in 'throw something into the water', 'send someone to school', 'sit on a chair'. The same is true for the examples given from Chimwi:ni in Kisseberth and Abasheikh (1977): 'spill water on something', 'bring, send, write something to somebody'.

On the basis of this evidence, though admittedly incomplete, it seems that there is a good basis for the following hypotheses:

(H1) In languages in which Subj/Obj can be assigned to Loc and Temp, this is in principle restricted to Loc and Temp arguments and σ_1 satellites.

(H2) In the exceptional cases in which σ_2 satellites can receive Subj/Obj function, this is under the external pressure of some rule (such as relativization) which is constrained to Subj and/or Obj terms.

To the extent that these hypotheses are correct they can be used as an additional criterion for distinguishing σ_2 satellites from σ_1 satellites and arguments with similar semantic functions.

These hypotheses seem to offer a possible explanation for some 'difficult' passives in other languages as well. In Ancient Greek, for example, there are some cases which are traditionally described as passives, but whose Subjects are not evidently Goals (cf. also Metz 1988). An example of a passive Subject with the semantic function of Duration is the following:

(80) *Ede*   *treis*   *menes*
      already   three.NOM.PL   months.NOM.PL
      epitetrierarchento   *moi*
      be.triërarch.beyond.the.legal.time.MP.3PL   me.DAT
      "I have been a triërarch already three months beyond the legal time"
      (Demosth. 50,23)

An active counterpart (with the same meaning) is found in Demosthenes 50,36:

(81) *Epitetrierarcheka*   *tettaras*
      be.triërarch.beyond.the.legal.time.ACT.1SG four.ACC.PL
      menas
      months.ACC.PL
      "He had been a triërarch four months beyond his legal time"

The passive construction in (80) suggests that the Duration term *treis menes* is
closely associated with the predicate, and has the status of either an argument
or a σ_1 satellite. This close association could in this case have been reinforced
by the fact that the Duration term has the accusative case form, which is also
the normal case form for Goal arguments.

3.2.1.2. Predicate formation. There are strong indications that predicate
formation rules may not only affect the arguments of the input predicate, but
also the σ_1 satellites associated with the nuclear predication. On the other
hand, σ_2 and higher satellites seem to fall outside the scope of predicate
formation rules. Consider the following three phenomena:
(i) Incorporation:
Incorporation can be described as a form of predicate formation through which
nominal predicates are incorporated into (derived) verbal predicates. Compare:

(82) a.   John goes **to school**
      b.   John **school**-goes

The formation of the derived predicate in (82b) can be described as a process
through which a nominal predicate corresponding to a Direction satellite is
incorporated into the predicate. Across languages, certain satellites can be more
easily incorporated than others. We expect that those satellites can be most
easily incorporated, which have the closest relation to the nuclear predication.
As a working hypothesis we may assume that only σ_1 satellites can be

incorporated.

Across languages we find the following types of incorporation:[14]

(83) **Incorporated nominal corresponds to argument**
    a. Goal   John bird-catches (= catches birds)
    b. Agent   man-drawn car (= drawn by men)
    c. Force   fuel powered engine (powered by fuel)
    d. Processed   it is snow-falling (snow is falling)

(84) **Incorporated nominal corresponds to satellite**
    a. Instrument John knife-cut the meat (= with a knife)
    b. Direction   John school-went (= to school)
    c. Manner   You must quiet-sit (= quietly)
    d. Speed   John fast-ran to the station
    e. Location   John chair-sits in the garden

Most of the examples of (84) clearly involve σ_1 satellites. Only the incorporation of nominals with Location function might be reason for some doubt. Note, however, that in a construction such as:

(85) John sits on a chair in the garden

it is the 'inner' Location represented by *chair* which can be incorporated rather than the 'outer' Location represented by *garden*. Thus, we do not expect constructions of the form:

(86)   *John garden-sits on a chair.

This is fully parallel to what we found in the case of Subj/Obj assignment: Locations can only be incorporated when they entertain a close bond with the predicate, such that the resulting compound predicate designates a specialized SoA rather than an unmodified SoA located at some place.

This can also be seen in a number of verbs in Dutch which feature an incorporated locative nominal:

(87) a. *paalzitten*   = pole sitting, a record breaking game
     b. *waterskiën* = water skiing, a special kind of skiing, not simply 'skiing on water'
     c. *ijszeilen*   = ice sailing, a special kind of sailing

d. *wadlopen*   = (mud) flat walking, a special kind of walking
e. *schoolblijven* = school staying, not simply 'staying in school', but
                    'staying after school' (for punishment)

(ii) Valency reduction:

σ_1 satellites can also be involved in predicate formation when a valency reduction rule removes a σ_1 satellite instead of an argument. In Risselada (1987) it is argued that the middle-passive in Ancient Greek, which has a number of different uses (e.g. direct reflexive, indirect reflexive, pseudo-reflexive, pseudo-passive and passive) can be accounted for systematically by a set of valency reduction rules. In most cases, of course, the term which is removed by a valency reduction rule is an argument, but in the case of the Indirect Reflexive Predicate Formation Rule the Beneficiary is removed and implied in the predicate frame of the new predicate:

(88) **Indirect reflexive predicate formation rule**
  input: $pred_{VAct} (x_1)_{Ag} (x_2)_{Go} (y_3)_{Ben}$
  output: $pred_{VMp} (x_1)_{Ag} (x_2)_{Go}$
  meaning: 'x_1 performs $pred_V$ in his own interest'

Mp (middle-passive) is the formal marker of the reduced nature of these derived predicates. An example is:

(89) *Ho stratos   paraskeuazetai tas naus*
  the army.SUBJ prepares.MP the ships.GO
  "The army is preparing the ships for itself"

Risselada (1987: 131-132) suggests that the French example

(90) *Jean s'   est cassé la jambe*
  John REFL is broken the leg
  "John has broken his leg"

(cf. Vet 1985) can be analysed in a similar way as involving reduction of the σ_1 satellite Beneficiary, where *se* is the reduction marker involved in various types of valency-reducing predicate formation rules.

These facts suggest that the domain of predicate formation rules is not the nuclear predication, but the core predication, i.e. the nuclear predication extended by σ_1 satellites.

(iii) Satellite absorption:
The term 'satellite absorption' has been used in two senses within the context
of FG. First, it has been used to indicate the process through which a satellite
gets absorbed into the predicate in some predicate formation rule (Kahrel
1985). Compare:

    (91) a.   Mary washes these clothes
        b.   *These clothes wash
        c.   These clothes wash easily

The valency reduction rule which removes the Agent argument of transitive
wash at the same time requires that something is added to the derived
predicate. Where this something is a satellite such as *easily*, we may say that
this Manner satellite has been 'absorbed' into the derived predicate in the
process of predicate formation, so as to become an argument. We assume that
satellites will be more easily absorbed in this way when they are more closely
associated with the nuclear predicate.

    The second sense in which 'satellite absorption' has been used is to indicate
the historical process through which an original satellite gets reinterpreted as
an argument of the predicate to which it was originally more loosely attached.
This process has been assumed (Pinkster 1988a; Mulder 1988) to underlie the
phenomenon that in Latin and Greek certain two-place predicates have non-
accusative second arguments. The facts are as follows.

    In Latin, with verbs like *dolere* "to grieve for", the constituent which refers
to the source or cause of the emotion is either marked by an ablative case form
or by an accusative case form (cf. Pinkster 1988a):

    (92) a.   *Qui sociorum   iniuriis ...   doleat*
            who allies.GEN.PL wrongs.ABL.PL deplores.3SG
            "Who deplores our allies' wrongs'" (Cic.*Ver*.3,6)
        b.   *Meum casum   luctumque   doluerunt*
            my   misfortune.ACC.SG sorrow.ACC.SG.and grieved.3PL
            "They grieved for my misfortune and sorrow" (Cic. *Sest*. 145)

Although in Classical Latin both the ablative in (92a) and the accusative in
(92b) are best considered second arguments, from a historical point of view
iniuriis in (92a) could be considered as a satellite of Cause or Source, which
normally has an ablative case form. The use of the ablative for coding a second
argument could then be understood by assuming that the satellite has gradually

been absorbed into the predicate frame, creating a two-place predicate *dolere* while retaining its original case form. The use of the accusative can then be seen as due to the Principle of Formal Adjustment (Dik 1985): the new two-place predicate adjusts its formal expression to the prototypical expression model for second arguments, viz. the accusative case form.

A similar development can according to Pinkster be assumed for compound verbs like *antecellere* "to surpass", which occur with either a dative or an accusative second argument. In this case a Beneficiary would have been absorbed into the predicate frame.

Mulder (1988: 235) defends a similar hypothetical scenario for the development of Ancient Greek non-accusative second arguments:

(93)		relation to predicate	semantic function	expression
	phase 1	satellite	non-Goal	non-accusative
	phase 2	2nd argument	non-Goal	non-accusative
	phase 3	2nd argument	Goal	accusative

A difference between Latin and Greek in this respect is, that in Greek even some of the predicates which are in the presumed phase 2 allow Subject assignment to the second argument, while in Latin such Subject assignment is not allowed.

Again, it could be assumed that historically, those satellites which are most closely associated with the nucleus will be more easily absorbed into the nuclear predicate frame.

3.2.1.3. Semantic constraints on the occurrence of satellites. A third fact which points to the argument-like behaviour of σ_1 satellites lies in the restrictions on their occurrence, which were already mentioned in 3.1.4 above. In general, satellites seem to be more constrained in their occurrence, the closer they are to the nucleus of the clause. Most σ_2 satellites occur freely with any type of SoA. When they are sensitive to [+control] SoAs (as is the case for Purpose and Reason (both σ_2 satellites)), they may nevertheless occur freely with *any* such SoA.

For the occurrence of σ_1 satellites more specific constraints must often be formulated. For example, Risselada (1987: 130) points out that intrinsically benefactive verbs in Greek, such as 'eat' or 'drink', which refer to [+control] SoAs, can nevertheless not be extended by a Beneficiary. In Dik (1975: 97) a subcategorization of Manner adverbs is given according to the specific types of

SoAs with which they may occur. Similar subcategorizations are given in Platt and Platt (1972) and Allerton and Cruttendon (1978). From these subcategorizations it is clear that rather specific semantic features of both predicate and Manner adverb are essential for describing the privileges of occurrence of 'inner' satellites. A last example of such more specific restrictions is provided by satellites of Source, Direction and Path, which are mainly restricted to movement predicates.

A further argument can be derived from the uses of the Latin ablative case. The ablative case is used for both 'outer' and 'inner' satellites with various semantic functions. Especially the occurrence of σ_1 satellites in the ablative is strongly dependent on the semantics of the nuclear predication.[15]

On the basis of such facts as these it could be argued that a predicate frame has a number of implied slots for σ_1 satellites which may but need not be filled. Moreover, the type of SoA is a property of the whole core predication (including the σ_1 satellites) rather than a property of only the nuclear predication. Thus, the following constructions have the same nucleus but describe two different SoA types ([+co][+dyn][-tel] in (94) and [+co][+dyn][+tel] in (95)), as evidenced by the different possibilities of adding σ_2 satellites:

(94) John drove from Amsterdam to Paris *for hours/in five hours

(95) John drove along the highway for hours/*in five hours

We saw in this section that 'inner' (σ_1) satellites in many ways behave differently from 'outer' (σ_2) satellites, are closer to arguments, and are more strongly associated with the semantics of the nuclear predication. This corresponds to the overall semantic difference between σ_1 and σ_2 satellites as conceptualized in this paper: σ_1 satellites specify additional features of the nuclear SoA, while σ_2 satellites serve to 'localize' the (specified) SoA in relation to temporal, spatial, and cognitive parameters.

3.2.2. *Ordering and position differences.* Differences in the ordering and position of predicate and predication satellites are extensively discussed in Quirk et al. (1985: 511-512). They note that what we call predication satellites are relatively free to occur in either sentence-initial or sentence-final position, as opposed to predicate satellites, which cannot freely occur in initial position:

(96) a.   She kissed her mother **on the cheek**
      b.   ?**On the cheek,** she kissed her mother

(97) a.   She kissed her mother **on the platform**
b.   **On the platform**, she kissed her mother

These ordering differences can be interpreted as 'iconically' reflecting the relative scope differences between the satellites, in the sense that 'outer' or 'higher' satellites take 'inner' or 'lower' satellites in their scope. Further evidence for such a reflection of scope differences is found in the ordering of predicate and predication satellites relative to the predicate:

(98) a.   She kissed her mother **on the cheek on the platform**
b.   **On the platform**, she kissed her mother **on the cheek**
c.   ?*She kissed her mother **on the platform on the cheek**
d.   ?***On the cheek**, she kissed her mother **on the platform**

3.2.3. Paraphrase possibilities. In English, predication (σ_2) satellites allow for a paraphrase by means of corresponding nouns, as in the following examples (from Mackenzie and Hannay 1982):

(99) a.   I met Sheila in the park
b.   The place that I met Sheila was the park

(100) a.   I met Sheila at three o'clock
b.   The time that I met Sheila was three o'clock

Such paraphrases are not possible with predicate (σ_1) satellites:

(101) a.   I approached the lion with great caution
b.   *The way that I approached the lion was great caution

(102) a.   I cut the meat with a knife
b.   *The instrument that I cut the meat was a knife

Predication satellites allow a paraphrase with *occur, take place,* or *happen,* whereas predicate satellites do not:

(103) The event of John's travelling took place
      in Europe
      last summer
      frequently
      although he was ill
      because he hadn't had a holiday for years...

(104) The event of John's travelling took place
      *to Italy
      *by train
      *for Mary...

Again, these differences can be interpreted as reflecting the higher degree of
independence of σ_2 satellites with respect to the content of the predication.

3.3. Proposition (σ_3) vs. Illocutionary (σ_4) satellites

The difference between proposition satellites and illocutionary satellites resides
in the fact that the latter specify or modify the illocutionary force of an
utterance, whereas the former modify the propositional content. Since
propositions are within the scope of the illocution, we may expect that the
differences between the two groups of satellites center around their behaviour
with respect to the illocution. That this is indeed the case can be derived from
some of the features which Greenbaum (1969) lists for illocutionary satellites:
(i) They may appear in front of questions:

(105) Seriously, how do I look?

(ii) Many may appear in front of imperative and optative clauses:

(106) Honestly, let's not tell him about it

In contrast, proposition satellites never occur in these positions:

(107) *Hopefully, how do I look?

(108) *Probably, let's not tell him about it

Proposition satellites in general presuppose the speaker's positive commitment to the truth of the proposition he presents. These satellites are therefore largely restricted to declarative sentences. They can be said to operate inside the illocutionary layer. Illocutionary satellites, on the other hand, operate outside the illocutionary layer, which is shown in their relative freedom to occur with any kind of sentence type.

3.4. Negation

As we have already seen in 3.1.3, predicate and predication satellites (σ_1 and σ_2 respectively) fall within the scope of the tense and (objective) modality operators as well as within the scope of (sentence) negation. In this section we examine more in detail the behaviour of the four satellite classes with respect to negation and show that negation provides useful criteria for distinguishing the different subcategories.

Before dealing with the behaviour of the satellites proper it is useful for our discussion to make some observations about the interpretation of negation in sentences without satellites. In doing so, we use some elementary concepts of model-theoretical semantics. Compare:

(109) a.   Mary danced
      b.   Mary did not dance

In model-theoretical semantics (109a) is usually interpreted as follows: the referent denoted by *Mary* ([Mary]) belongs to the extension of the predicate *dance* ([dance]): in other words, [Mary] 0 [dance]. The negation (109b) indicates that Mary does not belong to the extension of the predicate *dance*: [Mary] $\emptyset$ [dance]. For sentences containing a two place predicate:

(110) a.   Mary hit the cat
      b.   Mary did not hit the cat

the interpretation is that in (110a) the pair <[Mary], [cat]> belongs to the extension of the predicate *hit*, that is the set of all the pairs of individuals between which a hit-relation holds: <[Mary], [cat]> 0 [hit]. Sentence (110b) can be interpreted as <[Mary], [cat]> $\emptyset$ [hit], that is, the pair consisting of the referents of *Mary* and *the cat* does not belong to the set of pairs between which a hit-relation holds.

For our discussion it is important that while in nuclear predications sentence negation affects the relationship between the argument(s) and the predicate, this is not the case in sentences containing a predicate satellite (core predications). Compare:

(111) a.   John died of pneumonia
      b.   John did not die of pneumonia

In (111b), at least in the dominant reading[16], John's dying is not negated. Rather, the negation affects the relationship between the nuclear predication (*John died*) as a whole and the Cause satellite. In (111a) the addressee is invited to accept the truth of *John died* and to accept pneumonia as being the cause of this event. In (111b) the addressee can safely admit that John died, but the speaker blocks the possibility to ascribe John's death to pneumonia. (111a) can be interpreted as: the SoA denoted by the nuclear predication ('John died') belongs to the set of events which are caused by pneumonia, whereas (111b) states that the SoA ('John died') is not a member of the set of events which are caused by pneumonia.

The other subcategories of predicate satellites can all be interpreted in the same way. For example:

(112) Mary did not dance elegantly

Here the negation indicates that the predicate *elegant(ly)* cannot be applied to the nuclear predication (*Mary danced*), or equivalently: the SoA denoted by *Mary danced* is not a member of the set of SoAs to which the predicate *elegant* can be truthfully applied. The interpretation of (113) is analogous to that given for (111b) and (112):

(113) John did not accompany Mary as her lawyer

Here the interpretation is that John accompanied Mary, but not as her lawyer. As in (111b) and (112) the negation does not affect the nuclear predication, but the predicate satellite *as her lawyer*.

In all the examples discussed so far the predicate satellites can be semantically interpreted as (second-order) predicates which take the nuclear predication of the sentence as their argument.[17] It is a general property of such predicate satellites that they are primarily affected by negation.

Let us now turn to the second category distinguished above, that of predication (σ_2) satellites. The point to be examined here is whether the behaviour of this type of satellite differs from that of predicate satellites. Compare the following examples:

> (114) a.   John arrived at eight o'clock
> b.   John did not arrive at eight o'clock
> c.   At eight o'clock John did not arrive

The most striking difference with predicate satellites is that the (nuclear) predication can now be taken to be negated, i.e. fall within the scope of the negation: (114b) may mean that John arrived but that this event did not take place at eight o'clock, or that there was no event of John's arriving taking place at eight o'clock at all (the latter is the only interpretation of (114c)). In 3.2.2 it was already pointed out that predication satellites have greater freedom of occurrence than predicate satellites; they can be placed in front of the nuclear predication, in which case they do not fall within the scope of the negation in negative sentences such as (114c). A different intonational pattern may have the same effect in sentences such as (114b).

The fact that in (114) there are two negative sentences that correspond with one positive sentence has raised the question whether the positive sentence is structurally ambiguous. Kraak (1966: 156ff), for example, explains the existence of the two readings of the negative sentence by admitting that the corresponding positive sentence is structurally ambiguous. This ambiguity would be due to a different distribution of Focus.[18] Consider such a pair as:

> (115) a.   *Fred reisde   met de   trein vanwege   de   regen*
> Fred travelled with the   train because.of the   rain
> "Fred travelled by train because of the rain"
> b.   *Fred reisde   niet met de   trein vanwege   de   regen*
> Fred travelled not with the   train because.of the   rain
> "Fred did not travel by train because of the rain"

Sentence (115b) can be interpreted in at least two ways: (i) Fred travelled by train, but not because of the rain; (ii) Fred did not travel by train and did so because of the rain. Kraak admits two other readings: (iii) the 'strong' one we mentioned in note 16 ('Fred did not travel at all, not by train and not because of the rain') and (iv) one in which Fred travelled but not by train and not because of the rain. In our opinion these two interpretations, and especially the latter one, are highly improbable.

The analysis we propose is as follows. We adopt for (115a) the following structure:

(116)   extended predication

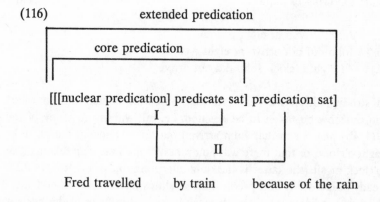

Fred travelled   by train   because of the rain

The readings (i) and (ii) of (115b) correspond to the negation of the relations II and I, respectively. In the latter case it is said that Fred does not travel by train. If relation II is negated, it is claimed that Fred travels by train, but not because of the rain. The nuclear predication refers to a SoA ('Fred travelled') which is said to belong to the SoAs which take place by train. The core predication refers to a SoA ('he travelled by train') which is said to pertain to the set of SoAs which take place (or do not take place) because of the rain. We agree with Kraak that the different possible interpretations of (115a) and (115b) correspond with different Focus assignments. (115b) could be used to answer the following questions:

(117) a.   By which means of transport did Fred travel because of the rain?
            I do not know, but he did not travel by train.
      b.   Because of what did Fred (did Fred not) travel by train?
            Because of the rain.

The reason why predication satellites can combine with a positive or negative core predication may be that circumstances expressed by predication satellites such as *because of the rain* can influence somebody's behaviour in a positive or a negative sense: both cancelling activities which were previously planned and doing things which were not planned because the rain creates a new situation. In the case of predicate satellites it is more difficult to imagine how these might specify something which would deny the validity of the nuclear predication. Consider an Instrument satellite such as that in:

(118)((He did not kill the duckling) with an axe)

Such a construction can hardly be interpreted as 'he used the axe for not killing the duckling'. This shows that *with an axe*, as a predicate satellite, is an integral part of the specification of the SoA, rather than providing some kind of setting for the SoA as already established in the predication.

All predication satellites combine with negative or positive core predications, but also with positive or negative nuclear predications:

(119) a. Mary left because of the rain
b. Mary did not leave because of the rain

Depending on the distribution of Focus, (119a) may answer the following questions:

(120) a. What did Mary do because of the rain
(**left** is Focus in (119a))
b. Because of what did Mary leave?
(**because of the rain** is Focus)

In the same way (119b) can answer the following questions:

(121) a. What did Mary not do because of the rain?
(She did not leave)
b. Because of what did Mary leave?
(I don't know, she did not leave because of the rain)

In these cases either the nuclear predication (or at least its predicate) carries Focus, or the predication satellite. In core predications the nuclear predication (or its predicate, or one of its arguments) never carries Focus.

As far as proposition satellites and illocutionary satellites are concerned we can be brief. Neither of them can fall within the scope of negation, but the (nuclear, core or extended) predication they combine with can be positive or negative (with the corresponding Focus distributions). (Cf. Quirk et al. 1985.) For example:

(122) a. In my opinion we should do it/should not do it
b. We should not do it in my opinion

(122b) does not allow the interpretation that we should do it, but not in my opinion. In the same way, illocutionary satellites (*frankly*, *since you ask me*) cannot fall within the scope of the negation. The same explanation can be given for the fact that proposition satellites such as *possibly*, *probably* do not have negative counterparts (**impossibly*, **improbably*).

From these facts we can conclude that negation can be used as a criterion for distinguishing predicate satellites from predication satellites: the latter combine with negated predications, the former do not. The two satellite types have in common that they can both themselves be negated. Negation can also be used to distinguish proposition and illocutionary satellites from the rest (they never fall within the scope of the negation), but negation cannot serve as a criterion to distinguish between proposition satellites and illocutionary satellites since they show the same behaviour with respect to negation.

4. Other parameters

In the preceding sections we have tried to demonstrate that the position satellites occupy within the hierarchical structure of the clause to a large extent determines their behaviour. The hosting layer of the clause was the parameter along which we tried to arrive at a typology of satellites. This is not the only parameter that is relevant for such a typology, and we will discuss two more in this section. The first of these concerns the internal complexity of satellites. The second concerns the restrictive/non-restrictive opposition.

4.1. The internal structure of satellites

Satellites can have different degrees of internal complexity, as can easily be demonstrated by means of the following examples:

(123) Mary danced **beautifully**

(124) Mary danced **because she didn't want to talk to John**

The complexity of the Manner satellite *beautifully* in (123) is that of a mere predicate, the complexity of the Reason satellite *because she didn't want to talk to John* in (124) is that of a finite sentence.

Degrees of *internal* complexity of satellites can be defined in terms of the same hierarchical clause model (see 2.1) that was used earlier to define the satellite types in terms of what may be called their *external* complexity, the layer of the clause they attach to.

The construction with the highest degree of complexity is the whole clause structure. It contains a construction with a lower degree of complexity: a proposition. This proposition again contains a construction with a lower degree of complexity: a predication. Within the predication one finds two units of still lower complexity: predicates and terms. By peeling off layers from the hierarchical model of the clause one encounters all types of construction that can provide the structure of a satellite. It may be useful to give a formal definition of the several constructions mentioned here:

(125) clause	$(E_I: [ILL (S) (A) (X_I: [etc.] (X_J))] (E_I))$
proposition	$(X_I: [(e_I: [pred_\beta (x_I: [etc.] (x_I))] (e_I))] (X_I))$
predication	$(e_I: [pred_\beta (x_I: pred_N (x_I))] (e_I))$
term	$(x_I: pred_N (x_I))$
predicate	$pred_\beta$

A *predicate* designates a property or relation, a *term* an individual, a *predication* designates a SoA, a *proposition* a potential fact, and a *clause* designates a speech act. Not only are these different layers, both formally and semantically, relevant for the construction of main clauses, they also constitute a typology of emdedded constructions.[19]

This typology can be applied to the satellite types we have been concerned with. Consider the following series of examples:

(126) John met Peter **repeatedly**

(127) John met Peter **on the platform**

(128) John met Peter **after leaving the train**

(129) John met Peter **because he wanted to talk to him**

The satellites in (126)-(129) have all been classified as predication satellites (σ_2). They do not differ with respect to the layer that hosts them, but they do differ with respect to their internal complexity. The Frequency satellite *repeatedly* in (126) has the internal complexity of a predicate. It designates a property (repeated) of the SoA described in the main clause. The Location satellite *on the platform* in (127) has the internal complexity of a term. It designates an *individual* (the platform), on which the SoA described in the main clause is situated. The Time satellite *after leaving the train* in (128) has the internal complexity of a predication. It designates a SoA (John's leaving the train) with respect to which the SoA described in the main clause is located in time. The Reason satellite *because he wanted to talk to him* in (129) has the internal complexity of a proposition. It designates the propositional content ('I want to talk to Peter') that motivated the occurrence of the SoA described in the main clause.

Just as we can distinguish between several types of predication satellites by looking at their internal complexity, so can we distinguish between several types of predicate satellites, proposition satellites, and illocutionary satellites. The following table gives an overview of the possibilities by cross-classifying satellites according to the two parameters discussed so far: external structure (ext) and internal structure (int). Note that this table is not intended to give an exhaustive listing of all satellites discussed in the preceding sections, but to give one illustrative example of each satellite type that results from combining the two parameters.

(130) Internal and external structure of satellites

ext \ int	$pred_\beta$	x	e	X
$pred_\beta$	Manner	Beneficiary	Force	--
e	Frequency	Location	Circumstance	Reason
X	Attitude	Source	Evidence	Motivation
ILL	Manner	Beneficiary	Condition	Reason

Apart from providing a second parameter for the classification of satellites, the specification of the internal complexity of a satellite predicts the kinds of distinctions that can be expressed within it, such as (in)definiteness in the case of satellites that have the internal complexity of a term, temporal distinctions in the case of satellites that have the internal complexity of a predication, and propositional attitudes in the case of satellites that have the internal complexity of a proposition.

4.2. Restrictive and non-restrictive satellites

Sometimes a distinction is made between restrictive and nonrestrictive satellites (e.g. Rutherford 1970; Quirk et al. 1985; Hannay and Vester 1987; Hengeveld 1989). Rutherford (1970) as a matter of fact uses these terms to make the distinction between our σ_2 and σ_3/σ_4 satellites. Most of his tests have already been discussed in 3.1 above. Quirk et al. (1985) only devote one paragraph to the topic, since, as they say, the distinction largely overlaps with their distinctions between adjuncts, disjuncts, etc. The opposition restrictive vs. nonrestrictive is, in their opinion, only relevant for their adjuncts (our σ_1 and σ_2 satellites). In fact all their examples of nonrestrictive adjuncts are of the σ_2 type. Disjuncts (σ_3 and σ_4 satellites) are necessarily nonrestrictive. In Hannay and Vester (1987) the examples with either a restrictive or a nonrestrictive adverbial clause are all of the σ_2 type; the same applies to Hengeveld (1989).

The interaction between satellite type and restrictiveness may thus be represented as follows:

(131)   restrictive   nonrestrictive

σ_1 $\pi_2 e_1$: [pred x_1 x_2 σ_1] (e_1)   -

σ_2 $\pi_2 e_1$: [predication]: σ_2 (e_1) $\pi_2 e_1$: [predication] (e_1), σ_2 (e_2)

σ_3 - $\pi_3 X_1$: [ext pred] (X_1), σ_3 (X_2)

σ_4 - $\pi_4 E_1$: [proposition] (E_1), σ_4 (E_2)

Predicate satellites (σ_1) necessarily contribute to the specification of the SoA: they are necessarily restrictive. Predication satellites may either restrict the nature of the SoA through providing it with time/space coordinates, or provide additional information to the SoA as already defined. Higher-level satellites necessarily provide additional information, pertaining to the speaker's evaluation of the (nature or occurrence of the) SoA, or to the communicative intentions with which the SoA is presented to the addressee. This is in accordance with the fact that the task of *representing* the SoA ends at the level of the extended predication.

The distinction restrictive vs. nonrestrictive can also be interpreted as a difference in scope: restrictive satellites fall under the scope of the corresponding operators; nonrestrictive satellites do not fall under the scope of these operators. We thus find confirmation for the status of the negative operator discussed in 3.4 above: predicate satellites are necessarily within the scope of negation, predication satellites may be within or outside the scope of the negation, and higher-level satellites necessarily take the negation in their scope.

5. Conclusion

We argued in this paper that the layered structure of the clause, as proposed in Hengeveld (1989), provides a natural framework for the subcategorization of satellites. On mainly semantic grounds, we made a fourfold distinction between:

(132) a. **Predicate satellites (σ_1):**
Predicate satellites specify additional properties of the SoA desiganted by the nuclear predication.
b. **Predication satellites (σ_2):**
Predication satellites serve to localize the SoA as defined in the core predication with respect to temporal, local, and cognitive dimensions.
c. **Propositional satellites (σ_3):**
Propositional satellites specify the attitude of the speaker vis-à-vis the fact designated by the proposition.
d. **Illocutionary satellites (σ_4):**
Illocutionary satellites specify or modify the illocutionary force of the speech act in which the proposition is presented.

We then showed that this division into four layers correlates with a variety of differential coding and behavioural properties of satellites, and provides a natural place for many observations which have been made in the literature on adverbial constituents.

Negation was shown to interact in interesting ways with this layering of satellites. Finally, it was noted that satellites can be further subcategorized on the basis of their internal structure, and that the restrictive/non-restrictive contrast is distinctive only for predication satellites.

Many problems concerning the place of satellites in the layered model of the clause remain to be explored. For one thing, we have hardly touched the problem of the relations between different satellites at the same layer (e.g., the relations between Temporal and Local satellites, both predication satellites).

Also, certain theoretical issues have been left unresolved. For example, the question whether satellites can be analysed as predicates over the units which they take in their scope (as proposed in Vet 1986), or should be regarded as some type of modifiers different from predicators (as in Dik 1989).

In spite of these open ends, however, we believe that we have demonstrated that the layered clause model provides for a more adequate typology of satellites, and conversely, that the natural way in which a variety of distinctions can be captured in this conception of clause structure reinforces the validity of the clause model itself.

Notes

1. We are grateful to the editors of this volume for critical remarks which led to improvements of the text.

2. See Hengeveld (1989) for a more elaborate description of this model. The status of the illocutionary component in (4) is based on Hengeveld's analysis. Compare Dik (1989) for a slightly different view. In the present paper we take the layered structure of the clause as described here as given, and consider what implications this would have for the analysis of satellites. Obviously, the layered model itself is under discussion as well (see, for example, Bolkestein 1989).

3. Compare the distinctions made in Dik (1989).

4. Bolkestein (1989) argues that predications may contain temporal satellites without having a tense operator. This might lead to a reconsideration of the analysis presented here.

5. In Hengeveld (1989) a fifth satellite type is distinguished at the level of the clause, which is used in order to account for the expression of interclausal relations. We restrict ourselves to the level of the clause here.

6. Most of the definitions given in the following sections are taken from Dik (1989).

7. Combination of two spatial setting satellites is possible only when one of them specifies a subregion of the other, as in *in Rome on the Forum, in Amsterdam near the central station*, etc. These might well be analysed as internally complex single satellites.

8. For formal differences between Reason and Cause satellites in Latin, compare Pinkster (1988b) and Bolkestein (this vol.).

9. For the German data, see Bartsch (1972, 1976).

10. For discussion of this example, see Levinson (1983: 256).

11. This difference between *quoniam* on the one hand and *quod/quia* appears to be relevant only in classical literary Latin.

12. See Dik (1978) and the discussion in Dik (1989).

13.   Note that the verb takes the 'instrumental' voice when Subj is assigned to Temp. This is
      also reported for Kalagan.

14.   For general discussion of incorporation see Mardirussian (1975), Dik (1980), Anderson
      (1985).

15.   See Vester (1983) for what this implies for the relations between satellites of Manner,
      Cause, and Instrument, which in Latin can all be expressed in the ablative.

16.   It is sometimes admitted that sentences such as (112) have another, 'strong' reading,
      paraphraseable as: 'Mary did not dance elegantly, because she did not dance at all'. In this
      interpretation the negation does have the nuclear predication in its scope. This kind of
      reading, however, is quite exceptional in normal usage. We will return briefly to this point
      at the end of this section.

17.   In Vet (1986) it is argued that (certain) satellites can also be analysed as second-order
      predicates in the underlying structure of the clause. In Dik (1989) the satellites are as-
      sociated as modifiers or specifiers with the layer which they take in their scope. We leave
      this difference unresolved here, since it does not affect the main theme of this paper.

18.   On the interaction between negation and Focus, see also Bossuyt (1983).

19.   See Hengeveld (this vol.) and Bolkestein (this vol.) for applications of this typology.

References

Allerton, D.J. and A.Cruttenden
   1974   "English sentence adverbials: Their syntax and their intonation in British English".
          Lingua 44: 133-168.
   1978   "Syntactic, illocutionary, thematic and attitudinal factors in the intonation of adverbials".
          Journal of Pragmatics 2: 155-188.

Anderson, Stephen R.
   1985   "Typological distinctions in word formation". In T.Shopen (ed.), 3-56.

Auwera, J.Van der and L.Goossens (eds.)
   1987   *Ins and outs of the predication*. Dordrecht: Foris.

Bartsch, Renate
   1972   *Adverbialsemantik*. Frankfurt: Athenäum.
   1976   *The grammar of adverbials*. Amsterdam: North-Holland.

Barwise, J. and J.Perry
   1983   *Situations and attitudes*. Cambridge: MIT-Press.

Bell, Sarah J.
1983   "Advancements and ascensions in Cebuano". In D.M.Perlmutter (ed.), 143-218.

Bellert, I.
1977   "On semantic and distributional properties of sentential adverbs". *Linguistic Inquiry* 8: 337-351.

Bolkestein, A.Machtelt
1989   "Latin sentential complements from a functional grammar perspective". *Cahiers de l'Institut de Linguistique de Louvain* 15: 41-52.
fc.   "Causally related predications and the choice between parataxis an hypotaxis in Latin". In R.Coleman (ed.), *Papers from the 1987 international conference on Latin linguistics* (provisional title). Amsterdam: Benjamins.

Bolkestein, A.Machtelt, Casper De Groot and Lachlan Mackenzie (eds.)
1985a   *Syntax and pragmatics in functional grammar*. Dordrecht: Foris.
1985b   *Predicates and terms in functional grammar*. Dordrecht: Foris.

Bossuyt, Alain
1983   "Historical functional grammar: An outline of an integrated theory of language change". In S.C.Dik (ed.), 301-325.

Cole, Peter and Jerrold M.Sadock (eds.)
1977   *Syntax and semantics, vol.8: Grammatical relations*. New York: Academic Press.

Dik, Simon C.
1975   "The semantic representation of manner adverbials". In A.Kraak (ed.), *Linguistics in The Netherlands 1972-1973*. Assen: Van Gorcum, 96-121.
1978   *Functional grammar*. Amsterdam: North-Holland. (3rd printing: 1981, Dordrecht: Foris).
1980   *Studies in functional grammar*. London: Academic Press.
1985   "Formal and semantic adjustment of derived constructions". In A.M.Bolkestein et al. (eds.) 1985b, 1-28.
1989   *The theory of functional grammar, pt.1: The structure of the clause*. Dordrecht: Foris.

Dik, Simon C. (ed.)
1983   *Advances in functional grammar*. Dordrecht: Foris.

Dryer, Matthew S.
1983   "Indirect objects in Kinyarwanda revisited". In D.M.Perlmutter (ed.), 129-140.

Gary, Judith Olmsted and Edward L.Keenan
1977   "On collapsing grammatical relations in universal grammar". In P.Cole and J.M.Sadock (eds.), 83-120.

Greenbaum, Sidney
1969   *Studies in English adverbial usage*. London: Longmans.

Hannay, Michael and Elseline Vester
  1987 "Non-restrictive relatives and the representation of complex sentences". In J.Van der Auwera and L.Goossens (eds.), 39-52.

Harder, Peter
  1989 *Tense, semantics and functional grammar*. Working Papers in Functional Grammar 30. (Revised version published in this volume.)

Hengeveld, K.
  1989 "Layers and operators in functional grammar". *Journal of Linguistics* 25: 127-157. (Earlier version published as: Working Papers in Functional Grammar 27.)

Kahrel, Peter
  1985 *Some aspects of derived intransitivity*. Working Papers in Functional Grammar 4.

Keenan, Edward L.
  1972 "Relative clause formation in Malagasy (and some related and not so related languages)". In P.M.Peranteau et al. (eds.), 169-189.
  1976 "Towards a universal definition of 'subject'. In C.Li (ed.), 303-333.

Kisseberth, Charles W. and Mohammad Imam Abasheikh
  1977 "The object relationship in Chimwi:ni, a Bantu language". In P.Cole and J.M.Sadock (eds.), 179-218.

Kraak, A.
  1966 *Negatieve zinnen: Een methodologische en grammatische analyse*. Hilversum: De Haan.

Levinson, Stephen C.
  1983 *Pragmatics*. Cambridge: Cambridge UP.

Li, Charles N. (ed.)
  1976 *Subject and topic*. New York: Academic Press.

Mackenzie, J.L. and M.Hannay
  1982 "Prepositional predicates and focus constructions in functional grammar". *Lingua* 56: 43-57.

Mardirussian, G.
  1975 "Noun incorporation in universal grammar". *Papers from the Regional Meeting of the Chicago Linguistic Society* 11: 383-389.

Metz, G.
  1988 *Het Griekse passivum: Semantische en pragmatische aspecten van subject toekenning in het Grieks*. MA-Thesis, Free University of Amsterdam.

Mirikitani, Leatrice
1972 *Kapampangan syntax*. Oceanic Linguistics Publication 10.

Mulder, H.
1988 "Non-accusative second arguments of two-place verbs in Ancient Greek". In A.Rijksbaron et al. (eds.), 219-236.

Peranteau, Paul M. et al. (eds.)
1972 *The Chicago which hunt: Papers from the relative clause festival*. Chicago: Chicago Linguistic Society.

Perlmutter, David M. (ed.)
1983 *Studies in relational grammar vol.1*. Chicago: University of Chicago Press.

Perlmutter, David M. and Paul M.Postal
1983 "Towards a universal characterization of passivization". In D.M.Perlmutter (ed.), 3-29.

Pinkster, Harm
1984 *Latijnse syntaxis en semantiek*. Amsterdam: Grüner.
1988a "Non-accusative second arguments of two-place verbs in Latin". *Cuadernos de Filología Clásica* 21: 235-245.
1988b *Lateinische Syntax und Semantik*. Tübingen: Francke Verlag.

Platt, John T. and Heidi K.Platt
1972 "Orientation of manner adverbials". Paper, Monash University.

Quirk, R., S.Greenbaum, G.Leech and J.Svartvik
1972 *A grammar of contemporary English*. London: Longman.
1985 *A comprehensive grammar of the English language*. London: Longman.

Rijksbaron, Albert
1976 *Temporal and causal conjunctions in Ancient Greek*. Amsterdam: Hakkert.
1986 *The pragmatics and semantics of conditional and temporal clauses: Some evidence from Dutch and Classical Greek*. Working Papers in Functional Grammar 13.

Rijksbaron, A., H.A.Mulder and G.C.Wakker (eds.)
1988 *In the footsteps of Raphael Kühner*. Amsterdam: Gieben.

Risselada, Rodie
1987 "Voice in Ancient Greek: Reflexives and passives". In J.Van der Auwera and L.Goossens (eds.), 123-136.

Rutherford, W.E.
1970 "Some observations concerning subordinate clauses in English". *Language* 46: 97-115.

Shopen, Timothy (ed.)
   1985   *Language typology and syntactic description, vol.3: Grammatical categories and the lexicon*.
          Cambridge: Cambridge UP.

Vester, Elseline
   1983   *Instrument and manner expressions in Latin*. Assen: Van Gorcum.
   1988   "Enkele opmerkingen over de plaatsing van temporele bijzinnen". In A.M.Van Erp
          Taalman Kip, D.den Hengst and J.J.L.Smolenaars (eds.), *Propemptikon:Afscheidsbundel
          W.J.H.F. Kegel*. Amsterdam: University of Amsterdam, 116-120.

Vet, Co
   1985   "Passive, reflexive, and causative predicate formation in French". In A.M.Bolkestein et
          al. (eds.) 1985b, 49-69.
   1986   *A pragmatic approach to tense in functional grammar*. Working Papers in Functional
          Grammar 16.
   fc.   "Les constructions causatives et réfléchies en français". *Actes du XVIIIe Congrès
          International de Linguistique et Philologie Romane*.

Sentential Complements in Functional Grammar: Embedded Predications, Propositions, Utterances in Latin

A. Machtelt Bolkestein
University of Amsterdam

0. Introduction[1]

Hengeveld (1987, 1988, 1989a, b, this vol.) and Dik (1989, fc.) suggest that predicates which govern sentential complements, such as English *to say, to believe, to know, to regret, to see, to be probable* etc. should be subcategorized according to the type of entity represented by their sentential complements. These different types of entities supposedly correspond to the various layers distinguished in the hierarchically organized layered structure ascribed to utterances: the basic distinction is that between (from the bottom up) predication, proposition and utterance (or clause). This threefold distinction is assumed to be universally relevant, for example with respect to explaining differences in coding regularities and/or behavioural properties of the various types of complements.

In this paper I will, on the basis of a discussion of data from classical Latin, investigate to what extent the distinctions which appear to be relevant for the description of independent sentences are indeed relevant (necessary and sufficient) in order to account for the systematic differences in coding and/or behaviour found to exist between sentential complements as well. This question can obviously only be answered if, on the basis of clear criteria, we are able to determine unambiguously with what type of entity we are dealing in the case of specific matrix predicates. This will turn out to be quite problematic in certain cases. This implies that the question of possible criteria (i.e. how to operationalize the notions involved) will in fact form the bulk of this paper. The answer to the first part of my question (are the distinctions involved necessary) will turn out to be positive, that to the second (are they sufficient) will prove negative.

Before discussing several classes of embedding predicates in Latin and some problems they raise, I will briefly give some more details concerning the nature of the layered structure alluded to.

1. Layers and complements

In recent publications in Functional Grammar (FG) (Hengeveld 1987, 1988, 1989a, b, this vol.; Dik this vol., 1989: ch.12, fc.) the structure underlying independent sentences is analyzed as consisting of (at least) four hierarchically ordered layers, each of which represents a different 'type' of entity in the sense of the distinction between 'different order' entities presented in Lyons (1977). The highest, outermost layer (which might be called a fourth order entity, not as such distinguished in Lyons) is that of the sentence as product of a speech act, an utterance exchanged or exchangeable between two speech participants in some communicative situation. This layer (the 'clause' layer, in a formal representation of the underlying structure represented by the variable E) contains a so-called 'propositional' layer which represents the sentence as a possible fact, a content which may have a positive or negative truth-value. This propositional layer (representing a third order entity, symbolized by the variable X) in its turn contains a lower layer, that of the sentence as referring to a State of Affairs (SoA), an event entity situated in time and space (Vet 1986). This layer is called that of the ('extended') predication (symbolized by the variable e). This extended predication in its turn contains a so-called 'core' predication, which represents a potential (or virtual, sometimes also called 'dynamic') SoA. The core predication, lacking tense and Locational and Temporal satellites, does not in itself actually refer to a specific event situated in time or space. Minimally it consists of a nucleus formed by a predicate plus its required argument terms (the latter symbolized by the variable x).[2]

Each of the layers distinguished may be expanded by its own type of satellites (see Dik et al. this vol.): in the case of the two outermost layers E and X, which represent the sentence in its interpersonal function, such satellites would, for example, correspond to various types of disjunct adverbials in other approaches, such as Quirk et al. (1985). Furthermore, each layer possesses its own type of operators. The utterance layer E contains, for example, those operators which modify, mitigate or reinforce the basic illocutionary force of the sentence (see Risselada 1990 and Vet this vol. for two different ways to account for some pragmatic phenomena on this level). The propositional layer X includes, among other, those operators which express the speaker's evaluative attitude towards the propositional content, or the degree to which he commits himself to the truth of the proposition involved. And, finally, on the level of the extended predication layer e we find operators such as those responsible for verbal tense, which situate the SoA in time, and operators for objective modality. Operators of a particular level have satellites of that level within their scope; and operators of a higher level have operators and satellites of a lower level within their scope.

Sentence type in FG is viewed as a grammaticalization of the basic, universally relevant illocutionary functions (ILL) declarative (DECL), imperative (IMP) and interrogative (INTERR). Dik (1989) considers such illocutionary qualifications to have the status of operators and to belong to the highest level, that of the sentence-as-utterance. Hengeveld (1989a: 148) on the other hand speaks of the proposition as being an argument in a basic illocutionary frame: in this view ILL itself does not have the status of an utterance operator. (I will return to this difference below.)[3]

For more discussion of the hierarchically ordered layered structure I refer to the papers mentioned and various contributions in this volume. A discussion of the relevance of distinguishing at least two different level satellites in the area of causal relations between clauses in classical Latin, on the basis of various differences in coding and in behaviour between the two types of causal satellites is to be found in Bolkestein (fc.). Pinkster (1984, 1988) gives a survey of various other disjunct satellite types in classical Latin.

Both Hengeveld (1989a: 144ff, 156) and Dik (1989, fc.) suggest that the distinctions set out above are relevant not only for a satisfactory description of independent sentences, but for a description of sentential complements as well. This claim supposedly holds not only in the case of finite and infinitival complements, but also in the case of other constructions which represent higher order arguments, such as various types of nominalizations and participial and gerundial constructions.

In other words, such complements may represent different types of entities, in the sense of different layers of the hierarchically ordered underlying structure, namely utterances, propositions, or predications respectively. The necessity of furthermore distinguishing between extended predications with and without tense for a satisfactory description of complement types, on the basis of behavioural or coding differences between them, is not discussed in Hengeveld (1988), but the need to do so will be demonstrated below. The type of embedded entity appears to be determined by the specific semantic properties of the governing predicate, which, consequently, must be specified for these properties in the lexicon.

In this paper I will show that the distribution of different level operators and satellites provides the main criterion that enables us to distinguish between complement types: if a complement contains a higher level element, then it must be an entity of that level itself. Furthermore, tense of the embedded predicate and pronominalization patterns may also offer evidence with respect to the status of a complement, as we shall see.

2. Data from Latin complements

The system of Latin complement clauses exhibits several phenomena which offer support for the relevance of distinguishing certain basically different types of complements, which can be related to the different layers of the layered structure described in 1. First I will discuss evidence provided by the behaviour of the class of verba dicendi or predicates of speech (discussed in somewhat different terms in Bolkestein 1976a, b, 1977, 1986). I will argue that ILL is present in their complements, even though they are not utterance-entities. Subsequently I will treat complements of verba affectuum or verbs of emotion (Bolkestein 1981b, 1986), which pose a problem of classification by perhaps being able to govern both propositions (without ILL) and predications. Furthermore, complements of the subclass of verbs of happening will be discussed: they demonstrate the need for distinguishing factive predications from non-factive predications. A survey of the array of syntactic constructions which are possible for higher order complements in Latin may be found in Pinkster (1984, 1988), who does not, however, systematically treat the question what possible semantic differences underlie the various formal realizations.[4]

2.1. Evidence from verbs of speech: E vs. X plus ILL

In traditional grammars of Latin (for example Kühner-Stegmann 1912; Szantyr 1965) it is generally acknowledged that for a certain subclass of verbs of speech it makes sense to differentiate complements referring to an order and complements referring to a statement, or, in our terminology, between IMP and DECL complements. This distinction (sometimes formulated in terms of different meanings of the governing predicate, and sometimes in terms of different meanings of the complements itself) is useful in order to account for differences in behaviour between the two types and for the differences in construction which correlate with this. Thus the verb dicere "to say" may govern two constructions, an infinitival so-called Accusativus cum Infinitivo (AcI) clause and a finite clause introduced by the subordinating conjunction ut and the verb in the subjunctive mood. The two types of complement with dicere are illustrated in (1a) and (1b) respectively:

(1)   a.   *Milites*   *abisse*   *dixit*
            soldiers.ACC leave.INF.PF say.PF.3SG
            "He said that the soldiers had left"
       b.   *Dixit*   *ut*   *milites*   *abirent*
            say.PF.3SG   SUB soldiers.NOM   leave.SUBJ.3PL
            "He said that the soldiers should leave"

The two are clearly not synonymous. Describing the difference in terms of a difference in sentence type of the complement clauses is justified on account of the fact that the first type of clause behaves like an independent declarative sentences in certain crucial aspects (which I will not illustrate in detail here - see Bolkestein 1976a, b): it may for example contain truth value specifying and other attitudinal adverbials, and it is not sensitive to any semantic restrictions, e.g. on the tense operator of the predicate of the complement (perfect tense in (1a)), or on the controllability of the SoA designated. The second type of complement, illustrated in (1b), shares all its properties with independent imperative sentences: the requirement that the SoA be controllable for the addressee, restrictions on tense, incompatibility with certain types of (disjunct) adverbials and compatibility with some particles which occur in independent imperative sentences as well (see also Pinkster 1984, 1988). The restrictions on tense and on the occurrence of various proposition level disjuncts can be accounted for if we assume that IMP sentences and clauses do not contain a propositional layer at all, but only a predicational one (Hengeveld 1989a: 154, 1989b: 244).

The variation illustrated in (1) is shared by a number of verbs of speech in Latin, but not by all. Thus verbs like *negare* "deny, say that not" or *confiteri* "to admit, confess" occur only with DECL complements (in the AcI), whereas verbs like *imperare* and *iubere* "to order" occur only with IMP ones (both in the AcI and as *ut*-clause), as an investigation of the semantic properties of the complements summed up above would show. See (2)-(4):

(2)   a.   *Milites*   *abisse*   *negabat*
            soldiers.ACC leave.INF.PF deny.IMPF.3SG
            "He denied that the soldiers had left"
       b.   **Negabat*   *ut*   *milites*   *abirent*   (cf. (1b))
            deny.IMPF.3SG   SUB soldiers.NOM   leave.SUBJ.IMPF.3PL

(3) a. *Imperavit   ut   milites   abirent*
        order.PF.3SG SUB soldiers.NOM   leave.SUBJ.IMPF.3PL
        "He ordered that the soldiers should leave"

    b. *Milites   *abisse*   *imperavit*   (cf. (1a))
        soldiers.ACC   leave.INF.PF order.PF.3SG

(4) *Milites*   *abire*   *imperavit*
    soldiers.ACC leave.INF.PR order.PF.3SG
    "He ordered that the soldiers should leave"

As far as the relation between construction (coding) and meaning (sentence type, basic illocutionary function) of the complements is concerned, the above examples show that there is a certain correlation, although this is not simply a matter of one-to-one correspondence. On the one hand, the AcI construction is reserved for declarative complements in the case of the neutral class which allows for both DECL and IMP complements, such as *dicere*, and it is the only construction found in the case of the subclass represented by *negare* "to deny" (in other words, there are no verbs of speech in Latin with which DECL complements may have the form of *ut* clauses). On the other hand, the IMP clauses governed by the subclass to which *imperare* "to order" belongs (which never governs DECL clauses) may have the form not only of *ut* clauses (as to be expected), but also of AcI constructions (as (4) illustrates). Leaving interrogative complements out of consideration, this means that the picture of the relation between form and meaning in the case of verbs of speech in Latin may be visualized as in (5) (cf. Bolkestein 1976a):

(5)

subclass		sentence-type complement	form complement
I	*negare* "to deny"	DECL	AcI
II	*dicere* "to say"	DECL	AcI
		IMP	*ut*
III	*imperare* "to order"	IMP	AcI/*ut*

Thus, as (5) shows, within the semantic class of verbs of speech there is a partial relation between coding and underlying properties, due to the fact that DECL complements are never coded as *ut* clauses. And both coding and behavioural properties show that it makes sense to distinguish the complements of such matrix predicates according to their basic illocutionary function (ILL) as DECL or IMP (and of course INTERR, here left out of account).

In Bolkestein (1986) it was therefore suggested that embedded predications with such matrix verbs should be specified as representing 'speech', perhaps by means of a term operator specifying the type of entity which the embedded clause represents. Within the 'layered structure' account we could reformulate this by stating that complements of verbs of speech represent the highest order entity, including a basic ILL. At the same time, this tells us something about the status of ILL in the layered structure as a whole, in view of some other restrictions which manifest themselves in the case of such complements.

Hengeveld (1988, 1989a: 147) argues that verbs of speech may govern two different types of complements: when they introduce direct speech they govern entities of the highest layer (in other words, utterances), as in (6a), and when they govern indirect speech, as in (6b), they are taken to govern entities with the status of a proposition:

(6) a. He said: "I will come"
     b. He said that he would come

It is, of course, necessary to differentiate the complements in (6a) and (6b) (I treat the direct speech in (6a) as a complement in spite of its having the internal properties of an independent sentence), since indirect speech can certainly not contain all 'extra-clausal' material which is possible for direct speech, as is shown in (7):

(7) a. *John said that now/well, Peter had left
     b. *John said that yes, but Peter had left
     c. *John requested him to come on, leave

In Dutch, the list of expressions excluded from indirect speech includes various types of comparable sentence starters and interjections such as *nee, nou* "no, well", *nou, eh* "well, eh", *(ja) maar* "(yes) but", evaluative expressions such as *fijn* "great", or *jammer* "a pity", attention drawing expressions such as *kijk* "look", and curses like *Jezus*, etc. In Latin too not all direct speech material may occur in the corresponding indirect speech constructions. This includes the particle introducing unfulfillable wishes (*utinam*), concessive statements (*sane*), vocatives and other attention drawing expressions such as *ecce* "look", and several idiomatic expressions making explicit or mitigating IMP (*sis, sodes, amabo*, all

78 A. MACHTELT BOLKESTEIN

meaning something like "please" and *age* "come on").[5]

Yet, as argued above the data from Latin demonstrate that the basic illocutionary functions DECL and IMP are present in complements which represent
indirect speech. This implies that this distinction should not be situated (as
proposed in Dik 1989) as an operator on the highest (the sentence as speech
product) layer of the underlying structure (on which - or above which -
presumably extra-clausal elements such as *now, well, yes, but* and *come on*
figure), but at another level below that, as implied in Hengeveld (1988: 22, 24).
Otherwise we would have to assume that indirect speech complements represent
the same type of entity as direct speech complements do.

On the other hand, in Latin and in other languages indirect speech
complements may well contain other disjunct expressions, not only some which
presumably should be analyzed as satellites of the propositional level, but also
some which should be analyzed as belonging to the utterance level. Thus, DECL
complements may contain expressions specifying subjective epistemic modality
such as modal verbs (*must* in (8c)) or adverbs (*surely* in (8a)), which are
analyzed as belonging to the propositional level, and other disjuncts, such as
evaluating adverbials (cf. (8b)). Moreover, both DECL and IMP clauses may
contain certain types of *if-* and *since*-clauses (cf. (8c)), which to my opinion
should be analyzed as satellites on the illocutionary level (Bolkestein fc.; Dik
1989: ch.12; Dik et al. this vol.):

(8) a.   John said that surely Peter had left
     b.   John said that fortunately Peter had left
     c.   John said that, since/if the car had gone, Peter must have left

In Latin, causal clauses introduced by *quoniam* "since" (which are more or less
the equivalent of English *since* clauses) should be analyzed as belonging to the
highest level of the layered structure (Bolkestein fc.), on the basis of the fact
that such clauses (i) cannot be focalized, (ii) are outside the scope of subjective
epistemic modality (like the *since* clause within the complement clause in (8c)),
and (iii) are outside the scope of the basic illocutionary force. They may be
used to explain the subjective epistemic modality of the main clause (cf. (9a))
or to justify its DECL or IMP illocutionary force (cf. (9b)) (see Dik this vol. on
the possibility of *if*-clauses to do so as well).[6] This implies that they are attached
to a higher level than that of the proposition. The above three claims do not
hold in the case of lower level causal satellites introduced by *quia* "because"
(cf. (9c)): sentence (9d) illustrates that causal satellites introduced by *quia* fall
within the scope of subjective epistemic modality, and should therefore be

analyzed as being attached to a lower layer than *quoniam* in (9a-b):

(9) a.   *Quae dea   est?   Bonam   esse   oportet quoniam*
          what goddess be.3SG good.ACC be.INF ought   since
          quidem   est   abs   te   dedicata
          PARTICLE   be.3SG   by   you   enshrined
          "What goddess is she? She must be benign since you enshrined
          her" (Cic. *Dom.* 110)

     b.   *Quoniam   nox   est,   discedite*
          since   night be.3SG leave.IMP
          "Since it is night, go home"

     c.   **Quia   est   abs   te   dedicata   bona esse   oportet*
          because   be.3SG by   you   enshrined good be.INF ought

     d.   *Istum equum emeris   oportet (ideo)   quia*
          that horse   buy.PF.2SG ought   therefore because
          pulcher   est
          beautiful be.PR.3SG
          "You must have bought that horse because it is beautiful"

It is not hard to find instances of Latin *quoniam* clauses within complements of
verbs of speech, justifying the basic declarative or imperative illocutionary force
of such complements. An example is the IMP complement of *rogare* "to request"
in (10):

(10) *Rogabat*   *ut*   *quoniam*   *sibi*   *non*   *subvenisset,*
     request.IMPF.3SG that since   REFL   not   help.PLPF.3SG
     mortem suam   ne   inultam   esse pateretur
     death his   not   unrevenged be   suffer.SUBJ.IMPF.3SG
     "He requested that, since he had not come to help him, he should not
     let his death be unrevenged" (see Cic. *Div.* 1, 27)

(Other instances are Cic. *S.Rosc.* 6, Caes. *Civ.* 3.25.2 and Plaut. *Truc.* 402). In
(10) the causal clause justifies the illocutionary act of requesting, and would
consequently have to be classified as a satellite attached to the highest layer
according to the analysis of Dik et al. (this vol.).

The conclusion to be drawn from the above observations is that, because
they can contain such illocutionary force justifying satellites, indirect speech
complements of verbs of speech represent entities *somewhere in between*
propositions plus basic ILL on the one hand and direct speech utterances on

the other. Further evidence in favour of this conclusion (which I will not further illustrate with Latin examples here) is the capability of such complements to contain non-restrictive relative clauses and parenthetical clauses which have to be interpreted as having the matrix Agent as their source, and not the speaker of the sentence as a whole.

In this respect, complements of verbs of speech differ from complements of other matrix predicates which in Hengeveld (1989a: 147) are mentioned as governing entities with the status of propositions, such as the one place predicates *to be undeniable, to be true, be a fact*:

(11) a.   ??It was undeniable that frankly Peter had left
     b.   ??It was true that, since the car had gone, Peter had left

To my opinion, the sentences in (11) are only interpretable if the disjunct expressions *frankly* and *since...* are taken as being the speaker's own comment, added parenthetically. This means that some proposition-like complements, such as those in (8) and (10), may contain elements belonging to higher levels than the propositional layer, whereas other proposition-like complements, such as those in (11), may not contain such elements. Consequently, the distinction between the two types of X-like complements should be represented in the lexical entry of the matrix predicate alongside the distinctions already proposed (cf. 1.).

2.2. Verbs of mental activity

The behaviour and coding of complements of the semantic class of verbs of mental activity, such as *to think, to know* etc. raises a problem. In Hengeveld (1989a) and Dik (1989) this subclass of predicates is assumed to govern propositions as well. For Latin such verbs (including the class of verbs of 'considering', 'deciding' and 'wishing') are discussed in Bolkestein (1977). As opposed to the matrix expressions in (11), complements of this class seem to mirror those of verbs of speech in almost all respects, both in coding and in behaviour and in the relation between the two, apart from having two different subclasses which allow two semantic types of complement (cf. (5) above):

(12) subclass   semantic type   form
                                       complement   complement

I	*putare* "to think"	'decl'	AcI
IIa	*cogitare* "to consider"	'decl'	AcI
		'non-decl'	*ut*
IIb	*decernere* "to decide"	'decl'	AcI
		'non-decl'	*ut*/AcI
III	*velle* "to want"	'non-decl'	*ut*/AcI

I have provisionally used the labels 'declarative' vs. 'non-declarative' type of complements here. As in the case of verbs of speech, the former are never expressed by an *ut* clause. Like DECL propositions they may contain expressions indicating subjective epistemic modality and various disjunct adverbials, up to the property of allowing for the presence of satellites which seem to belong to the illocutionary level (Bolkestein 1989).[7] Thus if we replace *it was true* in (11b) by *she thought/knew/considered*, the *since* clause will simply be interpreted as having the matrix Subject as its source, and consequently as part of the complement. However, whether or not such complements should actually be analyzed as containing ILL is unclear. They do not refer to some product of speech being exchanged between a speaker and an addressee, unless one conceives of thought as internalized speech. Moreover, although the 'non-declarative' complements occurring with predicates such as *cogitare* "to consider" or *decernere* "to decide" seem to require controllable SoAs, and thus share this semantic restriction with IMP predications, complements of verbs which allow only non-declarative complements, such as for example *velle* and *cupere* "to want, wish", do not share this controllability restriction with independent and embedded IMP clauses. However, they do have in common the fact that the embedded verbs themselves do not have independent temporal reference (which is not to say that they do not have morphological tense-endings, of course): they necessarily are always conceived of as situated at some point in time following that referred to by the matrix predicate. In Latin, the embedded verb will not carry a future tense ending in such complements, as opposed to verbs in DECL and 'declarative' complements in which all tenses are possible, with their independent referring function. In other words, just like IMP complements they designate virtual SoAs, not situated in a particular time by means of verbal tense. Thus they might be analyzed as representing core predications rather than extended predications. However, temporal satellites, which belong to the level of the extended predication in the layered structure analysis, are not excluded (with the restriction that the point in time to which they refer is compatible with the 'virtual' nature of the complement). This suggests that within extended predications a distinction must be made between those in which tense variation with corresponding differences in reference is possible, and those in which it is not. For those matrix predicates which govern the latter type but where these complements are not classifiable as IMP complements, a specification as to the nature of the predication type, e.g. as virtual, is required in the lexical entry. Hengeveld (1989a: 143, 1989b: 239) recognizes a predication operator 'non-actual' for this purpose.

I will now turn to another class of embedding predicates, which offer a problem for analysis, that of verba affectuum or verbs of evaluation and emotion.

2.3. Verbs of evaluation: X- and e-type complements

Predicates of evaluation in Latin may govern various constructions, one of which they share with verbs of speech, namely the AcI construction. The possibilities are exemplified in (13a-c):

(13) a. *Socios   abisse   dolebat*
         allies.ACC leave.PF.INF regret.IMPF.3SG
         "He regretted that the allies had left"

     b. *Dolebat   quod socii   abierant*
         regret.IMPF.3SG   SUB allies.NOM   leave.PLPF.3PL
         "He regretted that the allies had left"

     c. *De   hostibus   profectis   gaudebat*
         about   enemy.ABL   depart.PART.ABL rejoice.IMPF.3SG
         "He rejoiced about the departure of the enemy"

In (13a) we are dealing with an AcI clause, in (13b) with a finite clause introduced by the subordinating conjunction *quod* and in (13c) with a prepositional phrase where the preposition *de* introduces a so-called dominant participle (DP) construction with the noun *hostibus* "enemies" in the ablative case form (required by the preposition *de* "about") as head to a perfect tense participle *profectis* "departed", which like any ordinary adjective agrees with this head in caseform, gender and number.

2.3.1. Factive vs. non-factive SoAs. In Bolkestein (1981b, 1986) it is pointed out

that the two constructions exemplified by (13b) and (13c) are reserved for so-called 'factive' complements, that is, complements which designate a SoA which is presupposed to be actually realized (in the past, present or future, depending on the tense reference of the finite or infinitival predicate or of the participle involved). (First arguments with the semantic function Cause of causative verbs in Latin such as *terrere* "to frighten" or *efficere (ut)* "to cause (that)" may also be realized in these two constructions.) Furthermore the two constructions are unacceptable for complements of verbs of speech in classical Latin, whether declarative or imperative (see however Szantyr 1965: 576 for late Latin developments). Cf. (14a). They are also not found as expressions for other complements that might be analyzed as representing propositions rather than SoAs, such as those governed by verbs of thinking and predicates like *verisimile est* "it is likely", as in (14b):

(14) a. *Milites   abeuntes   dixit*
        soldiers.ACC   leave.PART.PR.ACC say.PF.3SG
     b. *Verisimile est   quod milites abeunt*
        likely   be.3SG SUB soldiers leave.PR.3PL

It was suggested that in order to distinguish factive complements from other types of complements and to account for the possibility to apply the DP formation illustrated in (13c), the underlying structure should contain a term operator specifying the factivity of the entity involved (this solution was opted for rather than other ones, because Latin does not possess a predicate with the meaning 'be a fact' or a noun with the meaning 'fact'). The more 'thing'-like nature of realized events as compared to 'content of speech' was taken to facilitate nominalization of the predication, whereas such a process cannot apply to indirect speech complements in many languages.

Reformulating this insight in agreement with the layered structure analysis, one might say that the possibility of applying the rule which 'nominalizes' the embedded predication as a DP construction (i.e. as a noun phrase) is sensitive to whether the complement represents an e-type (a second-order) entity as opposed to a proposition. Furthermore, it is also sensitive to whether this predication represents a SoA which is presupposed to be realized (and therefore necessarily situated in time and referred to by the tense of the predicate involved). Consequently it is useful to somehow distinguish such entities in the underlying structure. What we need for this is not only the general distinction between propositions and predications, but also a distinction between factive predications and non-factive predications. Non-factive predications are virtual predications, and, as pointed out in the previous section, virtual predications may be extended by temporal satellites as well as factive ones may. (I want to point out that I treat the notion 'factive' as signifying 'event presupposed to be realized', and not 'proposition presupposed to be true'. In other words, it applies to a predication entity. The notion is used in a confusing number of senses.)

Hengeveld (this vol.) mentions some implications of the hierarchical ordering of the layers for the applicability of a nominalization rule. He predicts that if nominalization of a higher layer is possible, it will certainly be possible of a lower layer. In Latin the cut off point is apparently situated between propositions and predications. Lower level entities may indeed be nominalized. However, in Latin the construction selected for non-factive, 'virtual' predications is different from the one chosen for factive (and consequently tensed) ones, using a different nominalizing construction (a special verbal noun (a gerund - GER) or adjective (a gerundive - GERV)). See (15a-b). Some matrix expressions may occur with both the DP (cf. (15d)) and the construction for virtual SoAs (cf. (15c)), with a clear difference in meaning. (See also Pinkster 1984: 98, 1988.)

(15) a. *Nos*   *hortatur*   *ad*   *abeundum*
          us.ACC exhort.PR.3SG   to   leave.GER.ACC
          "He exhorts us to leave"

   b. *Cupido urbis*   *relinquendae*
          wish   city.GEN   leave.GERV.GEN
          "The wish to leave the city"

   c. *Pudor   relinquendi*   *equites*
          shame   leave.GER.GEN   cavalry.ACC
          "A feeling of being ashamed to leave the cavalry" (Liv. 39.49.2)

   d. *Pudor   non   lati*   *auxilii*
          shame   not   bring.PART.PF.PASS.GEN help.GEN
          "A feeling of shame about not having brought help" (Liv. 21.16.2)

In (15a) and (15c) the virtual action is expressed by a gerund, a verbal noun (in the accusative and genitive case form, respectively) which does not situate the SoA in time, but designates a non-actual, virtual SoA. In (15b) the NP *urbis relinquendae* consists of a head noun *urbis* "city" in the genitive case form (required by the governing noun), modified by a gerundive, a verbal adjective which agrees with its nominal head, and here used 'dominantly' (in a way quite similar to the tensed participle in (13c) and (15d)). This verbal adjective also does not carry tense but designates a virtual action.[8] Note that, like in (15a), the presumably imperative content of a direct speech exhortation (the verb *hortari* "exhort, admonish" may also govern an imperative finite clause introduced by *ut*, cf. 2.1) is apparently 'nominalized' as a verbal noun. Does this nominalization still represent an entity plus ILL here, or should we analyze such complements of *hortari* as containing only the extended (but tenseless, see above) predication? The latter solution seems preferable in view of the impossibility to add operators or satellites of the propositional or illocutionary level explicitating or modifying for example the basic ILL in the case of (15a). As I have pointed out such elements may be present in DECL and IMP complements of verbs of speech (see the discussion concerning (10) above).

As the above examples show, complements referring to factive SoAs and complements designating virtual SoAs are coded differently in Latin. Consequently, this difference between two types of extended predications should be represented as well as the distinction between higher layers. Note that the presence of the tense operator alone does not suffice, because DECL (X) type complements also contain this predication operator. Thus the implicational relation between factivity and tensedness does not hold both ways.

2.3.2. Distinguishing propositions from predications. For each subclass of matrix predicates the question should be raised as to the semantic equivalence of different constructions. This brings us back to the criteria by which the different types of entities are to be differentiated. We have seen above that differences in the distribution of certain types of illocutionary layer elements show that it makes sense to distinguish direct speech from indirect speech complements of verbs of speech, whether or not the latter are analyzed as E-level or as X-level entities; and that the distribution of other elements, especially satellites of the illocutionary and propositional level distinguish complements with and without ILL.

With respect to verbs of emotion in English, such as *to dislike, to deplore, to surprise,* Hengeveld (1989: 148) and Dik (1989: ch.12.1) point out that they may govern either propositions or predications, and that these two types of entities are sometimes distinguished by being coded differently. In some cases the nature of the complement may be ambiguous (cf. (16a)), in other cases, according to them, the construction used will disambiguate the two possibilities (cf. (16b-c)):

(16) a.   John disliked Peter's driving (X/e)
      b.   John disliked Peter's recklessly driving the car (the fact that, X)

    c.   John disliked Peter's reckless driving of the car (the way in which, e)

    d.   John did not dislike Peter's recklessly driving the car/Peter's reckless driving of the car

The more verbal type of nominalization in (16b) is claimed to be used in the case of propositions, whereas the different, less verbal type of nominalization in (16c), which exhibits a higher degree of nominalization (Mackenzie 1986), is used in the case of predications.

However, although the two constructions (16b) and (16c) indeed do not seem to be synonymous, I am not convinced that they do exhibit the difference between propositions and predications. In my opinion, both complements represent factive SoAs, and, consequently, predications and not propositions. This can be seen, for example, from the unchanging implications when the matrix verb is negated (cf. (16d)). However, they seem to differ in the degree to which they may exhibit tense variation and may be further extended by Time satellites (*Peter's yesterday having driven* being possible in (16b), but not in (16c)). Thus what seems to be involved here is a difference between referring extended predication vs. core predication, rather than that between predication and proposition.

Whatever is the case, the observation that verbs designating evaluation or emotion may govern not only (factive) predications but also propositions may still hold in the case of finite and infinitival complements. An expression like *I regret that...*, for example, may be used almost like a verb of speech with the meaning 'I regretfully inform you that..', or like a verb of mental activity in the sense 'I regretfully reflect that..'. The difference between two types of entities may betray itself by different patterns of pronominalization, as has been argued by Kuno (1987).

2.3.3. Layers and pronouns. The following pair (17a-b) exhibits forward and backward pronominalization between a constituent of the complement and a coreferential constituent of the main clause:

    (17) a.   That he_i was not very smart worried $John_i$ (the thought that or the fact that)

          b.   That $John_i$ was not very smart worried him_i (only the fact that)

(where identity of subscript indicates coreferentiality). The sentential complement in (17a) can be interpreted either as representing the content of John's thoughts or as referring to some SoA. The complement in (17b), on the other hand, which is the same construction, can only be interpreted as representing a SoA presented as a fact by the speaker of the sentence as a whole. Kuno (1987: 112ff) claims that the possibility of having the coreferential pronoun with cataphoric reference in the preceding complement clause in (17a) and the possibility of having a coreferential proper noun in (17b) - which normally would be excluded in complement clauses which represent the content of speech or thought of the coreferential matrix clause argument - is connected with whether or not the complement clause contains the content of the human participants' own thought, or some fact presented by the speaker as objectively known. In the former case we would be dealing with a propositional comple-ment, in the latter with a predicational complement. Other verbs of emotion, such as *to surprise, to please, to bother, to disturb*, with the same predicate frame, show similar behaviour.[9] Verbs of emotion with different patterns (e.g. with the human participant as first argument) such as *to deplore* also allow the two patterns for expressing the two coreferential items when the complement clause precedes the governing verb.

However, even some matrix predicates of which the complements cannot be analyzed as representing factive predications turn out to allow the pattern, as shown in (18a-b):

(18) a.   That he$_i$ could do the job was repeatedly denied/suggested/ claimed by John$_i$

b.   That John$_i$ could do the job was repeatedly denied/suggested/ claimed by him$_i$

The difference between (18a-b) cannot always be accounted for on the basis of the difference between an X-type entity in (18a) and an e-type entity in (18b), since e.g. *to suggest* and *to claim* are verbs of speech in both instances. Rather it is connected with the *de dicto* reading of *he* in (18a), i.e. with the matrix Agent as the source, and with the *de re* reading of *John* in (18b): in the latter the speaker of the sentence as a whole is the source of the proper name. Apparently the latter is possible for noun phrases even within X-type comple-ments, in spite of the fact that the whole complement clause itself cannot be analyzed as representing an e-type entity by which the speaker refers to a factive SoA.

In view of the possibilities demonstrated in (17), one might investigate whether in Latin the two sentential constructions possible with verbs of emotion as illustrated in (13a-b) represent the same type of entity (a factive SoA), or

two different ones. Differences in the distribution of reflexive and non-reflexive
pronouns in the two constructions could offer evidence for the latter alternative,
although the data from (18) should warn us to be careful about conclusions.
Other evidence would again be differences in the occurrence of the various
types of satellites and operators. I will discuss both criteria.

2.3.4. Layers and indirect reflexives in Latin. The rule that determines the
occurrence of indirect reflexive pronouns in Latin is quite straightforward: if the
complement clause presents the content of speech, thought, perception or
wishes of a main clause constituent (be it the Agent or an addressee in a three
place pattern), the coreferential constituent in the complement clause will be
realized as a reflexive pronoun. Moreover, coreferential items in causal satellite
clauses (of the predicational or the propositional level) and in relative clauses
which present information which forms part of the mental experience or
consciousness of a main clause constituent are also realized as reflexive
pronouns. The occurrence of such 'indirect' reflexives is excluded in the case of
causal satellites which belong to the utterance level (see the *quoniam*-clauses
discussed earlier), and in the case of non-restrictive relative clauses, both of
which are outside the proposition and its basic ILL. Consequently, they do not
represent the thought of a participant of the main clause, but have the speaker
of the sentence as a whole as their source. The same holds of course for
parenthetical phrases or clauses.

The possibilities for pronouns in causal satellite clauses in Latin are
demonstrated in (19):

(19) a.   *Caesar   castra   movit   quia   hostes*
           Caesar   camp   move.PF.3SG because enemy
           eum   secuti erant
           PRO   follow.PLPF.3PL
           "Caesar$_i$ moved camp because the enemy had followed him$_i$"

    b.   *Caesar castra movit quia hostes   se   secuti erant*
                                             3SG.REFL
           "Caesar$_i$ moved camp because the enemy had followed him$_i$"

    c.   *Quoniam   hostes   eum/*se   secuti sunt*
           since   enemy   him/*REFL   follow.PF.3PL
           Caesar castra   movebit
           Caesar camp   move.FUT.3SG
           "Since the enemy have followed him$_j$, Caesar$_i$ will move camp"

By using the non-reflexive pronoun *eum* "him" in (19a) the speaker himself takes the responsibility for the truth of the content of the causal satellite. By using the reflexive pronoun in (19b) the speaker indicates that the content of the causal satellite has played a role in the perception or thought of the main clause Agent. (I am not sure whether this may be interpreted as indicating that the causal satellite functions on the propositional level in (19a) and on the predicational level in (19b).) This cannot be the case with the higher level satellite exemplified by (19c), which contains the speaker's own justification for his declarative utterance. (The presence of a reflexive pronoun in example (10) above is due to other factors, namely to the fact that the whole complement is governed by a verb of speech.)

The distinction illustrated by (19a-b) reminds us of the *de re/de dicto* distinction made with respect to the complements of verbs of speech in (18). It is also similar to the distinction between e (predicational) and X (propositional) complements in the case of verbs of emotion (as in (17)): the speaker of the sentence as a whole may be responsible for naming a referent, be it a first order or a second order entity, or a matrix participant is the source.

As far as Latin verbs of emotion are concerned, the two constructions possible, the AcI and the finite construction introduced by *quod* (see (13a-b)), are sometimes assumed to exhibit a semantic difference (Perrochat 1932: 121ff; Kühner and Stegmann 1912: 277). The latter construction is claimed to emphasize the factive nature of the complement. The two constructions indeed seem to behave differently with respect to the distribution of non-reflexive pronouns. Both regularly occur with reflexive pronouns within the complement, but non-reflexives are excluded in the case of the AcI, and are not excluded in the case of the finite *quod* clauses, although examples are rare (and their interpretation open to discussion). Still, there are some indubitable instances of non-reflexives in complements introduced by the subordinating conjunction *quod*:

(20) *(Philosophi)   queruntur   quod eos   insimulemus*
     philosophers complain.PR.3PL   SUB PRO.3PL   suggest.SUBJ.PR.1PL
     omnia   incerta dicere
     everything vague   say.INF
     "The philosophers$_i$ complain that we suggest (according to them) that they$_i$ say that everything is uncertain" (Cic. *Ac.* 2,32)

(Other instances of non-reflexives are given in Bolkestein 1989.) The subjunctive mood of the main verb of the complement clause *insimulemus*, which itself is a verb of speech governing an AcI-clause, indicates that the speaker does not himself subscribe to the content of the *quod* clause, but considers it to be a false accusation. Such a use of the subjunctive mood is also possible in the causal clauses illustrated in (19), whether or not they contain reflexive pronouns. The pronoun *eos* "they" is coreferential to *philosophi* and might well have been a reflexive (*se*), the direct speech equivalent in that case being 'they suggest that we...' The trouble here is that the objective fact reading of the *quod* clause suggested by the non-reflexive is annihilated by the presence of the subjunctive mood, which shows that the content of the complement is only assumed to be the case by the matrix Subject. The pronoun itself is used as having the speaker as its source, and perhaps the whole clause should be analyzed as representing an e-type entity, with the narrator's own scepticism smuggled in at the same time.

The few other attested instances offer problems of interpretation as well. However, we might interpret the fact that they exist at all, and that *quod* clauses seem to be somewhat freer in their use of non reflexives than AcIs, as in itself compatible with a predicational status of the former rather than a propositional status of such complements. The occurrence of reflexives on the other hand shows that the matrix Subject may still be treated as the (perceiving) source.

Let us now see whether other diffences between the two constructions are found which would support the hypothesis that AcIs represent propositions whereas *quod* clauses represent factive predications.

2.3.5. Subjective epistemic modality and layers. A final criterion which might be used to determine whether complements represent predications (factive or non factive) or propositions is connected with the capability of containing operators or satellites expressing subjective epistemic modality, in the form of adverbials or of modal verbs. For example, sentences (17b) and (18b) do not allow such elements within the complement (cf. (21b)), whereas (17a) and (18a) do (cf. (21a)). Instances containing a causal satellite connected to the illocutionary layer are even less to be expected (cf. (21c)).

(21) a.   That he surely was not very smart worried John
      b.   ?That John$_i$ surely was not very smart worried him$_i$
      c.   ?John regretted that since the car had gone Peter had left

I have not found any attested instances of verbs of emotion in Latin in which the complement contains either *quoniam* clauses or such modal elements, as opposed to predicates of speech and thought (cf. 2.1. and 2.2.). The lack of expressions indicating subjective epistemic modality seems to agree with the observations made in Koktova (1986: 68ff) concerning restrictions on the distribution of various subclasses of disjunct adverbials in different types of sentential complements. As far as this criterion is concerned, there is, in other words, no positive evidence that verbs of emotion govern propositions.

The criterion offered by the distribution of such elements is also applicable to complements of verbs of happening or occurring in Latin, to which I will now turn. Such predicates may govern two different constructions. These complement constructions are not synonymous, but again demonstrate the necessity of distinguishing between factive and non-factive predications: whether the factive complements should not rather be classed as representing a DECL proposition is difficult to determine.

2.4. Latin verbs of 'happening'

In Hengeveld (1988) and Dik (1989: ch.12) predicates like *to occur* or *to happen* are claimed to govern predications rather than propositions. Latin predicates signifying 'to occur, to happen (to someone), to take place', such as *accidit*, *evenit*, *contingit* (with or without a dative case form Experiencer constituent), may govern two different complement constructions, as exemplified in (22a-b):

(22) a. *Accidit   ut   abiret*
        happen.PF.3SG SUB leave.SUBJ.IMPF.3SG
        "It happened that he left"
     b. *Accidit   perincommode   quod abibat*
        happen.PF.3SG unfortunately   SUB leave.IND.IMPF.3SG
        "It happened unfortunately that he left"
     c. *Accidit   perincommode   quod abierat*
        happen.PF.3SG unfortunately   SUB leave.PLPF.3SG
        "It happened unfortunately that he had left"

In (22a) we are dealing with a finite clause introduced by *ut* (and consequently with the verb automatically in the subjunctive mood), in (22b) with a finite clause introduced by the complementizer *quod* (with the verb normally in the indicative mood). In the handbooks of Latin it is pointed out that there is a difference in meaning between the two constructions. In the first case the event designated by the clause is only conceived of, and necessarily still to take place (the governing expression might be called an 'implicative' verb, but not a factive one, as the negation test would show), i.e. it is virtual, non-factive. In the second construction, which is almost always accompanied by an evaluative adverb (in (22b) *perincommode* "unfortunately"), the event is presented as a fact. (See Kühner and Stegmann 1912: 273ff.) In terms of the layer approach (22a) would represent an extended predication without an independently referring tense operator (see my remarks concerning IMP predications and non-declarative complements of verbs of deciding and wishing above), whereas (22b) would represent a factive extended predication (and factivity implies the presence of the tense operator). Statistically, the pragmatic status of the SoA expressed in the complement clause also differs: Rosén (1989) observes that the construction with *quod* usually contains a SoA already known from the context, whereas the *ut* clause usually introduces new information (in her terms: *quod* serves to 'de-rhematize' the SoA). In FG terms it might be said that in construction (22a) the complement is more often Focus (where I do not want to imply that newness and focality are the same), whereas the complement in construction (22b) is more often topical. Now, although factivity and topicality need not necessarily go together (see Bolkestein (1981) for some instances of focal factive complements, and Hengeveld (1989b: 263) for the proposal to treat factive predications on a par with definite terms), they will coincide more often than not, and the pragmatic difference observed supports the underlying semantic difference between factive extended predications and 'virtual' extended predications.

Another revealing difference between the two complement constructions, not pointed out in the handbooks, is the fact that in (22b) but not in (22a) the tense of the verb of the complement clause may independently refer to some orientation point in time, as in (22c). In (22c) the verb of the complement refers to a time before some orientation point in the past by means of the pluperfect; this would be impossible in construction (22a).

The status of complements of verbs of happening seems clear enough. However, sentences such as (22b) are rather similar to sentences in which the speaker specifies his personal evaluation of the content by means of attitudinal disjuncts, such as (23a). In the layer approach it is not quite clear whether such disjuncts are analyzed as satellites on the propositional or on the predicational level. In Dik (1989: ch.12) sentences such as (23a) are paraphrased as (23b). In Dik et al. (this vol.) they are paraphrased as (23c). The former suggests an analysis as a propositional, the latter as a predicational satellite:

(23) a.   Fortunately, John left
      b.   I think it is fortunate that John left

c.   It is fortunate that the leaving event took place

In spite of the resemblance, (23a) differs from (23c) in that only the latter may occur in an interrogative sentence, whereas the former may not. Interestingly, this property is shared by the paraphrase (23b). Furthermore, pragmatically, the clause *John left* in (23a), or one of its two constituents, will more frequently carry Focus than in the case of (23b-c). Moreover, in my opinion, in (23a) the main clause may contain an indication of subjective epistemic modality, whereas this seems less acceptable in (23b-c). Cf. (24a-c):

(24) a.   Fortunately, John must have left
      b.   ?I think it is fortunate that John must have left
      c.   ?It is fortunate that the leaving event must have taken place

The difference seems to indicate that the adverbial expression in (24a) is attached to a proposition, whereas the predicate *be fortunate* in (24b-c) applies to a factive extended predication.

In the case of the Latin verbs which signify 'to happen, to occur' we may ask ourselves whether the matrix expression when accompanied by an evaluative adverb resembles (22a) or (22c), that is, whether the complement in that case should be regarded as a proposition rather than a predication. As far as the distribution of pragmatic functions is concerned, it resembles (22c) rather than (22a): the complement clause frequently refers to an identifiable entity. A further argument in favour of analyzing the complement as being a predication rather than a proposition is that in Latin I have not found, neither in *ut* complements nor in *quod* complements of verbs like *accidit*, any expressions indicating subjective epistemic modality (let alone satellites introduced by *quoniam* "since"). Their equivalents in for example English also do not seem to be able to contain elements expressing subjective epistemic modality. Cf. (25a-b):

(25) a.   *It happened that John surely left/John must have left
      b.   *It happened fortunately that John surely left/must have left

If we accept that the possibility to express subjective epistemic modality is a criterion for proposition status, both complement types of the class of verbs signifying 'to occur, to happen' represent lower order entities, only differring in being non-factive or virtual vs. factive extended predications.

3. Conclusion

We have discussed several phenomena which can be used as behavioural criteria for the distinction between different complement types:
(i) Real extra-clausal elements do not occur in sentential complements of any class of verbs (2.1.).
(ii) Complements of verbs of speech (2.1.) and thought (2.2.) may contain satellites of a higher layer than the proposition, non-restrictive relative clauses and parentheticals.
(iii) Furthermore, basic ILL distinctions are relevant for complements of verbs of speech. (ii) and (iii) lead to the conclusion that they are propositions plus ILL. This suggests that in the layered structure an extra layer should be distinguished between E and X. Complements of verbs of mental activity resemble those of verbs of speech in allowing illocutionary satellites, but the relevance of ILL is dubious (2.2.).
(iv) Naturally, in view of the scope relations between operators and satellites of the utterance level and those of the propositional level, complements of verbs of speech and of thought, as opposed to lower level complements, also contain proposition operators and satellites, such as those expressing subjective epistemic modality (and of course all other material belonging to the lower levels of the layered structure).
(v) Not all complements which one would tend to classify as representing proposition complements seem to be equally well able to contain such elements.
(vi) Complements of emotion verbs do not contain either ILL specifications or modifiers of basic ILL, nor do they occur with proposition operators and satellites such as those indicating subjective epistemic modality. The distribution of such elements confirms the predicational status of complements of verbs of emotion (2.3.).
(vii) The same holds for verbs of happening (2.4.).
(viii) Extended predication complements may either have independent temporal reference, or they may lack the possibility to carry tensed verbs. In the first case they are factive, in the second non-factive or virtual. This distinction between different types of extended predication should be indicated in the lexical entry of the matrix predicate (2.3.1.).
(ix) Factive extended predications may exhibit different pronominalization or reflexivization possibilities both from proposition complements and from non-factive predication complements (2.3.3., 2.3.4.).
  This list of behavioural properties is probably not exhaustive.[10] I would

hypothesize, for example, that higher level entities might be more sensitive to differences in pragmatic status of their constituents, i.e. to the distribution of topical and focal information. In fact the restrictions upon the occurrence of the personal passive in Latin and on the occurrence of the so-called proleptic accusative in Latin (Bolkestein 1981a) and ancient Greek (Panhuis 1984) point into that direction.[11] Another difference, less easy to describe in linguistic terms, might be the presence of elements with a strong rhetorical or exclamative colouring of which the source is a matrix participant. This remains to be investigated.

With respect to coding properties, at first sight several forms may code different types of entities in Latin (e.g. AcI is found for DECL propositions, IMP predications, propositions without ILL, factive predications and non-factive, virtual, ones; *ut* clauses are found for IMP predications, propositions without ILL, and virtual predications). However, not only distinctions within entities plus ILL are systematically reflected (to a certain extent) in the form which the complement takes (DECL never becomes *ut*), but the distinction between factive predications vs. propositions is reflected by formal differences as well (only the former allow dominant participle formation in Latin). Moreover, factive extended predications and non-factive, virtual predications also differ as to the coding applied to them. This is quite clear in the case of complements governed by noun phrases in Latin, for example (virtual predications can only appear in the gerund or the dominant gerundive construction, not in the dominant participle). It does not seem implausible that such correlations will also be present in other languages.

Summarizing, on the one hand this means that the difference between the layers is mirrored by differences between complements: complements governed by different subclasses of matrix verbs may contain different types of elements, and different codings apply to them. On the other hand, for the purpose of classifying complement types, some refinement is called for: (i) the distinction between the illocutionary and the propositional layer seems less absolute than suggested by the model; (ii) the difference within extended predications between factive and non-factive ones should be recognized; and (iii) tense operators and satellites of time do not have the same distribution, and may not characterize the same level.

The relevance of the different layers of the hierarchical structure for a characterization of complement types appears from the distribution of operators and satellites belonging to these layers over different types of complements. If the different layers are universally relevant, one would expect behavioural differences such as those investigated here to occur in other languages as well.

However, the tripartite division into utterance entities, propositional entities and predicational entities, being insufficient for describing the complement system of a language like Latin, may be so for other languages as well, and consequently requires further elaboration.

Notes

1. At various stages of this paper I have gratefully profited from discussions with and comments by Casper de Groot, Kees Hengeveld, Caroline Kroon, Lachlan Mackenzie, Harm Pinkster, Jan Rijkhoff and Co Vet.

2. The notion that data from all levels are simultaneously relevant is comparable to the approach of Systemic Grammar, where utterances are also assigned structure at several levels (cf. Halliday 1985). In FG however, it is explicitly assumed that the levels involved are related in a hierarchical way. In Systemic Grammar it is less clear how the levels are related.

3. Several data from Latin suggest that factors from the speech act level should be incorporated into a grammatical description. For example, the choice of verbal mood in dependent question complements in archaic Latin seems to be influenced by a combination of the illocutionary function of the sentence as a whole and other properties of the speech situation (Stephens 1985). Similarly, assertive question sentences (which have the form of questions but the function of assertions) take a different form in indirect speech from 'real' questions for information (Orlandini 1981). From the interpretative point of view, Risselada (1990) argues that illocutionary force is much more often directly derivable from structural properties than is frequently assumed.

4. In traditional grammars of Latin there has been a tendency to assume a close relation between differences in form and semantic differences. Recently, Serbat (1988: 35) defends the opposite view. As will appear below, the truth is somewhere in the middle.

5. Certain forms of speech acts, especially those consisting of a combination of two clauses, cannot be embedded in the same form at all, even by the appropriate speech act describing verbs, such as warnings (*touch this and I'll hit you*), threats (*take this or I'll hit you*) or contingent promises (*touch this and it will open*) etc. Such linguistic entities can only be referred to in a different form (*I said that if you..., I would...*).

6. In sentences such as (9a) one could defend the view that the causal satellite, allthough being outside subjective epistemic modality, still falls within the declarative illocutionary force. This would imply that there are several proposition operators which are ordered hierarchically with respect to each other. However, where *quoniam* clauses justify IMP or INTERR clauses, it is undeniable that they fall outside the illocution.

7.   Verbs of mental activity differ in having one more subclass. This subclass may govern two
        semantic types of complements, which might be differentiated as 'decl' and 'non-decl', and
        two constructions, parallel to those in (5). However, the construction reserved for the
        declarative complements in (5) with this subclass may also be used for 'Imp' complements
        (alongside with the other construction).

8.   In Subject and Object function neither construction can be used; for expressing a virtual
        predication the infinitive will be used in such cases.

9.   Kuno (1987) does not distinguish between the two predicate frames of *to worry*, one in
        which the [+human] Experiencer argument is the second argument and one in which it is
        the first argument. In the last frame, the complement always represents the content of the
        thought of the matrix argument and is a proposition.

10.   An investigation of the two complement constructions possible with the Latin verb *admirari*
        "be amazed" (Cenacchi p.c.) suggests that in one of the two (the AcI) the content was
        often of a generic nature, whereas this was not found in *quod* clauses. Such a difference
        might be the consequence of the difference between propositional vs. predicational
        complements. Another difference might be the presence or absence of 'interactive' particles:
        the results of an investigation of Latin causal particles by Kroon (p.c., 1989) opens the
        possibility that such particles might be frequent in one type of complements (of E or X
        plus ILL level) but absent in another type (propositions without ILL, and factive and virtual
        predications).

11.   In classical Latin the constructions mentioned are blocked when the Focus of the sentence
        as a whole does not fall within the complement, but on a constituent of the main clause
        (Bolkestein 1981a). Whether or not similar factors play a role in the acceptability of
        comparable constructions in other languages, is an open question: I do not know of any
        recent corpus investigations of other languages in order to determine whether any kind of
        pragmatic factor is involved in the choice of construction.

References

Bolkestein, A.Machtelt
        1976a   "The relation between form and meaning of Latin subordinate clauses governed by verba
                dicendi". *Mnem* 29: 155-175, 268-300.
        1976b   "AcI and 'ut' clauses with verba dicendi in Latin". *Glotta* 54: 263-291.
        1977   "Syntaktische en semantische eigenschappen van komplementen van verba sentiendi in
                het Latijn". *Handelingen van het Vlaams Filologenkongres* 31: 112-120.
        1981a   "Embedded predications, displacement and pseudo-argument formation in Latin". In
                A.M.Bolkestein et al. 1981, 63-112.
        1981b   "Factivity as a condition for an optional expression rule in Latin". In A.M.Bolkestein et
                al. 1981, 205-233.
        1986   *Parameters in the expression of embedded predications*. Working Papers in Functional
                Grammar 8. (Reprinted in G.Calboli (ed.), 3-35. 1989.)
        1989   "Latin sentential complements from a functional grammar perspective". *Cahiers de*

l'Institut de Linguistique de Louvain 15: 41-52.

fc. "Causally related predications and the choice between parataxis and hypotaxis in Latin". In R.Coleman (ed.), *Papers from the 1987 international conference on Latin linguistics* (provisional title). Amsterdam: Benjamins.

Bolkestein A.M., H.A.Combé, S.C.Dik, C.De Groot, J.Gvozdanovic, A.Rijksbaron and C.Vet
1981 *Predication and expression in functional grammar.* London: Academic Press.

Calboli, G. (ed.)
1989 *Subordination and other topics in Latin: Proceedings of the Third Colloquium on Latin Linguistics, Bologna, 1-5 April 1985.* Amsterdam: Benjamins.

Coulmas, F.
1986 *Direct and indirect speech.* Berlin: Mouton.

Dik, Simon C.
1989 *The theory of functional grammar, pt.1.* Dordrecht: Foris.
fc. "Embedded predications from a typological point of view". Paper Workshop European Science Foundation 1987.

Fugier, H.
1989 "'Quod', 'quia', 'quoniam' et leurs effets textuels chez Cicéron". In G.Calboli (ed.), 91-119.

Halliday, M.A.K.
1985 *An introduction to functional grammar.* Baltimore: E.Arnold.

Hengeveld, Kees
1987 "Clause structure and modality in functional grammar". In J.Van der Auwera and L.Goossens (eds.), *Ins and outs of the predication.* Dordrecht: Foris, 53-66.
1988 *Layers and operators.* Working Papers in Functional Grammar 27.
1989a "Layers and operators in functional grammar". *Journal of Linguistics* 25: 127-157.
1989b "Illocution, mood and modality in a functional grammar of Spanish". *Journal of Semantics* 6: 227-269.

Koktova, Eva
1986 *Sentence adverbials in a functional description.* Amsterdam: Benjamins.

Kroon, Caroline
1989 "Causal connectors in Latin: The discourse function of 'nam', 'enim', 'igitur' and 'ergo'". *Cahiers de l'Institut de Linguistique de Louvain* 15: 231-244.

Kühner, R. and C.Stegmann
1912 *Ausführliche Grammatik der lateinischen Sprache, pt.2: Satzlehre.* (Reprint 1962.) Darmstadt: Wissenschaftliche Buchgesellschaft.

Kuno, S.
1987 *Functional syntax*. Chicago: The University of Chicago Press.

Lehmann, Christian
1988 "Towards a typology of clause linkage". In J.Haiman and S.A.Thompson (eds.), *Clause combining in discourse and syntax*. Amsterdam: Benjamins, 181-225.

Lyons, J.
1977 *Semantics*. Cambridge: Cambridge UP.

Mackenzie, J.Lachlan
1986 *The representation of nominal predicates in the fund: A new proposal*. Working Papers in Functional Grammar 25.

Orlandini, A.
1980 "On rethorical questions". In G.Calboli (ed.), *Papers in grammar, vol.1*. Bologna: CLUEB, 103-140.

Panhuis, Dirk G.
1984 "Prolepsis in Greek as a discourse strategy". *Glotta* 62: 26-39.

Perrochat, P.
1932 *Recherches sur la valeur et l'emploi de l'infinitif subordonné en latin*. Paris: Les Belles Lettres.

Pinkster, Harm
1984 *Latijnse syntaxis en semantiek*. Amsterdam: Grüner.
1988 *Lateinische Syntax und Semantik*. Tübingen: Francke Verlag.

Quirk, R., S.Greenbaum, G.Leech and J.Svartvik
1972 *A grammar of contemporary English*. London: Longman.
1985 *A comprehensive grammar of the English language*. London: Longman.

Rijksbaron, Albert
1976 *Temporal and causal conjunctions in ancient Greek*. Amsterdam: Hakkert.

Risselada, Rodie
1990 *Illocutionary function and functional illocution*. Working Papers in Functional Grammar 34.

Rosén, Hannah
1989 "General subordinators and sentence complements". In G.Calboli (ed.), 197-217.

Serbat, G.
1988 *Linguistique Latine et linguistique générale*. Louvain-La-Neuve: Peeters.

Stephens, L.
   1985 "Indirect questions in Old Latin: Syntactic and pragmatic factors conditioning modal
         shift". *Illinois Classical Studies* 10: 195-214.

Szantyr, A.
   1965 *Lateinische Syntax und Stilistik*. München: Beck.

Vet, Co
   1986 *A pragmatic approach to tense in functional grammar*. Working Papers in Functional
         Grammar 16.

Semantic Relations in Non-Verbal Predication

Kees Hengeveld

University of Amsterdam

0. Introduction[1]

The 'copula support hypothesis', advanced in Dik (1980), states that in those languages which make use of a copula the occurrence of that copula can be handled by means of a copula support rule. The hypothesis is based on the idea that non-verbal predicates can be represented in the lexicon in much the same way as verbal predicates. An example of a non-verbal predicate is given in (1), where the adjective *clever* is represented as a predicate with a single argument with zero function:

(1) $clever_A (x_i)_\emptyset$

Predications based on such a non-verbal predicate may serve as the input of a copula support rule, which inserts a copula under the relevant conditions. A somewhat adapted version of this rule is given in (2):

(2) **Copula support**
     input: $\pi \; predicate_\beta \; (\Omega\alpha_1)_\sigma$
     conditions: $\pi = ...$ (predicate operators)
                   $\beta = ...$ (predicate type)
                   $\Omega = ...$ (term operators)
                   $\alpha = ...$ (argument type)
                   $\sigma = ...$ (semantic function)
     output: $\pi \; copula_\gamma \; predicate_\beta \; (\Omega\alpha_1)_\emptyset$

The conditions to be specified in the rule are language specific: in some languages certain predicate operators (π) or term operators (Ω) will trigger copula support, in others properties of the predicate (β), the argument (α), or the semantic function of the argument (σ) will be relevant. Possibly some languages will not need a copula support rule at all. If they do, the copula type (γ) is relevant.

One of the implications of this approach is that the different meanings often attributed to the copula have to be accounted for in a way that does not make reference to the copula itself, since the copula is assumed to be a semantically empty supportive device. This paper is concerned with some of the problems related to this implication of the copula support hypothesis and can be outlined schematically as in (3).

(3)

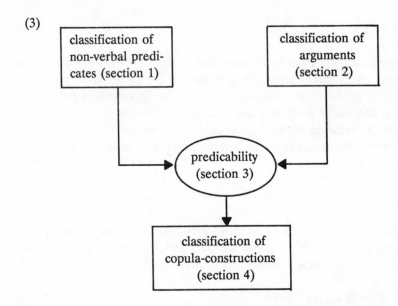

I will claim that in order to account for the semantics of all copula constructions it is necessary to have a classification of non-verbal predicates (ß), a classification of arguments (α), and a theory on the ways in which arguments and predicates may be combined with each other, for which I will use the notion of *predicability*, taken from ontological philosophy. The result should then be a classification of copula constructions which accounts for the various semantic shades and nuances of these constructions. I use the term *copula-construction* for any construction which can be assumed to be based on a non-verbal predicate, regardless of whether or not it actually contains a copula.

1. Non-verbal predicates

So far the different semantic relations expressed by non-verbal predication types have mainly been accounted for by means of a classification of non-verbal predicates. Dik (1980) recognizes two main categories of non-verbal predicates. The first category is formed by bare predicates, which can be either adjectival or nominal, as illustrated in (4)-(5) (Basque, Isolate, Lafitte 1944):

(4) *Piarres hil   da*
     Pierre dead COP.PRES.3SG
     "Pierre is dead"

(5) *Soldado zen*
     soldier COP.PAST.IMPF.3SG
     (lit. 'he was soldier')
     "He was a soldier"

Example (4) shows an adjectival predicate, example (5) a nominal predicate. The latter predicate can be applied in its bare form in Basque, but has to be rendered as a term in English. This brings me to the second category of non-verbal predicates recognized by Dik: predicates derived from terms by means of a predicate formation rule of the format given in (6):

(6) **Term-predicate formation**
     input: $(\text{term})_{(\sigma)}$
     output: $\{(\text{term})_{(\sigma)}\}\ (x_1)_{\phi}$

This predicate formation rule accounts for constructions like (7)-(8) with their representations in (9)-(10):

(7) This book is a bestseller

(8) The chair is in the garden

(9) $\{(i1x_i\colon \text{bestseller}_N\ (x_i))\}\ (d1x_j\colon \text{book}_N\ (x_j))_{\phi}$

(10) $\{(d1x_i\colon \text{garden}_N\ (x_i))_{Loc}\}\ (d1x_j\colon \text{chair}_N\ (x_j))_{\phi}$

The predicate *a bestseller* in (7) is derived from a term without a semantic function. The class-membership relation expressed in this sentence is accounted for by means of the term operators on both the argument and the predicate term, as represented in (9). The predicate in (8) is derived from a term provided with the Locative semantic function, as represented in (10). The locative relation expressed in sentence (8) can thus be seen as residing in the locative character of the predicate. It will be clear that by varying the semantic function of the predicate term many different semantic relations can be accounted for, such as location, possession, and time. In (11) a somewhat simplified classification is given of the different semantic relations expressed in non-verbal predication that can be accounted for by varying the non-verbal predicate (cf. Dik 1980: 111):

(11) **A classification of non-verbal predicates**

non-verbal predicate	semantic relation
bare predicates: $\text{pred}_A\ (x_1)_\emptyset$ $\text{pred}_N\ (x_1)_\emptyset$	property assignment property assignment
derived predicates: $\{(x_i)\}\ (x_1)_\emptyset$ $\{(x_i)_{Poss}\}\ (x_1)_\emptyset$ $\{(x_i)_{Loc}\}\ (x_1)_\emptyset$ $\{(x_i)_{Temp}\}\ (x_1)_\emptyset$	classification possession location time

Although in this way many different meanings can be accounted for without reference to the copula, there still remain several constructions which exhibit shades of meaning not captured by the formalism. The sentences in (12)-(14) illustrate only one of the problematic cases:

(12) The table is in the next room

(13) The meeting is in the next room

(14) It is in the next room that we meet

The copula in (12) can be paraphrased as 'be located', the copula in (13)-(14)

can be paraphrased as 'take place', 'occur', or 'happen'. Although the difference may seem marginal, it is important enough to be formally reflected in some languages. Japanese (Altaic), for instance, uses different locative suffixes on the predicate depending on whether the argument refers to an individual or to an event, as illustrated in (15)-(16) (from Makino 1968):

(15) *Illinois daigaku-wa   Illinois syuu-ni   ar-ru*
     Illinois university   Illinois state-LOC COP
     "The University of Illinois is in the state of Illinois"

(16) *Olympics-ga Mexico-de   ar-ru*
     Olympics   Mexico-LOC COP
     "The Olympics will be held in Mexico"

The locative suffix *-ni* in (15) is used with arguments referring to entities with physical dimensions, the locative suffix *-de* in (16) is used with arguments referring to entities with temporal dimensions.

Spanish (Indo-Hittite) uses different copulas to make the same distinction[2], as illustrated in (17)-(18) (from Hengeveld 1986):

(17) *La   mesa   está   en la   sala 14*
     the table   COP in the   room 14
     "The table is in room 14"

(18) *La   reunión es   en la   sala 14*
     the meeting COP in the   room 14
     "The meeting is in room 14"

The copula *estar* in (17) is used for the location of individuals, the copula *ser* in (18) for the location of events.

The Turkish (Altaic) examples in (19)-(20), finally, show that the difference between these constructions does not reside in various meanings of the copula (from Lewis 1967, Gerjan van Schaaik p.c.):

(19) *Köpek   bahçe-de*
     dog   yard-LOC
     "The dog is in the yard"

(20) *Toplantï   26   numara-lï   oda-da*
       meeting   26   number-with room-LOC
       "The meeting is in room 26"

Neither of the two Turkish constructions makes use of a copula, yet the same semantic difference is present. This shows that in a typologically adequate approach the difference in meaning between the two constructions cannot be attributed to the copula, but must be interpreted as residing in the nature of the argument terms. What we need, then, besides a classification of non-verbal predicates, is a classification of arguments.

2. Arguments

In Hengeveld (1989) I argue for a hierarchical organization of the clause model in Functional Grammar (FG) and discuss the implications of such an approach for the treatment of subordinate constructions. My claim there is that arguments can be of four types of increasing complexity, depending on whether they refer to first, second, third or fourth order entities (see Lyons 1977: 442-447). The linguistic correlates of these ontological types occupy a prominent place in the model developed so far, which is given in (21) below.

The model in (21) consists of two levels, each containing several layers. The highest level is called the interpersonal level, as it is concerned with those linguistic means which are used by the speaker to evoke a certain communicative effect in the addressee. The lowest level is called the representational level, as it is concerned with those linguistic means which are used by the speaker to evoke a picture of an external situation in the addressee. The highest level is structured on the basis of an abstract illocutionary frame, which specifies relations between a speaker (S), an addressee (A) and the processed message unit or content (X). The lowest level is structured on the basis of a predicate frame, which specifies a property of an individual or a relation between several individuals (x). Starting from the outermost layer the schema in (21) states that within a speech act (E) a propositional content (X) is processed, within which reference is made to an external situation (e) in which some individuals (x) participate. All except the outermost layer in (21) can be provided with their own operators, which will not be dealt with here.

(21) **General structure of the simple utterance**

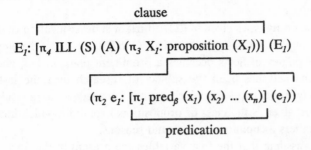

clause

$$E_I: [\pi_4 \; ILL \; (S) \; (A) \; (\pi_3 \; X_I: \; \text{proposition} \; (X_I))] \; (E_I)$$

$$(\pi_2 \; e_I: [\pi_1 \; \text{pred}_\beta \; (x_I) \; (x_2) \; ... \; (x_n)] \; (e_I))$$

predication

E_I:	speech act	π_I:	predicate operators
X_I:	propositional content	π_2:	predication operators
e_I:	event	π_3:	proposition operators
x_I:	individual	π_4:	illocution operators

The representation of a simple utterance thus contains four different types of variable, each referring to a different kind of entity. I have listed these entities in (22):

(22) **A classification of entities**

entity	order	clause correlate
individual	first	$(x_I: \; \text{pred}_N \; (x_I))$
SoA	second	$(e_I: \; \text{predication} \; (e_I))$
propositional content	third	$(X_I: \; \text{proposition} \; (X_I))$
speech act	fourth	$(E_I: \; \text{clause} \; (E_I))$

The x-variable refers to a first order entity or *individual*. First order entities can have colour, size, and weight, can be touched, can be located in space, and can typically be evaluated in terms of their existence. The e-variable refers to a second order entity or *state of affairs* (SoA). Second order entities can be witnessed and regretted, can be located in space and time, and can typically be evaluated in terms of their reality.[3] The X-variable refers to a third order entity or *propositional content*. Third order entities can be known and forgotten, asserted and denied, can be located in neither space nor time, and can typically be evaluated in terms of their truth. The E-variable, finally, refers to a fourth order entity or *speech act*. Fourth order entities can be uttered and understood, they locate themselves in space and time, and can typically be evaluated in terms of their felicity.

For each of the entity-types given in (22) a further subclassification could be given. The 'typology of entities' given in Dik (1987) is in fact a typology of individuals, the typology of SoAs occupies a prominent place in FG, and the typology of speech acts has been the subject of research over the last few decades. The only entity type for which to my knowledge no full subclassification has been given is the class of propositional contents, which includes such diverse members as opinions, wishes and reasons.

The reason to assume that the four variables are present in the underlying representation of every utterance is that anaphoric reference can be made to any of these variables after the production of an utterance, as illustrated in (23)-(26):

(23) A: Come here, please!
     B: Is that an order? (AE_i)

(24) A: He's a liar
     B: That's not true! (AX_i)

(25) A: John won't come
     B: That's a pity! (Ae_i)

(26) A: Yesterday I saw a boy with a scar on his face
     B: That must have been my brother! (Ax_i)

In (23) anaphoric (A) reference is made to the preceding speech act E_i, in (24) to the content X_i presented in the preceding speech act, in (25) to the external situation e_i to which reference is made within that content, and in (26) to one of the participants x_i in that external situation.

While demonstrating that the different parts of the utterance can be referred to separately, these examples show at the same time that every one of these parts can be made the argument of a higher predicate. The nature of an argument term is determined entirely by the higher predicate. Some illustrations from the verbal and non-verbal domains are given in (27):

(27) verbal   non-verbal

$say_V (x_1)_{Ag} (E_1)_{Go} (x_1)_{Rec}$ $question_N (E_1)_\phi$
$know_V (x_1)_\phi (X_1)_{Go}$ $true_A (X_1)_\phi$
$see_V (x_1)_\phi (e_1)_{Go}$ $stupid_A (e_1)_\phi$
$give_V (x_1)_{Ag} (x_2)_{Go} (x_3)_{Rec}$ $green_A (x_1)_\phi$

With respect to the expression of the four types of argument there are two possibilities. One is to extract the corresponding clause units from (21), as listed in the second column in (28). Apart from this there seems to be a limited possibility to describe all types of entity by means of nouns, as is indicated in the third column in (28):

(28) **Variables and restrictors**

variable	restrictor		
E_1	clause (E_1)	or	$pred_N (E_1)_\phi$
X_1	proposition (X_1)	or	$pred_N (X_1)_\phi$
e_1	predication (e_1)	or	$pred_N (e_1)_\phi$
x_1	$pred_N (x_1)_\phi$		

With respect to the first possibility, the expression of arguments by means of the corresponding clause units, the difference between the four kinds of argument has some formal reflection in several languages. Nama Hottentot (Hagman 1973) uses nouns for first order arguments, nominalizations for second order arguments, has a specialized complementizer for third order arguments and a quote particle for fourth order arguments. The situation is not as clear-cut in English, although examples (29)-(32) seem to point at a situation not very different from the one obtaining in Nama Hottentot:

(29) His question was **"Where are you going?"**   (quote)

(30) It's true **that I don't like you**   (finite complement)

(31) It's stupid **to drive without a license**   (non-fin.compl.)

(32) **The grass** is green   (noun)

With respect to the second possibility, the expression of arguments by means of nouns, compare the following sentences:

(33) It was a big mistake **to visit him**

(34) **The visit** was a big mistake

In (33) the argument position of the non-verbal predicate *a big mistake* is restricted by the non-finite predication *to visit him*, in (34) it is restricted by the noun *visit*, as in representations (35)-(36) of (33)-(34) respectively:

(35) $\{(e_i: \text{mistake}_N (e_i): \text{big}_A (e_i))\} (e_j: [\text{visit}_V (x_i)_{Ag} (x_j: \text{him} (x_j))_{Go}] (e_j))_\phi$

(36) $\{(e_i: \text{mistake}_N (e_i): \text{big}_A (e_i))\} (e_j: \text{visit}_N (e_j))_\phi$

Nouns such as *mistake* and *visit* designate second order entities and may therefore be called, following Lyons (1977: 446), second order nouns. Similarly, nouns such as *idea* and *fact* designate third order entities and may be called third order nouns, and nouns such as *order* and *question* designate fourth order entities and may be called fourth order nouns.

It will have been noted that nominalization is not used here as a criterion to identify arguments of any particular type. This is because in a typological perspective nominalization varies as to its domain of application. A tentative representation of this parameter is given in (37) in terms of a hierarchy (see also Lehmann 1982: 76 and Foley and Van Valin 1984: 275ff).

(37) **The nominalization hierarchy (hypothesis)**
      $x_1 \quad > \quad e_1 \quad > \quad X_1 \quad > \quad E_1$
      first order nominalization
                  second order nominalization
                              third order nominalization
                                          fourth order nominalization

The hierarchy should be read in the following way: if a language allows third order nominalizations, it also allows second and first order nominalizations, or, in other words, if a language allows nominalized propositions, then it also allows nominalized predications and terms, etc.

I have no examples of languages with fourth order nominalizations[4], nor do

I have clear examples of languages without first order nominalizations. This leaves us with the following instantiations of the nominalization hierarchy:

(38) **Instantiations of the nominalization hierarchy**

	x_1	e_1	X_1	E_1
type I (example: Turkish)	+	+	+	-
type II (example: English)	+	+	-	-
type III (example: Mandarin)	+	-	-	-

To illustrate this table, consider the following examples:

(39) **The drive-r is ill** (x)

(40) **His driv-ing without a license** was a big mistake (e)

(41) ***His driv-ing without a license** is true (X)

English has first (cf. (39)) and second (cf. (40)) but no third (cf. (41)) order nominalizations. English can be considered a type II language.

Turkish (Altaic) is less restrictive than English in the domain of nominalization. Apart from first and second it also has third order nominalizations (cf. (42), from Lewis 1967). Turkish is a type I language.

(42) *Bir   parti kur-duğ-unuz*   *doğru   mu* (X)
INDEF party found-NMLZTN-POSS.2PL   true   INT
"Is it true that you have founded a party?"

Mandarin Chinese (Sino-Tibetan), finally, is more restrictive than English in the domain of nominalization. It has first order nominalizations (cf. (43), from Li and Thompson 1981) only. Mandarin is a type III language.

(43) *Mai qiche de   daban dou shi hao ren* (x)
sell car NMLZTN majorityall   COP good person
"Car sellers are mostly good people"

3. Predicability

Given that not only the predicate type but also the argument type is relevant for the definition of possible copula-constructions, the question remains in what way predicates and arguments may be combined. In order to answer this question I use the concept of predicability. This notion has been the subject of study in ontological philosophy (recent contributions being Sommers 1965, 1967; and Drange 1966), cognitive psychology (Keil 1979), and linguistics (Bickerton 1981). The definition of predicability can be given in different forms. I will start with an ontologically based definition in (44):

(44) **Predicability (extralinguistic, ontological)**
      The possibility of meaningful attribution of a property or relation P to
      an entity E: A property or relation P is predicable of an entity E if P
      can be meaningfully attributed to E.

This definition raises the question of what should be understood by meaningful attribution. Examples (45)-(47) may serve to illustrate the answer to that question:

(45) Grass is green

(46) Grass is blue

(47) Grass is at six o'clock

Example (45) can be seen as containing a true proposition, (46) as containing a false proposition. Example (47), on the other hand, is neither true nor false, but semantically anomalous. The difference between a false proposition and a semantically anomalous proposition is that the negative variant of a false proposition is a true proposition, whereas the negative variant of a semantically anomalous proposition is still a semantically anomalous proposition, as (48)-(49) show:

(48) Grass is not blue

(49) Grass is not at six o'clock

Drange (1966) uses the term *type crossing* for semantically anomalous propositions like (47) and (49). It should be noted that in order to determine whether a sentence contains a type crossing it should be taken litterally. In a metaphorical sense example (47) could well be acceptable, and in fact many metaphors can be seen as type crossings. I will return to metaphors after discussing the concept of linguistic predicability.

4. Copula constructions

If languages conformed fully to what is predicable in an ontological sense, we could apply the predicability test to the possible combinations of properties and relations with the four entity types and would then arrive at the classification of copula constructions given in (50). Each possible combination in (50) can be seen as expressing a semantic relation. A name has been given to each of these semantic relations.

(50) **Semantic relations in non-verbal predication**

β \ α	$(x_1)_\emptyset$	$(e_1)_\emptyset$	$(X_1)_\emptyset$	$(E_1)_\emptyset$
ascriptive constructions				
pred_N	role/status	--	--	--
$\{(x_i)_{Poss}\}$	possession	--	--	--
$\{(x_i)_{Loc}\}$	location	occurrence	--	--
$\{(\emptyset)_{Loc}\}$	existence	reality	--	--
$\{(e_i)_{Time}\}$	--	time	--	--
pred_A	prop. ass.	evaluation	judgment	--
classifying constructions				
$\{(x_i)\}$	classification	--	--	--
$\{(e_i)\}$	--	instantiation	--	--
$\{(X_i)\}$	--	--	explanation	--
$\{(E_i)\}$	--	--	--	interpretation

In the upper part in (50) it is stated that a role can be attributed to first order entities only, that possession is a relation between two first order entities, that both first and second order entities can have a location. Existence is seen here, following Dik (1980), as a subclass of location in the sense that existence can be viewed as being located at an unspecified location. The distinction made here between first order *existence* and second order *reality* is in fact a representation of the distinction made by Hannay (1985) between entity-existentials and SoA-existentials. Time can be attributed to second order entities only, and properties can be attributed to first, second, and third order entities. Most of these constructions have been illustrated in the preceding sections.

In the latter half of (50) it is indicated that first, second, third, and fourth order entities can be classified, but only in classes of their own type. Examples of these different forms of classification are (51)-(54):

(51) That man is my father   (first order)

(52) To spank is to love   (second order)

(53) What I mean is that I don't like you   (third order)

(54) His question was "Where are you going"   (fourth order)

If there were a complete correspondence between ontological distinctions and linguistic categories, I could stop here. This is, however, not the case. Many languages do not have all the constructions represented in (50), and many languages have some constructions beyond those represented in (50). This is because the definition of predicability used so far has an ontological basis, rather than a linguistic one. Let me therefore reformulate the definition for predicability in linguistic terms and contrast it with the definition given earlier:

(55) **Predicability (extralinguistic, ontological)**
      The possibility of meaningful attribution of a property or relation P to an entity E: A property or relation P is predicable of an entity E if P can be meaningfully attributed to E.

(56) **Predicability (intralinguistic, semantic)**
      The possibility of meaningful application of a predicate ß to an argument α: A predicate ß is predicable of an argument α if ß can be meaningfully applied to α.

Ontological predicability should be seen as language-independent, linguistic predicability as language-dependent. Given these two definitions, one can say that discrepancies may arise between the two senses of predicability. Sometimes languages are more permissive than ontology, and the result is a metaphor. In other respects languages may be less permissive than ontology, in which case the need for a periphrastic expression arises, as represented in (57):

(57) **Discrepancies in predicability-systems**

	metaphor	periphrasis
ontologically predicable	-	+
linguistically predicable	+	-

Let me illustrate both discrepancies. Periphrastic expressions arise where a language does not permit the direct expression of an ontologically predicable relation or property. Compare the following examples from English ((58)-60)), Vietnamese (Austric) ((61)-(63), from Liem 1969), and Abkhaz (Caucasian) ((64)-(66), from Spruit 1986, p.c.):

(58) You are beautiful   (x)

(59) It's stupid to drive without a license   (e)

(60) It's true that I don't like you   (X)

(61) *Ông.áy lanh lám*   (x)
      he   cold very
      "He is very cold"

(62) *Làm viec   này   hay*   (e)
      do   business DEM well
      "To do this work is good"

(63) *Ông.áy không phải là   lính*   (X)
      he   NEG   right COP soldier
      "He's not a soldier"

(64) *Də-bzəya-Ø-w-p'*   (x)
      he-good-Ø-PRES-IND
      "He is good"

(65) *Á-mc-hºa-ra*   *Ø-gaza-rá-Ø-w-p'*   (e)
    ART-lie-tell-INF   it-stupid-NOM-Ø-PRES-IND
    "To tell lies is a stupidity"

(66) *Yə-y-hºa-wa-z*   *Ø-c'ábərgə-Ø-w-p'*   (X)
    REL-he-say-PRES-REL it-true-Ø-PRES-IND
    "What he says is true"

In English adjectival predicates can be applied to nouns, predications and propositions, as is illustrated in (58)-(60). In Vietnamese adjectival predicates can be applied to nouns and predications, but not to propositions, as is illustrated in (61)-(63). The alternative used in Vietnamese to specify that a proposition is (not) true is the application of a modal-like element *phải* "right, indeed". In Abkhaz adjectival predicates can be applied to nouns only, as is illustrated in (64)-(66). The alternative used in Abkhaz in the case of predicational arguments is nominalization of the predicative adjective, as in (65), which turns an ascriptive into a classifying construction. In the case of propositional arguments there is no clear alternative, although the propositional content can be referred to indirectly, as in (66), where the headless relative refers to a propositional content.

In general, linguistic predicability seems to follow the hierarchy[5] given in (67).

(67) **The predicability hierarchy**

$$\text{pred}_\beta (x_I) > \text{pred}_\beta (e_I) > \text{pred}_\beta (X_I) > \text{pred}_\beta (E_I)$$

This hierarchy states that if a language can apply a predicate of a certain class to third order arguments, it can also apply a predicate of that class to second order and first order arguments. The adjectival cases from English, Vietnamese and Abkhaz are represented schematically in (68) and offer an illustration of the predicability hierarchy:

(68) **The predicability hierarchy in the adjectival domain**

language \ frame	$pred_A (x_1)_\emptyset$	$> pred_A (e_1)_\emptyset$	$> pred_A (X_1)_\emptyset$
English	+	+	+
Vietnamese	+	+	−
Abkhaz	+	−	−

The second possible discrepancy between the two notions of predicability mentioned in (57) arises where languages are more permissive than ontology, as in the case of a metaphor. By way of illustration I give two examples of type crossings or at least constructions which must once have been type crossings. First consider the Tagálog (Austric) examples in (69)-(70) (from Schachter and Otanes 1972):

(69) *May relos   si   Juan* $\{(x_i)_{Poss}\} (x_j)_\emptyset$
COP watch   TOP Juan
"Juan has a watch"

(70) *May gagawin   si   Juan* $\{(x_i)_{Poss}\} (e_i)_\emptyset$
COP do.PROSP TOP Juan
"Juan has something to do" or "Juan is going to do something"

Example (69) is a regular possessive construction with a first order argument. Example (70) is identical to (69) except for the fact that it has a second order argument.[6] The subject is said to own a not yet realized SoA, which is ontologically non-predicable, but linguistically acceptable. The resulting meaning varies between a prospective and obligative meaning, the latter being quite similar to the English equivalent *have to*.

A second case of discrepancy, where it is the predicate term rather than the argument term that is of a type not predicted by schema (50), is illustrated by the Mandarin (Sino-Tibetan) examples (71)-(72) (from Li and Thompson 1981):

(71) *Lisi zai   hai-bian* $\{(x_i)_{Loc}\} (x_j)_\emptyset$
Lisi LOC sea-side
"Lisi is at the coast"

(72) *Lisi   zai   jieshi   wenfa* $\{(e_i)_{Loc}\}\ (x_j)_\emptyset$
      Lisi LOC explain grammar
      "Lisi is explaining grammar"

Example (71) is a regular locative construction in which both the argument term
and the predicate term designate first order entities. Example (72), discussed
in Hengeveld (1987), is identical to (71) except for the fact that the predicate
term designates a second order entity. The subject is said to be located in a
SoA, which again is ontologically non-predicable, but linguistically acceptable.
This locative metaphor has in fact entered the grammatical system of Mandarin
and is used to express durative aspect.[7]
   What may be concluded from these discrepancies is that the schema given
in (50) gives the *maximal* set of copula constructions, and that any violation of
this schema can be seen as a creative manipulation of linguistic categories.

5. Further perspectives

In 2. I have extracted information from a model for the utterance in order to
arrive at a classification of copula constructions. One might ask now whether
the classification arrived at has something to contribute in return to the clause
model. A final look at a pair of locative predicate frames, one with a first and
one with a second order argument, suggests that it has. Consider the predicate
frames in (73)-(74):

   (73) $\{(d1x_i\colon \text{room}\ (x_i)\colon \text{next}\ (x_i))_{Loc}\}\ (x_1)_\emptyset$

   (74) $\{(d1x_i\colon \text{room}\ (x_i)\colon \text{next}\ (x_i))_{Loc}\}\ (e_1)_\emptyset$

On the basis of the first predicate we can construe (75)-(76):

   (75) $(\text{Pres}\ e_i\colon [\{(d1x_i\colon \text{room}\ (x_i)\colon \text{next}\ (x_i))_{Loc}\}\ (dx_j\colon \text{table}_N\ (x_j))_\emptyset]\ (e_i))$
         "The table is in the next room"

   (76) $(dx_j\colon \text{table}_N\ (x_j)\colon \{(d1x_i\colon \text{room}\ (x_i)\colon \text{next}\ (x_i))_{Loc}\}\ (x_j)_\emptyset)$
         "The table in the next room"

In (75) the locative predicate is used predicatively, in (76) it is used attributively, i.e. as a restrictor. The copula in (75) is triggered by the presence of a tense

operator.

Similarly, on the basis of the second predicate, that in (74), we can construe (77)-(78):

(77) (Pres e_i: [{(d1x_i: room (x_i): next (x_i))$_{LocFoc}$} (Pres e_j: [meet$_V$ (dx_j: 1pl (x_j))$_{Ag}$] (e_j))$_{øTop}$] (e_i))
"It is in the next room that we meet"

(78) (Pres e_j: [meet$_V$ (dx_j: 1pl (x_j))$_{Ag}$] (e_j): {(d1x_i: room (x_i): next (x_i))$_{Loc}$} (e_j))
"We meet in the next room"

In (77) the locative predicate is used predicatively, in (78) it is used attributively. The copula in (77) is triggered by the (first) tense operator. Note that the predicative use of the locative predicate in constructions like (77) is possible only when it has a focal value.

The representation of the locative phrase in (78) is in fact that proposed for Locative and Temporal satellites in Vet (1986). The predicates needed for his approach to these satellites are those that take a second order argument. This is not the place to give a full account of this use of non-verbal predicates. It seems likely, however, that the classification of copula constructions arrived at has something to contribute to the description of clause structure as well.

Notes

1. I would like to thank Simon Dik, Hotze Mulder, and the editors of this volume for their comments and suggestions.

2. This is not the only difference between *ser* and *estar*. See Hengeveld (1986) for further details.

3. An individual exists if it is located someplace. A SoA is real if it occurred someplace, sometime.

4. In Lahu (Matisoff 1972) it is possible to nominalize entire independent sentences. It does, however, not follow from this fact that Lahu has fourth order nominalizations. Since the nominalizing particle in independent sentences may optionally be followed by modal adverbs, it is more likely that it is the proposition contained within the sentence that is nominalized.

5. A second predicability hierarchy can be defined in terms of the non-verbal predicate on which a non-verbal predication type is based. See Hengeveld (fc.) for discussion.

6. Cf. also Bolkestein (1983: 68-73); Seiler (1983: 54).

7. See Dik (1985) for a more systematic treatment of the use of locative metaphors in the expression of aspectual distinctions.

References

Bickerton, D.
  1981 *Roots of language*. Ann Arbor: Karoma.

Bolkestein, A.M.
  1983 "Genitive and dative possessors in Latin". In S.C.Dik (ed.), *Advances in functional grammar*. Dordrecht: Foris, 55-91.

Dik, S.C.
  1980 *Studies in functional grammar*. London: Academic Press.
  1985 *Copula auxiliarization: How and why?*. Working Papers in Functional Grammar 2.
  1987 "A typology of entities". In J.van der Auwera and L.Goossens (eds.), *Ins and outs of the predication*. Dordrecht: Foris, 1-20.

Drange, T.
  1966 *Type crossings*. The Hague: Mouton.

Foley, W.A. and R.D.Van Valin
  1984 *Functional syntax and universal grammar*. Cambridge: Cambridge UP.

Hagman, R.S.
  1973 *Nama Hottentot grammar*. PhD-thesis, Columbia University.

Hannay, M.
  1985 *English existentials in functional grammar*. Dordrecht: Foris.

Hengeveld, K.
  1986 "Copular verbs in a functional grammar of Spanish". *Linguistics* 24: 393-420.
  1987 *A functional analysis of copula constructions in Mandarin Chinese*. Working Papers in Functional Grammar 23.
  1989 "Layers and operators in functional grammar".*Journal of Linguistics* 25: 127-157. (= Revised version of: Working Papers in Functional Grammar 27).
  fc.   "Non-verbal predicability". In J.van der Auwera and M.Kefer (eds.), *Grammar and meaning*. The Hague: Mouton.

Keil, F.C.
  1979 *Semantic and conceptual development: An ontological perspective*. Cambridge: Harvard

UP.

Lafitte, P.
1944   *Grammaire Basque: Navarro-labourdin litteraire*. Bayonne: Librairie Le Livre.

Lehmann, C.
1982   "Nominalisierung: Typisierung von Propositionen". In H.Seiler and C.Lehmann (eds.), *Apprehension: Das sprachliche Erfassen von Gegenständen, Teil I: Bereich und Ordnung der Phänomene*. Tübingen: Narr, 66-83.

Lewis, G.L.
1967   *Turkish grammar*. Oxford: Clarendon Press.

Li, C.N. and S.A.Thompson
1981   *Mandarin Chinese*. Berkeley: University of California Press.

Liem, N.D.
1969   *A contrastive analysis of English and Vietnamese, vol.2: Vietnamese grammar*. Canberra: The Australian National University.

Lyons, J.
1977   *Semantics*. Cambridge: Cambridge UP.

Makino, S.
1968   "Japanese 'be'". In J.W.M.Verhaar (ed.), *The verb 'be' and its synonyms, vol. 3*. Dordrecht: Reidel, 1-19.

Matisoff, J.
1972   *The grammar of Lahu*. Berkeley: University of California Publications in Linguistics.

Schachter, P. and F.T.Otanes
1972   *Tagalog reference grammar*. Berkeley: University of California Press.

Seiler, H.
1983   *Possession as an operational dimension of language*. Tübingen: Narr.

Sommers, F.
1965   "Predicability". In M.Black (ed.), *Philosophy in America*. London: George Allen & Unwin Ltd., 262-281.
1967   "Types and ontology". In P.F.Strawson (ed.), *Philosophical logic*. Oxford: Oxford UP, 138-169.

Spruit, A.
1986   *Abkhaz studies*. Dissertation, University of Leiden.

Vet, C.
  1986   *A pragmatic approach to tense in functional grammar*. Working Papers in Functional
          Grammar 16.

Asymmetries in the Use of Tense and Modality

Co Vet

University of Groningen

0. Introduction[1]

In many languages the meaning or the function of a certain class of sentence depends on the choice of the Subject and the tense form. It is well-known, for example, that the speaker can realize a performative speech act only if the sentence he/she utters is in the present tense and has a first person Subject (evidently it has to contain an appropriate predicate too). It has been shown recently (Martin 1987; Anderson 1986) that this combination (i.e. present tense + first person) gives rise to special meanings in sentences expressing the speaker's attitude (modality/evidentiality). Compare for example:

(1) a.   I hear Mary won the prize
     b.   He hears Mary won the prize

(1a) is semantically equivalent to 'I know it because I have heard it' whereas (1b) cannot be paraphrased as 'He knows it because he has heard it' (Anderson 1986).

Since the source of this kind of asymmetry is clearly of a pragmatic nature, it cannot be dealt with in a purely syntactic framework. A recent proposal by Hengeveld (1988, 1989) offers the possibility of taking into account illocutionary factors in the structure of underlying sentences, thus enabling the grammar to deal with an important class of phenomena (mainly modality and evidentiality).

In the first section of this paper I will modify Hengeveld's proposal slightly, to make it agree with the general format adopted by Dik (1978) for terms, and by Vet (1986) for predications. In section 2 this structure will be used to analyse asymmetry phenomena in English and French (respectively, *hear* and the modal uses of the future tense).

1. Terms, propositions and utterances

In Vet (1986) it was shown that the format used in Functional Grammar (FG) for the representation of terms can also be used for the representation of propositions. In this paper I will use this general format for the representation of utterances.

Let us first consider the structure of terms as it is proposed by Dik (1978):

(2) $book_N$ (x_1)

(3)   term operator x_i: $book_N$ (x_i)

(4)   term operator x_i: $book_N$ (x_i): $restrictor_1$ (x_i): $restrictor_2$ (x_i):.....

The structure underlying a term is formed by applying a nominal predicate, for example that of (2), to a variable which is introduced (bound) by a term operator (an article, a demonstrative) (see (3)). The application of the predicate *book* to x_i means that the concept 'book' is realized in the entity referred to by x_i. As a conceptualized entity it can now be identified by the interlocutor. The structure of (4) illustrates the way in which more predicates (adjectives, for example) can be applied to the reference marker (x_i) indicating that more concepts are realized in the entity for which it stands. For example:

(5) $d1x_i$: $book_N$ (x_i): red_A (x_i)
      "the red book"

where d1 is the term operator (d stands for 'definite' and 1 for 'singular').

Whereas terms refer to individuals in the discussion domain, sentences can also be considered as referring to specific portions of the world, namely time-space regions, on which the concept they express is realized (see Bartsch 1986). In the representation of sentences tense is conceived of as an operator introducing the variable standing for a specific time-space region (e):

(6)   tense operator e_i: $\{pred_V (x_1).....(x_n)\}$ (e_i)

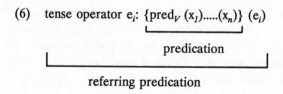

In (6) the status of the predication is analogous to that of the nominal predicate in the structures underlying terms. If the predication is applied to a space-time variable e (e_i in (6)), this results in a 'conceptualized space-time region' (see Bartsch 1986). The 'referring predication' of (6) refers to such a conceptualized space-time region. A referring predication refers to a State of Affairs (SoA) in the real world or in some possible world. The tense-operator gives information about the position of the SoA with respect to the speech moment (or some other reference point).

As an example, let us consider (7), the representation of which is given in (8) according to the principles specified above:

(7)   Peter walked

(8)   Past e_i: {walk$_V$ (d1x$_i$: Peter (x$_i$))$_{Ag}$} (e$_i$)

(8) reads as follows: there is a specific time-space region e_i, which is anterior to the speech moment and on which the concept 'walk (Peter)' is realized.

Note that the structure of (6) or (8) can also be extended by restrictors, for example:

(9)   Peter walked yesterday

(10) Past e_i: {walk$_V$ (d1x$_i$: Peter (x$_i$))$_{Ag}$} (e$_i$): yesterday$_{Time}$ (e$_i$)

Structures such as (8) and (10) only represent the referring function of the sentence and do not take into account its content function. In other words sentences can not only be regarded as expressions which refer to a SoA but also as information units which are transmitted by the speaker to the addressee. In line with Hengeveld's terminology I will call these entities 'propositions' and represent them by the variable X:

(11) **Proposition structure**
      X_i: [tense operator e$_i$: {pred$_V$ (x$_1$).....(x$_n$)} (e$_i$)] (X$_i$)

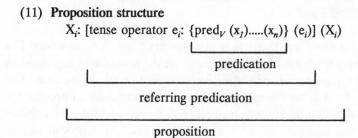

                              predication

                          referring predication

                              proposition

In natural language there is always somebody, the speaker, who guarantees that the proposition expressed by the sentence is true. If he or she does not accept responsibility, or only assumes a restricted responsibility for its truth, this is explicitly indicated in the form of the sentence itself. Thus, in order to be able to represent an utterance, we have to relate the proposition to some speech act by which the speaker assumes this responsibility. I propose to represent the illocutionary force of the speech act realized by the speaker as an operator (δ_{ILL}) which binds the proposition (factuality) variable X_i:[2]

(12) **Clause structure**

$$\delta_{ILL}\ X_i:\ [\text{tense operator}\ e_i:\ \{\text{pred}_V\ (x_1)\ldots(x_n)\}\ (e_i)]\ (X_i)$$

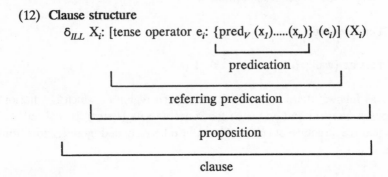

In (12) the clause represents an utterance. The operator (δ_{ILL}) provides linguistic information about the illocutionary force of the utterance. It binds the variable X_i, which stands for the factuality of the proposition. The element ILL can for example take the values DECL or INT; in that case the expression rules of the grammar produce a declarative and an interrogative sentence type respectively:[3]

(13) a. $\delta_{DECL}\ X_i:\ [\text{Past}\ e_i:\ \{\text{walk}_V\ (d1x_i:\ \text{Peter}\ (x_i))_{Ag}\}\ (e_i)]\ (X_i)$
         "Peter walked"
     b. $\delta_{INT}\ X_i:\ [\text{Past}\ e_i:\ \{\text{walk}_V\ (d1x_i:\ \text{Peter}\ (x_i))_{Ag}\}\ (e_i)]\ (X_i)$
         "Did Peter walk?"

In (13a) δ_{DECL} means that the speaker presents the proposition as a fact. The formula can be paraphrased as 'I guarantee that the proposition expressed by the sentence I am pronouncing/ writing corresponds to a fact in the world that I have in mind'. In (13b) the speaker invites the interlocutor to provide the value of X_i: does the proposition correspond to a fact or not? The illocutionary operator can thus be conceived of as a linguistic marker which provides a clue for the interlocutor as to how he/she has to understand the nature of the speech act the speaker wants to perform by uttering the sentence.

The illocutionary operator can be realized in different ways. In its unmarked form (cf. (13a-b)) it gives rise to the basic sentence types (interrogative, declarative). In this case δ remains unspecified. Many languages have grammatical and/or lexical means to either modify the degree of factuality of a proposition or to mitigate the illocutionary force of a proposition (mood, modal adverbs, predicate frames). We will see that these expressions can either be regarded as explicitating the value of δ or that of ILL.

In the rest of this paper the scope of the negation will play an important role in my argumentation (see also Dik et al. this vol.: 3.4). It is generally assumed in FG that negation (Neg) has only the predication in its scope, in other words, Neg lies itself within the scope of the tense operator. The negation of (14), for example:

(14) Peter did not answer that question

occupies the following position in the underlying structure

(15) δ_{DECL} X$_i$: [Past e$_i$: {Neg answer$_V$ (Peter (x$_i$))$_{Ag}$
      (that question (x$_j$))$_{Go}$} (e$_i$)] (X$_i$)

Neg indicates that the relation *answer* does not hold between x$_i$ (*Peter*) and x$_j$ (*that question*). The position of the negation in the sentence structure implies that any element of the sentence that cannot be negated has to belong either to the tense operator or to the illocutionary operator. See for example *peut-être* in (16b):

(16) a. *Pierre   ne   viendra   peut-être   pas*
          Pierre   not   will-come   perhaps   not
          "Perhaps Pierre will not come"
      b. **Pierre ne viendra pas peut-être*
          "Pierre will not perhaps come"

(16b) is unacceptable without a comma pronunciation between *pas* "not" and *peut-être* "perhaps". This shows that *peut-être* cannot lie within the scope of Neg and, consequently, cannot pertain to the predication of the sentence. Since its function is to modify the degree of factuality of the proposition, it has to be assumed that it occupies the position of δ_{ILL} in (12). Note that *peut-être* cannot be used in interrogative sentences so that the value of ILL in δ_{ILL} has to be DECL.[4] *Peut-être* indicates the value of δ. In other words I conceive of *peut-être* as a kind of declarative operator, which assigns the value 'possible' to X_i. The representation of (16a) is then as follows:

(17) peut-être$_{DECL}$ X_i: [Fut e_i: {Neg venir$_V$ (Pierre $(x_i))_{Ag}$} (e_i)] (X_i)

The elements which do not belong to the proposition are necessarily related to the speech act. Consequently they are directly connected with the speaker's position in time and space (the hic and nunc of the speaker) as well as to his/her person ('I'). Many if not all of the asymmetries I will discuss in the next section can be explained by this fact.

2. Some cases of asymmetry

In this section I will give two illustrations of the way in which the structure of (12) can be used to explain the syntactic and semantic particularities of the verb *hear* in English and of the future tense in French.

2.1. The verb 'hear' in English

Consider the following examples:

(18) a.   I heard that Mary won the prize
      b.   I hear (that) Mary won the prize

(19) a.   Peter heard that Mary won the prize
      b.   Peter hears (that) Mary won the prize

(20) a.   I did not hear that Mary won the prize
      b.   *I do not hear (that) Mary won the prize

(18a-b) show that the verb *hear* can be used in the past and the present tense, apparently without much difference in meaning. In fact the tense in (18b) is not a 'real' present tense because it does not indicate that the process of hearing overlaps the speech moment. Instead (18b) has to be interpreted as referring to a process of hearing in the past, just like (18a). It is interesting that this (pseudo-) synonomy disappears as soon as we replace in (18b) the first person by the second or third person, as is shown by (19a-b). More interestingly, only (18a) is compatible with the negation whereas the non-past variant is not (see (20a-b)).

What can be concluded from these observations? First, according to my criteria, it must be assumed that *hear* in (18b) lies outside the scope of both the negation and the tense operator. The most plausible explanation seems to be that *I hear* in (18b) occupies the position of δ_{ILL}. It would then be interpreted as a kind of evidential marker (hearsay): (18b) can indeed be paraphrased as 'I declare, because I heard it, that the proposition expressed by the sentence I am uttering is a fact'.

The underlying representation of (18b) would then be as follows:

(21) $[\text{hear (I)}]_{DECL}$ X_i: $[\text{Past } e_i: \{\text{win}_V \text{ (Mary)}_{Ag} \text{ (the prize)}_{Go}\} \text{ (}e_i\text{)}]$ (X_i)

Anderson (1986) regards the behaviour of *I hear* in (18b) as the beginning of a grammaticalisation process, which in the long run may reduce the grammatical status of *I hear* to a prefix or a particle, which will be accompanied by a parallel reduction of its form. He gives examples from Maricopa and Makah where evidential markers have developed in this way from perception verbs.

It is true that expressions which can occupy the position of the illocutionary operator have very restricted grammatical possibilities. We have already seen that they cannot be negated. Adverbs which function as an illocutionary operator either combine with declarative or interrogative mood, or if they combine with both moods they have different meanings (cf. *peut-être* and *perhaps*; see also note 4). If illocutionary operators have the form of a predicate frame (*I hear*) they are always contructed according to the same schema (declarative mood, present tense, first person Subject and, with some predicates, a second person indirect object). Parenthetical expressions such as *I hear, I guess*, etc. show the same type of restriction and probably also belong to the set of expressions which can function as an illocutionary operator. In that case (22):

(22) Mary won the prize, I hear

can be regarded as an alternative realization of (21).

2.2. Future tense in French

The future in French has its 'normal' temporal use in sentences such as:

(23) *Le   président   Bush se   rendra   à Moscou   (au   mois*
     the   president   Bush REFL   will.go   to Moscow   (in   month
     de mai)
     of Mai)
     "President Bush will go to Moscow (in May)"

The representation of (23) is straightforward:

(24) δ_{DECL} X_i: [Fut e_i: {se-rendre$_V$ (Bush $(x_i))_{Ag}$ (Moscou $(x_j))_{Dir}$} (e_i):
     au mois de mai (e_i)] (X_i)

However, grammars of French also distinguish so-called modal uses of this
tense form:

(25) *On   sonne.   Ce   sera   le   facteur.*
     they   ring   that   will.be   the   postman
     "There is a ring (at the door). It will be the postman."

(26) *Pierre   n'est   pas   là.   Il aura   manqué le   train.*
     Peter   not-is   not   here   he will.have   missed   the   train
     "Peter is not here. He will have missed the train"

Unlike the future tense of (23), the future and future perfect of (25) and (26)
do not indicate that the SoA referred to by the sentence is posterior to the
speech moment. Instead the speaker makes a conjecture about what may be the
case at the speech moment on the basis of the information provided by the first
sentence. However, he/she postpones giving a final judgement about its truth
until more evidence becomes available. Thus, the future tense in (25) and (26)
suspends (Suspend) the truth value (X_i) of the proposition. The representations
of the second sentences of (25) and (26) are as in (27a-b):

(27) a.   Suspend$_{DECL}$ X_i: [{Pres e_i: {{(être) le facteur (x_j)} $(ce(x_i))$}
          (e_i)] (X_i)
     b.   Suspend$_{DECL}$ X_i: [Pres Perf e_i: manquer$_V$ (il $(x_i))_{Exp}$ (le train$_{Go}$
          $(x_j))$} (e_i)] (X_i)

An expression rule will transform Suspend into Fut. A second expression rule will map Fut onto the verbal predicate of the predication and provide it with the future tense ending. Without Suspend the speaker would express his/her commitment to the truth of the propositions at the speech moment and then would have worded them as (28a-b), which justifies the presence of Pres and Pres Perf in (27a-b):

(28) a. *On   sonne. C'est   le   facteur.*
        they ring   that-is the postman
        "There is a ring (at the door). It is the postman"
    b. *Pierre n'est   pas là. Il a   manqué le   train.*
       Peter   not-is not here he has missed the   train
       "Peter is not here. He has missed the train"

Note that Suspend does not combine with interrogative mood:

(29) **Pierre n'est   pas là. Est-ce qu'il   aura   manqué*
      Peter   not-is not here is-that that-he will.have   missed
      le   train?
      the   train
      "Peter is not here. Will he have missed the train?" (*Suspend$_{INT}$ X$_i$)

In the framework developed so far, the reason for this incompatibility is easy to find: INT(terrogative) already indicates that the speaker does not know the factuality value of X$_i$ (see (13b)). It is therefore impossible to suspend the value of X$_i$ by means of Suspend, since it is already undecided because of the presence of INT.

    A different use of the future, also called 'modal' by the grammarians, is illustrated by (30) (an utterance used in a shop):

(30) *Ce   sera   tout, Madame?*
     that will.be all   Madam
     "Anything else, Madam?"

The meaning of this sentence is as in (31):

(31) *C'est   tout, Madame?*
     that.is   all   Madam
     "Anything else, Madam?"

The only difference is that (30) is polite and (31) is less so. Again the future tense of (30) does not indicate that the SoA is posterior to the speech moment. It does not temporarily suspend its factuality value either, since in that use it was incompatible with INT(errogation), as we have seen above, in (29).

On the basis of this difference it may be concluded that the future tense in (30) belongs to another class of operators, whose function is to mitigate (Mtg) the illocutionary force of the speech act (here INT(terrogation)). The representation I propose for (30) is as follows:

(32) $\text{Mtg}_{INT} X_i$: [Pres e_i:{ {(être) tout$_N$ (x_j)} (ce (x_i))} (e_i)] (X_i)

Again an expression rule will translate Mtg as Fut.

The explanation for the use of the future tense form as an operator which mitigates the illocutionary force of an utterance may be that in its temporal use the future presents the SoA as cut off from the speaker's present. Apparently it is this feature of the future that is exploited as a mitigating device. Note that its use in (25) and (26) seems closer to the temporal use than that of (30), since in (25) and (26) the judgement about the factuality of the proposition is postponed until further evidence will be available. In (30) any idea of posteriority is absent. The weakening of the temporal meaning of the future tense form may have followed the following historic development according to the general schema proposed by Hengeveld (1989: 142):

(33) $\text{Mtg}_{ILL} X_i$ > $\text{Suspend}_{DECL} X_i$ > Fut e_i [> deontic modal auxiliary
                                           (Latin *habere* + infinitive)]

where '>' means 'developed from'. However, I will not deal with this aspect of the future tense form here. Instead I will discuss another case illustrated by (34):

(34) *Je vous demanderai   une   bienveillante   attention*
     I you will.ask   a   kind   attention
     "May I have your kind attention, please?"

This sentence is ambiguous: it can refer to a future SoA or to a mitigated speech act realized at the speech moment. It is interesting that only the future reading is possible if (34) is negated or if *je* "I" is replaced by a second or third person (pro)noun:

(35) a. *Je ne   vous demanderai   pas   une   bienveillante   attention*
         I not   you will.ask   not   a   kind   attention
         "I will not kindly ask your attention"
     b. *Elle vous demandera   une   bienveillante   attention*
         she you will.ask   a   kind   attention
         "She will kindly ask your attention"

This clearly shows that *je demanderai*, in its mitigating reading, is outside the scope of both the negation and the tense operator.

From the analyses I have proposed so far it will be clear that the future tense, in its mitigating function (Mtg), occupies the δ-position of the illocutionary operator (δ_{ILL}) so that the predicate frame *demander (je)(vous)* "request-from (I) (you)" has to be regarded as an instantiation of ILL(ocution). However, the problem is that in (34) *une bienveillante attention* does not have the form of a predication. However, this expression does not represent a prototypical term either. In contrast to, for instance, *une chaise* "a chair" which denotes an object, *une bienveillante attention* refers to a SoA which can be controlled by the addressee of (34) (*vous* "you"). This explains why the substitution of *une bienveillante attention* by *une chaise* would lead here to a rather odd result since *une chaise* cannot be controlled. What expressions like *une bienveillante attention* have in common with predications is that they imply reference to a SoA and not to an individual. The difference with prototypical terms such as *une chaise* could then be accounted for by adopting for nominal or nominalized expressions referring to a SoA such as *attention* an e-variable (instead of an x-variable).[5] In the lexicon *chaise* and *attention* would then be listed in the following way:

(36) a. $\text{chaise}_N (x_1)$
     b. $\text{attention}_N (e_1)$

The presence of the category-marker N ('noun') in (36b) would then allow for *attention* to be used as a nominal predicate by the rules of term formation:

(37) $i1e_i$: $\text{attention}_N (e_i)$: $\text{bienveillant}_A (e_i)$
     "une bienveillante attention"

(where i in i1e$_i$ stands for 'indefinite' and 1 for 'singular').

Sentences such as (34) can now be represented according to the general schema of (12) since expressions such as *une bienveillante attention* can now function as a predication. The structure underlying (33) can be given the following form:

(38) Mtg [demander$_V$ (je)$_{Ag}$ (vous)$_{Rec}$]$_{REQU}$ X$_i$: [{i1e$_i$: attention$_N$ (e$_i$): bienveillant$_A$} (e$_i$)] (X$_i$)

Thus in uttering (34) the speaker (*je*) makes a mitigated (Mtg) request (*demander (je)*) addressed to the Recipient (*vous*) to attend to the realization of a SoA consisting of the addressee's kind attention. The same schema can be used for utterances such as:

(39) *Une bienveillante attention, s'il vous plaît!*
     a   kind   attention if-it you please
     "May I have your kind attention, please?"

which can be represented as follows:

(40) [s'il vous plaît]$_{REQU}$ X$_i$: [{i1e$_i$: attention$_N$ (e$_i$): bienveillant$_A$} (e$_i$)] (X$_i$)

The future tense form not only appears in utterances expressing a request, it can also be used to mitigate a declaration, as in:

(41) *Je vous dirai qu'une phrase négative présuppose*
     I you will.say that-a sentence negative presupposes
     l'existence d'une phrase positive
     the-existence of-a sentence positive
     "I'd say that a negative sentence presupposes the existence of a positive sentence"

In this case the e-element embedded in the illocutionary frame is a proposition, but the function of the future tense form is the same as in (34) (mitigation) and, similar to *demander (je)* in (34), *dire (je)* also expresses overtly the illocutionary value of the utterance. This shows that the mechanism underlying these speech acts is the same in both cases, which justifies the generalization I proposed for (34).

3. Conclusion

If the analyses proposed in this paper are accepted, sentences of natural language can be categorized according to the extent to which the elements they contain pertain to the domain of the illocution and to the domain of the (referring) predication (cf. Palmer 1983). The sentence types we have discussed can be classified as follows:

(42) illocutionary domain   e-domain
      δ ILL   referring predication

i.   - $DECL$ X_i Past e_i: {hear$_V$ (Peter) (Past e_j: {win$_V$
                                     (Mary) (the prize)} (e_j)} (e_i) (18a)

iia.   Suspend $DECL$ X_i Pres e_i: {{(être) le facteur} (ce)} (e_i)
       expression rule: Suspend -> Fut   (25)

iib.   Mtg INT X_i Pres e_i: {(être) tout {(ce)} (e_i)
       expression rule: Mtg -> Fut   (30)

iiia. peut-être $DECL$ X_i Fut e_i: {Neg venir (Pierre)} (e_i) (16a)

iiib. [hear (I)] $DECL$ X_i Past e_i: {win (Mary) (the prize)} (e_i) (18b)

iv.   Mtg [demander(je)]$_{REQU}$ X_i (i1e$_i$: (bienveillante attention) (e_i))
       expression rule: Mtg -> Fut   (34)

In category (i) the information about the illocutionary force of the utterance is carried only by DECL(arative), which gives rise to specific word order and intonation. In (ii), part of this information is provided by Suspend and Mtg which are both realized as future tense. In (iii) the δ-position of the illocutionary operator is occupied by lexical material, an adverb (*peut-être*) and a predicate frame (*I hear*) which both obligatorily combine with DECL(arative). In (iv) the δ-position is filled by the mitigation marker Mtg whereas the value of ILL ('request') is indicated by a predicate frame (*je demande*).

The illocutionary part of the utterance is invariably related to the speech event. This means that elements which pertain to this domain never cause a shift in time reference, as we have seen above, and that the pronouns which pertain to this part are always in the first person (Agent) or in the second person (Recipient).

From a pragmatic point of view the division of (42) is of paramount importance since it provides clues as to the way in which the interlocutor has to interpret the speaker's intentions with respect to the information conveyed by the e-component of the sentence.

Notes

1. Research for this paper was done during a stay at N.I.A.S. (Netherlands Institute for Advanced Study). I am grateful to Machtelt Bolkestein, Kees Hengeveld and Jan Nuyts for their valuable comments on an earlier version of this paper, and to Ann Simpson for correcting my English.

2. This schema is inspired by Hengeveld (1989), but differs from it in that the speech act is not obligatorily represented in the clause by an abstract illocutionary frame ((ILL (speaker) (addressee)(X_i)). Another difference is that δ_{ILL} assumes the functions of Hengeveld's proposition operator π_3 and illocution operator π_4.

3. I will not deal here with imperative sentences, which have a different underlying form. See Hengeveld (this vol.).

4. In Dutch the equivalent of *peut-être*, *misschien* "perhaps", can be used in declarative and interrogative sentences. For example:

    (a) *Piet   heeft   misschien heimwee*
    Peter has   perhaps homesickness
    "Maybe Peter is homesick"

    (b) *Heeft Peter misschien heimwee?*
    has   Peter perhaps homesickness?
    "Am I right in supposing that Peter is homesick?"

    In (b) *misschien* seems to indicate that the speaker is not quite sure if his/her question is justified. The temporal adverb *soms* "sometimes" offers an even clearer example of a meaning shift when it is used in an interrogative sentence. Compare, for example:

    (c) *Marie krijgt   soms   brieven   van   Peter*
    Mary receives sometimes letters   from   Peter
    "Mary sometimes receives letters from Peter"

    (d) *Krijgt   Marie soms   brieven   van   Peter?*
    receives Mary sometimes letters   from   Peter
    "Marie receives letters from Peter, doesn't she?"

In (d) the adverb *soms* does not mean 'now and then' but rather indicates that the speaker has inferred from the context that it might be the case that Marie receives letters from Peter.

5.   This solution was suggested to me by Simon Dik (p.c.).

References

Anderson, L.B.
    1986   "Evidentials, paths of change, and mental maps: Typologically regular asymmetries". In W.Chafe and J.Nichols (eds.), *Evidentiality: The linguistic coding of epistemology*. Norwood: Ablex, 273-312.

Bartsch, R.
    1986   "On aspectual properties of Dutch and German nominalizations". In V.Lo Cascio and C.Vet (eds.), *Temporal structure in sentence and discourse*. Dordrecht: Foris, 7-39.

Dik, S.C.
    1978   *Functional grammar*. Amsterdam: North-Holland.

Hengeveld, K.
    1988   "Illocution, mood and modality in a functional grammar of Spanish". *Journal of Semantics* 6: 227-269.
    1989   "Layers and operators in functional grammar". *Journal of Linguistics* 25: 127-157.

Martin, R.
    1987   *Langage et croyance: Les "univers de croyance" dans la théorie sémantique*. Brussels: Pierre Mardaga.

Palmer, F.R.
    1983   "Semantic explanation for the syntax of the English modals". In F.Heny and B.Richards (eds.), *Linguistic categories: Auxiliaries and related puzzles, vol.2*. Dordrecht: Reidel, 205-217.

Tasmowski, L.
    1980   "Un 'devoir' opérateur". *Travaux de Linguistique* 7: 43-58.

Vet, C.
    1986   *A pragmatic approach to tense in functional grammar*. Working Papers in Functional Grammar 16.

Tense, Semantics and Layered Syntax

Peter Harder

University of Copenhagen

0. Introduction: Some basic assumptions[1]

In this paper I shall try to make some points about semantics in a layered syntax of the kind that is emerging within Functional Grammar (FG), and illustrate them within the area of tense. The principles on which this account is based can be stated as (1)-(4) below:

(1) Linguistic *signs* are basic elements from a semantic point of view. When we want to say that something has the status of linguistic meaning, it must therefore be attached to a linguistic expression, i.e. 'coded in the linguistic expression as such', cf. Dik (1989: ch.1). The word 'content' will be used for the coded, linguistic meaning attached to a linguistic expression. 'Content' and 'expression' as used below correspond to 'signifié' and 'signifiant', respectively.

(2) Linguistic meaning cannot be understood with *information* as the common denominator (if information is seen as description of a state obtaining in some world). Like the kind of meaning usually described as illocutionary, all linguistic meaning is basically a form of communicative action and hence functional in nature. At sub-sentence level the action potential of linguistic expressions can be seen as taking the form of *instructions* for building a mental model (cf. Johnson-Laird 1983) and using it in various ways.

(3) Linguistic expressions have semantic content because of linguistic *conventions*, holding in the speech community in virtue of Searlian constitutive rules: *cheval* means 'horse' because using that expression counts as an instruction to invoke a mental (sub-)model of a horse (as an aspect of the total process of understanding the message of which this word forms part).

(4)   Apart from the minimal signs (lexical and grammatical), the con-
        ventions assigning semantic content to expressions also apply to
        complex signs, i.e. combinations of minimal signs. A complex expression
        may therefore owe part of its content to minimal signs and part of it
        to (diachronically and hierarchically) superimposed conventions
        applying to combinations. To be complete, a linguistic description must
        cover both types of meaning assignment.

The first two principles define a conception of semantics according to which it
is the communicative function that a linguistic expression is conventionally
designed to serve that constitutes its meaning (= semantic content). We have
been used to thinking of communicative function only on the level of full-blown
speech acts, but in bringing about a speech act, each linguistic item in the
utterance should be seen as having a sub-function that contributes to the total
speech act. These sub-functions can, as indicated, be seen as instructions to be
processed by the addressee (cf. Davies and Isard 1972).

According to this view informative meaning (= descriptive or ideational
meaning), which is obviously a very important type of meaning, can be seen as
a subtype of communicative function, but not vice versa. If all meaning that is
attached to utterances is paraphrased in terms of information, some of it will
be misunderstood, seen from a linguistic point of view (although such a
paraphrase will be useful for other purposes). Linguistic meaning is (according
to (3)) attached to expression elements in virtue of conventions upheld by
constitutive rules; to take part in the language game as played in a particular
speech community, one must know these rules.

The main source of (4) is Pawley and Syder (1983), although I use their
point in a slightly different manner. They focus on the fact that whole phrases
and utterances are lexicalized as the appropriate ways of putting things, so that
in practice it is unusual for a speaker to code his speech all the way from
minimal elements up to complete sentences. Instead, speakers use chunks of
varying size which they may combine and modify at considerably lower
processing cost. My point, however, is that in describing meaning we need to
cover both minimal options and conventional combinations, because meaning,
as attached by lexicalized conventions, may belong at more than one level.

1. Sentences as signs: On content and expression in syntax

That all sentence constituents from the morpheme level upwards are signs with a content side and an expression side must be considered a commonplace, after the anti-semantic tendencies in American linguistics have lost ground in the last decades. Nevertheless, the implications of this circumstance for syntactic theory are rarely considered explicitly. Since the views expressed below on tense in a layered syntax depend on some of these implications, they will be spelled out first.

The basic principle is very simple. Syntax deals with the combination of linguistic items into more complex linguistic items. Since the items combined are signs, syntax deals with both expression and content at the same time. If we only think in terms of *distribution* of signs, there is no point in worrying about keeping the two sides apart, since we cannot get one side without the other - the two sides of a sign must always co-occur. But where Bloomfield and followers could be satisfied with accounting for distribution, this is not satisfactory if we take seriously the views on which FG is based. In answering the question "What is the relationship between pragmatics, semantics, and syntax", Dik (1989: 7) says:

> pragmatics is seen as the all-encompassing framework within which semantics and syntax must be studied. Semantics is regarded as instrumental with respect to pragmatics, and syntax as instrumental with respect to semantics. In this view there is no room for something like an 'autonomous' syntax. On the contrary, to the extent that a clear division can be made between syntax and semantics at all, syntax is there for people to be able to form complex expressions for conveying complex meanings, and such meanings are there for people to be able to communicate in subtle and differentiated ways.

In order to provide a description of language that lives up to this programmatic statement, we shall need to show more than how linguistic forms or rather signs are distributed. If complex expressions are instrumental with respect to complex meanings, as indicated in the quotation, we need to have both a theory for the formation of complex expressions (out of less complex expressions) and a theory for forming complex meanings out of less complex meanings. And if semantics takes priority, the latter rules must be more fundamental. But we need both types, or we shall be unable to provide an explicit description of the instrument-al relationship of which Dik is speaking.

What this means is that a semantic theory must have a combinatorial component, whose job it is to specify how content elements form complex wholes - just as the theory of linguistic expressions must have a combinatorial component describing the construction of complex expressions. The aspect of semantics that describes how content elements are combined into larger wholes I propose to call 'content syntax'; the rules for combining expression elements into complex expressions consequently belong under 'expression syntax'. A language user must be able to apply both types of rules at the same time, since he needs to build up both the complex meanings he wants to convey and the complex expressions necessary to convey them.

I therefore venture to suggest a modest adjustment in the descriptive framework of FG. What is missing is an explicit place for grammatical content elements in FG syntax, and for rules describing their combination into the complex meanings of which Dik speaks. To formulate the combination rules, however, requires essentially no more than a reinterpretation of the existing framework. I can illustrate this by reference to a simplified diagram of FG (taken from Dik 1989: 46):

(5)   underlying clause structure
          ↓
       expression rules
          ↓
   linguistic expressions

In this diagram, what I would call expression syntax - linear order, affixation etc. - is essentially covered by the expression rules that mediate between underlying clause structure and linguistic expressions. It follows, then, that what is covered by the underlying clause structure must be content syntax according to the picture I have tried to outline - as, in fact, I think it is. I think the perspective offered by the layered model is precisely that it provides a framework for studying the way natural language structures its semantic content elements into full clause meanings.

This is slightly at variance with the understanding expressed in the comment Dik attaches to the diagram rendered as (5). There, the underlying structure is said to be "a complex abstract structure in which several levels or 'layers' of formal and semantic organization have to be distinguished" (Dik 1989: 46). The difference, of course, is in seeing layered structure as involving both formal and semantic organization. The pattern of thinking that involves a postulate of underlying *form* appears to me unnecessary here, since the relationships accounted for in the layered model would seem to be all semantic in nature.

Seeing the layered model as a framework for content syntax will also enable us to be completely explicit about the relationship between syntax and semantics. In arguing against autonomous syntax in the quotation above, Dik made a point of stressing that we could not make a clear division between syntax and semantics except to the extent that syntax was instrumental in relation to semantics. If we distinguish between rules for combining expression elements and rules for combining content elements, we can say that content syntax is a part of semantics (the part that describes the organization of complex meanings). Expression syntax, on the other hand, is outside of semantics; and it is expression syntax which is instrumental in relation to content syntax, cf. the quotation. In that respect syntax is just like the lexicon - where word expressions are instrumental with respect to word meanings.

2. On the semantic content of operators

Since the layered model can be seen as a framework for the organization of content, the only place where an adjustment is really necessary is in the recognition of simplex content elements as part of grammar. This involves the status of operators in the theory. Since Dik (1989: 15ff) uses definiteness as a paradigm example of the type of reasoning that motivates an operator in FG, and definiteness is essential to the semantics of tense, I shall try to show what the adjustment involves in relation to his discussion of definiteness as an operator.

Dik begins by considering the possibility of accounting for definiteness in terms of the syntactic structure matching the English definite article. This account, Dik points out, would undergeneralize both intralinguistically (because pronouns and proper names are also definite) and cross-linguistically (because definiteness can also be marked by an affix, as in Danish). "The notion definite article is too concrete to yield a typologically adequate account of definiteness", Dik (1989: 16) concludes, and he suggests positing the more abstract operator d, which can then be mapped into different forms of expression, as in his diagram (3), rendered below as (6):

(6)   English: d[house]   = the house
         d[John]   = Ø John
      Danish: d[hus]   = huset (Danish *hus* = "house")

The operator d enables the linguist to formulate rules affecting definite terms in a simple manner and provides an elegant means of accounting for all distributional features involved in this area. What I am suggesting is that the account would be even better if it included an explicit recognition of definiteness as a semantic item, a content element. This content element could then be seen as constituting the entire semantic content of the definite article, while being included in the content of other items such as pronouns and proper nouns.

To give substance to this suggestion, I shall offer a suggestion as to how this content element could be described (cf. (2) and (3) with respect to the format of semantic description):

(7)   Using a definite term counts as an instruction to identify[2] something in the world of discourse as being named (referred to) by the term in question.

But if Dik's description above would be left untouched by this amendment (as I think it would), why bother? Basically, because if it is in fact a content element which is responsible for the linguistic phenomena that are sensitive to the definiteness distinction, this should be reflected by the theory whose job it is to account for linguistic phenomena. To illustrate why an explanatory account of definiteness requires the explicit presence of semantic information, we can look at the status of proper names as carriers of the operator d in (6) above.

There are two related reasons why Dik's account as it stands is incomplete. First of all: that proper names should be d-marked is only a matter of contingent fact, as far as we can see from (6): the 'd' is something detachable from the name *John* itself, just as it is detachable from *house*. Secondly: if we want a complete semantic theory, and if proper names are part of the domain of linguistics, presumably we will have to say something about their semantic content as well. If the theory includes (6), however, there will be no direct link between the semantic account and the operator d in the theory.

The argument here is based on the assumption that proper names have something about them that makes them definite by nature. One way of focusing on this congenital definiteness is to consider the entity [John] in the formula d[John]. If we abstract definiteness out of a proper name, what is the nature of the object we have left? But the most fundamental reason for wanting an explicit semantic description instead of the bare d has to do with making the functional basis of FG explicit: the relations going from the use of definite terms (pragmatics) via their coded meaning (semantics) to their syntactic behaviour would seem to be cut off if we base our syntactic account on an uninterpreted d.[3]

On the other hand, if the d is regarded as a content element, this semantic element will provide a natural linking element - not only between linguistic structure and pragmatics, but also between linguistic items whose relationship would otherwise merely be a matter of contingent fact. To show how the definiteness of proper names could be accounted for through a semantic description of this kind, cf. (8):

(8)   Using the proper name PN of an individual x counts as an instruction to identify x as being named (referred to) by PN.

If we regard definiteness as a content element describable by (7), it will be immediately obvious why proper names are definite: they are coded as means of referring to uniquely specified entities. This is the reason why every proper name requires an individual naming convention, like a christening. Accordingly, they conform to the general description of definiteness given in (7).

There is also another reason why it is more revealing to view the d as a content element. The point of departure was the notion of 'definite article' in its syntactic position in front of the NP. Since definiteness occurred also (for example) as a suffix, we had to have a more abstract conception of it. But if definiteness always had the syntax of the English definite article, this argument would not apply. Again, positing the element d as in (6) appears to be a matter of contingent fact; if languages were more uniform on this point, we would not need it. However, if it is seen as a content element, it is of course necessary as part of linguistic description even if it happened always to be expressed in the same way.

If content elements are explicitly introduced as part of the items to which syntactic rules apply, it will also be possible to distinguish clearly between rules sensitive to semantic content and semantically empty rules. In languages like Latin nouns must be specified for gender, and in an argumentation which exactly parallels the one for definiteness above, one could argue that masculine nouns should be assigned an abstract 'm'. This m would then trigger the appropriate expression rules, which would also be quite diverse for different items. But in that case the 'm' would be just an abstract cover term for a number of different types of expression (generalizing over 'allomorphic' variation) rather than a content element. Correlation between gender and lexical content, it should be noted, does not mean that gender *has* content, if it is lexically fixed.[4]

I should like to conclude this criticism of FG by repeating that as far as I can see there is nothing in the descriptive aims and practices of FG that is incompatible with a modification of this kind. One example of FG description which, as far as I can see, can only be understood as an example of syntax operating in the manner argued here, is the discussion of 'stacking' as opposed to 'conjunction' of restrictors in a noun phrase (cf. Dik 1989: 118). As discussed by Dik, *a beautiful ancient house* is usually interpreted so that *beautiful* modifies the combination *ancient house*, while *ancient* modifies *house* (stacking) - while conjunction, where both adjectives separately modify *house*, would have to be indicated by special means (in writing, a comma, corresponding to intonation in speech). This would seem to be a clear case of syntax operating on the sides of expression and content simultaneously, with something essential getting lost if we had to speak of one syntactic structure only.

3. Tense operators as signs - and their syntax

I now turn to my area of investigation, which is tense in English, broadly conceived as comprising combinations of past, present, future and perfect forms (cf. also Davidsen-Nielsen 1984; Bybee 1985; Vikner 1985); alternative conceptions of the area will be considered in 5. below. I shall begin by summarizing some points made by Co Vet, since the description proposed in this paper is greatly indebted to his views. The basic model of tense forms that underlies this paper can conveniently be described by reference to a diagram set up by Vet (1981: 161), reproduced below as (9):

(9)

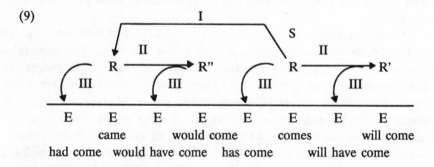

The main point of the diagram is to show that the traditional tripartition of the tenses into past, present and future does not reflect the linguistic facts, because future is secondary in relation to the distinction between past and present - it can be based on the past as well as the present. On the other hand, the future must be seen as primary in relation to the perfect: you cannot have a future which is based on a perfect tense, whereas you can have a perfect based on a future tense (what it means for one tense form to be 'based on' another will be clear from the discussion of scope relations later in this section).

In the diagram I indicates the first stage of the tense system (past or present), II the second stage (future), and III the third stage (perfect). The consequences of the three stages in terms of time reference are indicated with symbols inherited from Reichenbach (1947): S denotes the time of speech, E the time of the event denoted by the verb, and R the so-called point of reference. R was Reichenbach's innovation; it is most obviously useful in a case such as the past perfect, which Reichenbach used to explain the concept (cf. the form *had come* in the diagram: the event is located not only before S, but also before a reference point that is itself before S).

Later, Vet (1986) formulated an explicit account of tense in terms of operators, where he recognized that past and present must be given the status of 'superoperators', because they have the separate function in relation to the other tenses of indicating "whether the relationship expressed by tense holds between the state of affairs and the speech act [...] or whether it holds between the state of affairs and some already known point or interval before the speech event" (Vet 1986: 5). (More on this issue towards the end of this section.)

In working out a description of tense covering content as well as expression, it is interesting to note that tense has not typically been considered in this perspective, in terms of signs (exceptions are Langacker 1978; Bybee and Dahl fc.). One reason for this is that the prototypical sign is lexical, with expression in the form of a sequence of sound segments and a descriptive meaning that can be illustrated with a drawing. Tense deviates from the prototype by being grammatical, having an un-photogenic semantic content and expression in a number of different forms, including zero. Reference to form-meaning relationships within tense theory has usually been limited to observing that tenses are compositional in that past tenses contain the past tense morpheme, the future tenses contain a form of *will*, and the perfect tenses a form of *have* (cf. Vikner 1985; Comrie 1985). Apart from that treatments generally focus on one of the two sides, either the expressional morphology or the semantics.

Although the signs that we get out of our description may look rather messy, it must be kept in mind that it is only to be expected that grammatical signs should differ on both sides from lexical signs. One of the defining characteristics of grammatical items is that they 'operate upon' other items (cf. the term 'operator'). On this point there is a structural parallel between content and expression syntax: just as the contents of grammatical signs operate upon other content elements, so do the expression elements take the form of operations upon other expression elements. Therefore the FG terminology of 'expression *rules'* is intuitively attractive also in the sign-oriented approach suggested here.

Tense is a clear example of this. If we rephrase Vet's model in (9) to reflect the inventory of grammatical signs, we get the following four (cf. Harder fc.): past, present, future and perfect. If we forget about the rest of the clause for the time being (including other possible auxiliary elements), the skeleton of a content syntax of these four signs can be given as (10):

(10) **Past/Present** (Future (Perfect (**lexical verb**)))

Boldface indicates obligatoriness, the slash paradigmatic opposition. It will be seen that perfect operates on the lexical verb; future can operate either on the lexical verb or on the combination of perfect and lexical verb; past or present operates on either the lexical verb or any possible combination given above. The Chinese box organization typical of layered structure is apparent. To flesh out this account we need to describe the expression as well as the semantic content of each of the four items plus an account of the precise nature of the syntactic relations on both the content and expression sides.

To begin with expression: the future in English can be seen as expressed by *will* (cf. Davidsen-Nielsen 1988), and the perfect by *have*. The linear order of these expressions (including the lexical verb) can itself be seen as an expression element: the scope on the side of content is reflected in the linear order of the expressions, in the same way that obtained in the ordering of adjectives as a means for 'stacking' (cf. also Foley and Van Valin 1984: 223).

But as announced above there is more to the expression side than word forms and linear order. Each grammatical element contains, as part of its expression syntax, an operation that is to be performed on other expressions. The nature of this operation is interesting because it shows how expression rules make reference to content syntax: each element determines the form of the expression of the outermost verb inside its (semantic) scope. To begin with past and present, they are expressed *only* by means of changes in the form of the verb immediately inside their scope. The other sign expressions have this property in addition to expression in word form: *will* must be followed by the infinitive, and *have* by the past participle. The way these operations work can be illustrated by an example. In (11) we go through the expression rules in two stages: first, from content structure to the insertion of word expressions (given in their base form), and then from words in the base form via the operations to the appropriate word forms:

(11) Past (Fut (Perf (leave))) -> Past (will (have (leave)))
      -> would have left

It should be noted that scope relations as indicated by parentheses do not belong to the output of expression rules; they are part of content structure only, signalled by the linear order of words.

The distinction between the two types of expression parameter (word form and operation) is more than a matter of presence or absence of segmental elements. Even when the operation involves addition of segmental elements, the result of the operation does not follow the same ordering principles: past, when expressed segmentally, comes *after* the stem in English.

The operations can be characterized on various levels of generality. If the processes were regular, they could be expressed directly in phonological terms, but the highest level of syntactic generality in languages like English is achieved by stating it as a matter of selecting the appropriate form within the verbal paradigm (the 'word and paradigm' approach, cf. Hockett 1954). Abstract markers like those discussed above in connection with gender can then trigger morphological details.

As an example of historical change in morphological expression the case of the French 'futur' is illustrative in this context. The expression of future in English contains, as discussed above, a verb stem as well as an operation on the outermost verb within its scope. The construction that is now the French 'futur' was once expressed in a similar way, but the two elements underwent a process of coalescence: the verb stem expressing future merged with the verb that it operated upon to form a new stem that became part of the verbal paradigm. This process seems to have run parallel with a process on the content side, in which a deontic meaning was lost (on the relationship between inflectional expression and semantic bleaching, cf. Bybee and Dahl fc.). In present-day French the expression rule for 'futur', like the expression rule for past and present, involves only an operation, not an element with independent linear position. The expression rules, it may be noted, could be naturally formulated so that the 'futur' involves a selection of the future 'stem' of the verb immediately inside its scope, and then the past or present (as the outermost element) determines the corresponding set of forms of that stem. Cf. (12):

(12) Past (Fut (voir (Jean))) -> Past (verr- (Jean)) -> (verrait (Jean))
      -> *Jean verrait*

The content sides of the four signs[5] can be summarized as follows (for a fuller discussion, see Harder fc.):

(13) The use of the present tense counts as an instruction to identify WS,
      i.e. the world of discourse at the time S of speech, as the world to
      which the content inside its scope applies.

(14) The use of the past tense counts as an instruction to identify WP, i.e.
      the world of discourse at time P, $(P < S)$ as the world to which the
      content inside its scope applies.

(15) The use of the future counts as an instruction to understand the content
      inside its scope as applying to a time F ahead of the time identified (S
      or P).

(16) The use of the perfect counts as an instruction to understand the
      content inside its scope as applying to a time A anterior to time T (T
      = S, P or F), while understanding the anterior location (the 'being-
      anterior') of this content as a property of the world at time T.

In themselves, these formulations hopefully look merely like idiosyncratic
versions of what everybody knows about tense. We shall return to one feature
of the semantics of past and present, the definiteness aspect, in 4.; the main
interest here is in the implications of the layered syntax seen as organizing
explicitly specified semantic content elements.

The most intensively discussed aspect of tense semantics is no doubt the
structure of time reference, and the main interest of the account given here is
in the way it handles that aspect. It will be seen that each of the postulated
content elements in (13)-(16) contains an instruction about the temporal
location of its 'operand', involving the times symbolized by S, P, F and A. If we
forget about the other aspects of (13)-(16) for the moment, we can summarize
the time reference of the eight forms generated by the system as (17), again
taking *come* as the lexical verb:

(17) a. simple present: S (come)
      b. simple past: P (come)
      c. (present) future: S (F (come))
      d. past future: P (F (come))
      e. present perfect: S (A (come))
      f. past perfect: P (A (come))

      g.   (present) future perfect: S (F (A (come)))
      h.   past future perfect: P (F (A (come)))

If we return to the above example of the past perfect (e.g. *had come*), the content syntax accounts for its time reference by saying that past assigns the time P to what is inside its scope, so that (A (come)) is located at P. The perfect, in its turn, locates what is inside its scope at A, so (come) is located at A, anterior to P. If we compare the account implied in (17) with (9), it will be seen that (17) gives exactly the same system of time reference. Why bother, then, one may ask.

The distinguishing feature of the account given here is that it describes how complex time reference is built up through the cooperation of the minimal semantic elements of the language system. Reichenbach and a number of followers based their accounts on the concepts of reference time and event time (R and E in (9)). These notions have no evident relation to linguistic structure (for a fundamental reason, which will be discussed in 4.); they are set up as ways of symbolizing semantic intuitions *per se*. In the account given here each time is (an aspect of) a content element associated with an expression element, together constituting a linguistic sign. If we compare the account of past perfect here with the Reichenbachian account, the latter needs an extra theoretical construct in the shape of a reference point that suddenly pops up for linguistically opaque reasons. In contrast, we only need those time points that we would need anyhow in order to give each item semantic content.

Within the account given here, we can still formulate rules in terms of reference points; but the notion gets a different status. Since times other than P and S are defined only as 'after' or 'before', they need a 'reference point' if the addressee is to locate them. This reference time is determined as part of the job done by the content syntax: the 'outer' times serve as reference points for subsequent 'inner' times. This account has the advantage that each time can retain its identity in different combinations: the time signalled by 'past' is always simply P. In a Reichenbachian account, there is no such correspondence between linguistic structure and time reference. This could be seen as a reason for preferring the above version of Reichenbach's system to the numerous alternative versions that have been proposed (cf. e.g. Comrie 1981; Davidsen-Nielsen 1984; Vikner 1985; Declerck 1986). An account of time reference that follows automatically from a semantic description of the linguistic items involved and their syntax might be considered to have an edge over rival proposals, other things being equal.

Apart from founding the time reference expressed in (9) in the content syntax, the proposal made here modifies Vet's description on a few other points. Vet (1986) analyses the relationship between tense and predication as structurally analogous to the relationship between determiner and term; Hengeveld (1989) describes his layered model as a further development of this proposal. In terms of the account given here, it would only be the 'outermost' layer (past or present) which occupied the determiner-like position as obligatory element with scope extending over the rest of the predication (cf. Rijkhoff 1988 on term and determiner). This also fits in with the definiteness aspect of the content elements associated with past and present, the instruction to identify a time (as opposed to indicating its relative position), cf. 4. below.

The three-tier analysis suggested here can be seen as a logical extension of Vet's suggestion of giving past and present the status of 'super-operators'. In suggesting this notion Vet did not discuss what to do with combinations of future and perfect, although they are clearly part of the tense system in his account; the future would presumably have to be seen as a 'sub-superoperator'. Setting up a layered content syntax specifying where each content element belongs makes the prefixes superfluous.

Once the position of the future in the scope hierarchy is made explicit in this way, Vet's analysis of the 'near future' in French can also be taken a step further. Vet points out that the near future must be seen as structurally integrated in the tense system, because the auxiliary *aller* occurs only in the present and the past tense, and not in the future or perfect, as in **je suis allé avoir trente ans* or **j'irai avoir trente ans*. Vet's account, saying that near future only combines with 'super-operators', captures the position of the near future in relation to past and present ('outwards' in the structure). With the description suggested here, however, we can make its position in relation to the future and the perfect explicit by saying that the variety of French considered by Vet has a paradigmatic contrast at the second tier between two futures, so that this variety of French has a system structured as (18):

(18) **Past/Present** (Future/Near Future (Perfect (**lexical verb**)))

In addition to preserving Vet's analysis in relation to past and present, this also explains why the near future, although it cannot be combined with the perfect 'outwards' in the system, can take a perfect form inside its scope, as in *je vais avoir fini dans quelques minutes* (cf. Vet's 1986: 6 account). This paradigmatic contrast is a non-isomorphic feature of French, where the expression elements do not reflect the status of the content elements; this makes it difficult to capture elegantly unless the existence of a syntax of content elements is explicitly recognized.

A similar process is probably happening in the case of English *going to*. Although Jespersen (1924: 263) gave the form *I shall be going to* as exemplifying the 'after-future', he recognized the marginal status of both the notion and the form; if the form is cited as *gonna*, signalling the fused oral form (*I'll be gonna do it*), its grammaticality status is even more doubtful. Ultimately, the near futures may replace the 'proper' futures; but in the present state of English and French there are varieties in which the semantic contrasts give a clear-cut paradigmatic choice (cf. Vet 1984; Harder fc.).

4. Instructional semantics and auxiliaries

The view that semantic content should be understood in terms of communicative function, with instruction rather than information as common denominator, has not been central to the argument up to this point. The account of time reference makes the same descriptive claims as previous suggestions, and so we end up with the same points in time, although their relation with linguistic structure is different. On some points, however, the instructional view of meaning is crucial to the picture given here. Its implications should therefore be spelled out clearly.

The first point where the instructional view is essential is in relation to the definiteness element that was said to be part of the content of past and present. As pointed out in the introduction, it makes little difference apart from the principle itself whether we insist on viewing descriptive meaning as a (fundamental) subtype of instruction or not; but I shall argue that definiteness is one of those content elements which it is crucial to understand instructionally.

If definiteness is rephrased in terms of description or information, the best paraphrase will be essentially the theory of Russell (1905), which has been the basis for all subsequent logical accounts of definiteness. Its brief form is a paraphrase beginning 'there is one and only one...'. As a piece of information encoded in a linguistic utterance this makes little sense, because nobody talking about 'the window' would like to be understood as informing the addressee that there is a window (but only one). The sense in which existence and uniqueness are relevant to definite descriptions can only be understood on the basis of the instructional view: if the addressee is to identify the intended referent (as, according to (7), he is instructed to do), then there must exist one, and only one obvious candidate for identification in the context of speech.

Russell's account does not contradict this; rather, it addresses itself to a different issue, focusing on the relationship between a type of expression and the universe that is necessary to 'satisfy' it. That existence and uniqueness must be understood in relation to the process of identification is well-established in the literature; but the only description of its semantic content that accounts for this is one in which definiteness has the character of an instruction for the adressee. If it is viewed as a form of information, existence and uniqueness will stand as something the addressee is told about, which is intuitively unsatisfactory (as the whole issue of presupposition in the literature shows).

In looking at past and present, this instructional account of definiteness highlights an essential aspect of their meaning. The past tense has most generally been characterized as definite in the literature, in order to distinguish it from the present perfect. The choice between past and present is traditionally recognized to involve the same contrast found in other deictics, distinguishing here-now-this from there-then-that; and this description implies a parallel in definite reference.

However, the deictic contrast now/before tends to overshadow the element of definiteness in accounts of tense meaning. It is therefore worth emphasizing that both past and present involve an instruction for the addressee to identify a time as being referred to. Cf. (13) and (14). This element of identification is more basic to the semantics of past than its pastness. It has repeatedly been pointed out that past tense involves more than past time; in spite of this, however, the meaning of past tense is still most frequently described simply as involving occurrence before the time of speech.

An explicitly instructional account may help to avoid this unclarity. To demonstrate how, let us return to the system of points set up in (13)-(16) and look at it in relation to the account in terms of reference time and event time. Above it was argued that P, F, and A, while making the same claims as the Reichenbachian times, gave a better account of the relationship between linguistic structure and time reference. We shall now see that this is a consequence of the instructional - as opposed to an informational or descriptive - interpretation of meaning.

On the face of it, the notion of 'event time' is perhaps the most obviously necessary concept in accounting for time reference: tense informs us when the 'event' expressed by the clause took place. Yet this concept, like the concept of reference time, disappears in the account given above, and the reason for this is that viewing what is said in terms of 'event time' involves an informational approach to describing what is said. It describes, correctly, what we know when we have interpreted the statement. But if the instructional account is correct, this is not necessarily part of the linguistic content of the sentence. The times that are part of linguistic content tell the addressee how to understand what is said - but there is no special linguistic item reserved for telling *event* time. If we take a predication and put it inside the scope of past, past will indicate the event time - because it instructs the addressee about where to locate the predication in time. But if (in addition to past) we choose perfect, this element will occupy a position in the content syntax *between* the predication and past. Therefore it will be perfect that tells the addressee where to locate the predication, and hence points towards the event time. Since different linguistic elements may have the function of indicating event time (without being ambiguous), the concept 'event time' does not belong to the description of linguistic content, although it is basic if we describe the information conveyed. If we want to have a place in our theory for the concept 'event time', we may say that the tense element which takes the predication directly inside its scope thereby becomes the indicator of event time - but we add nothing but an extra term to the theory by doing this.

A similar shift in perspective will account for the recurrent tendency to describe past as meaning simply 'occurrence before now'. Once you have performed the instruction to identify a time before now as being referred to, what you get is information about an ocurrence before now. Hence, the traditional account of past is absolutely true as a description of the information conveyed. It is not accurate, however, as an account of linguistic content, because it loses the element of communicative action that is necessary to arrive at this information, and according to the instructional view this element is a basic part of what is coded as linguistic content. One issue where this perspective is observable in the analysis of past tense forms is the infelicity of using past tense out of the blue, beginning a conversation with a statement like *it rained*. As addressees we understand that it is meant to describe an occurrence before now, but since we cannot comply with the instruction of identification, this is not enough for the utterance to make sense.

Insisting upon an instructional view of linguistic content does not, of course, imply that an analysis of sentences as containers of information is *wrong*, only that linguistic content is not exhaustively analysable from this point of view. This raises the interesting question of the relationship between logical analysis and instructional meaning. An investigation of this issue would be oriented towards showing how the purpose of conveying information is achieved via instructions, and relating the linguistic 'process' account of meaning with the logical structure of the information that is the 'product'. For an account of tense and aspect in logical terms with many interesting parallels to the account given here, cf. Bartsch (1988).

In relation to the issue of functional logic, the point of view argued here would imply that the layered structure is indeed the most basic organization of linguistic content; no other representations are necessary to account for the semantic properties of sentences. The instructional view of semantic content, however, would mean that the layered structure was not directly interpretable as a means of storing world knowledge. Instead, the mental models worked out on the *basis* of the semantic clause structures would contain the information that the clause structure conveyed. To get from layered structures to mental models embodying world knowledge we would need some process-to-product conversion rules of the kind mentioned above.

5. Cross-linguistic perspectives

The description of tense above was founded on a view of the semantic organization of the clause in which operators were recognized as signs with semantic content. If, as implied in the instructional view, meaning is seen as action potential also at the level of linguistic signs, it is natural to see the use of each linguistic element as regulated by a very general pragmatic criterion for human action: what you do must make sense. From this criterion, which is basic in relation to both Grice's co-operative principle and its modern version in the form of relevance theory (cf. Sperber and Wilson 1986), may be derived a rock bottom default explanation of syntactic phenomena: syntax must organize semantic content in a way that makes sense. Looking at the content elements that have been discussed above, we can draw some tentative universal conclusions about the organization of tense based on this criterion alone.

To begin with past and present, their distinguishing feature is the element of time identification, as opposed to indications of *relative* time. This semantic distinction is sufficient to motivate a candidate universal saying that elements requesting time identification must take indicators of relative time inside their scope. A relative time is placed in relation to its point of reference - which must therefore be present as a precondition for relative time to make sense. Conversely, identified time within the scope of relative time seems equally senseless. As against this, if there was nothing in the semantics of tense other than relations of precedence, there would be no reason why these elements should not be combined arbitrarily, as sometimes found in logical accounts (cf. Bybee and Dahl fc.). Not all languages have identifying tense - but if they have it, it must (according to this account) take the broadest scope.

Looking at the future in relation to the perfect, we can predict that a 'pure' future - one in which *nothing* is said about the point of reference other than the 'being-ahead' of a future state of affairs (cf. Harder fc.) - cannot make sense inside the scope of a perfect. The perfect signals that what is inside its scope is anterior; and if it took the future inside its scope, it would put the future behind us. More technically, if nothing characterizes the reference point, it is impossible to conceive of a resulting state afterwards (cf. Bartsch 1988, where the future is treated as 'state before' in a parallel manner to the perfect as 'state after').

The criterion of making sense is the same that Schachter (1983) applied to the perfect in relation to progressive, showing why progressive must have the narrowest scope. Briefly speaking, the progressive indicates incompletion; and while it makes sense to be after an incomplete state of affairs (as in *John has been reading*), it is difficult to think of an incomplete state of being after something (as in **John is having read*).

Thus the English auxiliary system as described here presents a picture of fairly rigid structural rules solidly founded in a pragmatic criterion of sense-making; and to the extent that a language has the same content elements one might expect the same rules to apply. On one point the prediction made here diverges from an account suggested by Givón (1982, 1986). Since the discrepancy has to do with two important issues in accounting for auxiliary systems, it is worth outlining here. The issues involved are the relationship between content and expression and the relationship between synchrony and diachrony. The importance of diachrony in particular is emphasized by Bybee and Dahl (fc.).

Basing his account on creole studies by Bickerton, Givón argues that there is a universal auxiliary system containing the three elements (anterior) - (modal/irrealis) - (non-punctual). English, as Givón points out, diverges from this pattern with respect to 'anterior' (= perfect) in relation to 'modal-irrealis' (which includes future). Since Givón agrees with other authors in assuming that linear order generally reflects scope, he explains this divergence by putting it down to irregularities accumulated in the course of diachronic change.

In the account suggested here there is no mismatch between linear order and semantic scope in the English system. One reason for the difference in view may have to do with the semantics of the creole 'irrealis'. On this point, Givón's account is criticized by Bybee (1985: 199), who points out that Givón's own glossing suggests an interpretation in terms of 'intention', rather than future. In principle, however, there is an important point here: would the influence of historical factors typically be sufficient to preserve a mismatch between expression and content through the centuries, when it comes to linearity as a means of signalling semantic scope? Clear examples would be interesting.

Another divergence between Givón's account and the one suggested here is in the interpretation put upon the term 'scope'. Both accounts are oriented towards founding syntactic analysis in pragmatic factors, and Givón's argument for why the broad scope is natural for 'anterior' is based on its discourse function: in narratives, the anterior form is used to distinguish 'out-of-sequence' material from 'narrative backbone'. Givón describes scope relations between the auxiliaries by saying that the non-punctual only has scope over the verb, irrealis has scope over the proposition "while the anterior has the widest, *discourse* scope" (Givón 1982: 127).

I entirely accept Givón's description of the discourse function of the perfect; but this function is not dependent upon any particular scope relations within the semantic organization of the clause. According to (16), the perfect locates a state of affairs as anterior in relation to the time one is talking about. This precludes the state of affairs from carrying the action forward, since it puts the narrative into reverse.

According to the view argued here, Givón's mistake consists in trying to establish a direct link between linguistic expression and discourse function. Where coded semantic content is involved, its organization by the rules of content syntax must be taken into account if we are to get a complete picture of the relationship between linguistic expressions and their pragmatic function.

6. Content elements in the four-layered model

Finally, I will discuss the account of auxiliaries in terms of organization of individual content elements in relation to the model proposed by Hengeveld (1989, this vol.) and adopted in Dik (1989). The general principle of layered structure is the same in my approach as in Hengeveld's model, and as stated in 2. I think this is the fundamental principle of semantic organization in the clause. However, the layering between individual content elements does not follow automatically from the description embodied in Hengeveld's model. Rather, the four layers describe a 'macro'-level of clause organization: On each of the four layers the theory places several operators. Thus, both the progressive and the perfect are placed at the innermost layer, as π_1 (= predicate) operators. And if the future is classed as a tense (as in Dik 1989), both past/present and future belong at the level of π_2 (= predication) operators. This means that the four-layered model in itself does not specify scope relations as precisely as the account given here.

If both types of organization are required to describe semantic organization, the neatest fit would be one where we had a kind of micro-structure within the (macro)layers of Hengeveld's model; within each layer there would then be an internal layered structure between the operators, determined by their semantic content. To some extent, however, there may be problems in establishing a neat division into four distinct layers.

One case which may be inconvenient here is the perfect, which both semantically and positionally seems to occupy a middle position between tense (as a π_2 operator) and phasal aspect (as a π_1 operator). Although the perfect involves the internal properties of the state of affairs by denoting resultant state, it also involves external time relations by indicating anteriority. Moreover, to the extent that the property of resultant state becomes dominant, it ceases to be a prototypical perfect (cf. Dahl 1985). Therefore there would be a point in seeing it as being at once the tail end of tense and the beginning of aspect.

7. Conclusion

The account of tense given in this paper has simultaneously been an argument for a more explicit specification of the place of semantic content in syntax. The emphasis placed on individual content elements reflects a conviction that the syntactic behaviour of linguistic expressions is fundamentally (but, because of linguistic conventions, not totally) regulated by the language user's awareness of what job that expression will do for him.

The structural patterns formed by elements of the clause must be understood in that context. Models of clause structure represent general patterns of communicative functions, as described by Hengeveld (1989, this vol.). Such general patterns co-exist in every language with the cross-linguistic and diachronic vagaries of individual signs. To get a satisfactory description of the system of an individual language, we must approach it from both angles. This is true in principle of all systems, also the English one described above, where the semantic content elements are fairly clear-cut. But it is even more necessary where the system is semantically in a more tangled state. Thus in the frequent cases (cf. Bybee and Dahl fc.) where a present perfect gradually becomes more like a past tense, it will develop away from being composed of minimal signs as described above. Instead, it will develop more and more properties describable by a superimposed convention applying to the combination of present and perfect (cf. (4)). For a long period, it will be gradually taking over more and more of the domain of an earlier past tense; and it would be desirable to describe it at that particular stage of development where it is - instead of having just the universal categories of past and perfect. In such cases, there will be a tension between universal generalization and the muddiness of individual language stages. The approach based on individual content elements has a special mission in cases like that.

Notes

1.   I would like to thank Renate Bartsch, Simon Dik and Hartmut Haberland for helpful comments on an earlier version of this paper. Needless to say, they are not responsible for remaining errors in the presentation.

2.   The word 'identify' can be understood more or less broadly. Here, in order to distinguish between definite and indefinite reference, it must be understood narrowly: i.e. as involving an act of identification between the referent of the phrase and an entity in the world of discourse, which must either be already established (*the table* = the table we were talking about) or identifiable in the situation (*look at the tall one over there!*).

3.   The discussion on the relationship between syntax and semantics in FG is inspired by Janssen (1981). The semantic point of view adopted here, however, is different.

4.   Definiteness in proper names in some languages requires expression with the definite article. Like lexical gender, this is essentially a problem that belongs on the side of expression syntax only. Semantically, proper names are definite regardless of whether the rules of the language require marking or not. Hence, obligatory definite articles in front of proper names should not be treated in the same way as definite articles expressing a communicative choice, as in the choice between *the house* and *a house*. Cases like *was there a John in the class*? do not exemplify the word *John* used as a proper noun, but as a common noun meaning 'person called John'.

5.   Since there is a question of either the infinitive or the past participle following an auxiliary, there are really more than four minimal signs involved. Although the choice between infinitive and past participle has been treated as automatic here, according to (4) it is evident that a full account would have to discuss this issue as well. For two discussions of the roles of infinitive and participle, cf. Langacker (1978) and Bartsch (1988).

References

Anderson, L.B.
    1982   "The 'perfect' as a universal and as a language-particular category". In P.Hopper (ed.), 91-114.

Bache, C., H.Basbøll and C.E.Lindberg (eds.)
    fc.   *Tense - aspect - actionality: New data - new approaches.*

Bartsch, R.
   1988   *Tenses, aspects and their scopes in discourse*. ITLI Prepublication Series (Institute for
          Language, Logic and Information, University of Amsterdam) LP-88-07.

Bull, W.E.
   1960   *Time, tense and the verb*. Berkeley: University of California Press.

Bybee, J.L.
   1985   *Morphology: A study of the relation between meaning and form*. Amsterdam: Benjamins.

Bybee, J.L. and Östen Dahl
   fc.   "The creation of tense and aspect systems in the languages of the world". *Studies in
          Language*.

Comrie, B.
   1976   *Aspect*. Cambridge: Cambridge UP.
   1981   "On Reichenbach's approach to tense". *Papers from the Regional Meeting of the Chicago
          Linguistic Society* 17: 24-30.
   1985   *Tense*. Cambridge: Cambridge UP.

Dahl, Östen
   1985   *Tense and aspect systems*. Oxford: Blackwell.

Davidsen-Nielsen, N.
   1984   "Tense in Modern English and Danish". *Papers and Studies in Contrastive Linguistics* 20:
          73-84.
   1988   "Has English a future?" *Acta Linguistica Hafniensia* 2l: 5-20.

Davies, J. and S.Isard
   1972   "Utterances as Programs". In D.Michie and B.Meltzer (eds.), *Machine Intelligence, vol.7*.
          Edinburgh: Edinburgh UP, 325-339.

Declerck, R.
   1986   "From Reichenbach (1947) to Comrie (1985) and beyond". *Lingua* 70: 305-364.

Dik, S.C.
   1978   *Functional grammar*. Amsterdam: North Holland.
   1986   *On the notion 'functional explanation'*. Working Papers in Functional Grammar 11.
   1989   *The theory of functional grammar, vol.1*. Dordrecht: Foris.

Foley, W.A. and R.D.Van Valin
   1984   *Functional syntax and universal grammar*. Cambridge: Cambridge UP.

Givón, T.
   1982   "Tense-aspect-modality: The Creole prototype and beyond". In P.Hopper (ed.), 115-

163.
1986   *Syntax, vol.1.* Amsterdam: Benjamins.

Grice, H.P.
1975   "Logic and conversation". In P.Cole and J.Morgan (eds.), *Syntax and semantics, vol.3: Speech acts*. New York: Academic Press, 41-58.

Harder, P.
1976   *En strukturel og funktionel beskrivelse af bestemthed i moderne engelsk.* M.A.-thesis, University of Copenhagen.
fc.   "Verbal time reference in English: Structure and functions". In C.Bache et al.

Hengeveld, K.
1989   "Layers and operators in functional grammar". *Journal of Linguistics* 25: 127-157.

Heny, F. and B.Richards (eds.)
1983   *Linguistic categories: Auxiliaries and related puzzles.* Dordrecht: Reidel.

Hockett, C.F.
1954   "Two models of grammatical description". *Word* 10: 210-234.

Hopper, P.J. (ed.)
1982   *Tense-aspect: Between semantics and pragmatics.* Amsterdam: Benjamins.

Janssen, Th.M.V.
1981   "Montague grammar and functional grammar". In T.Hoekstra, H.van der Hulst and M.Moortgat (eds.), *Perspectives on functional grammar*. Dordrecht: Foris, 73-97.

Jespersen, O.
1924   *The philosophy of grammar.* London: Allen and Unwin.

Johnson-Laird, P.N.
1983   *Mental models.* Cambridge: Cambridge UP.

Langacker, Ronald W.
1978   "The form and meaning of the English auxiliary". *Language* 54: 853-882.

Montague, R.
1970   "Universal grammar". In R.H.Thomason (ed.), *Formal philosophy: Selected papers of Richard Montague*. New Haven: Yale UP, 222-246. (1974.)

Pawley, A. and F.H.Syder
1983   "Two puzzles for linguistic theory: Nativelike selection and nativelike fluency". In J.C.Richards and R.W.Schmidt (eds.),*Language and communication*.London: Longman, 191-226.

Reichenbach, H.
1947 *Elements of symbolic logic*. New York: The Free Press. (Reprint 1966.)

Rijkhoff, Jan
1988 *A typology of operators*. Working Papers in Functional Grammar 29.

Russell, B.
1905 "On denoting". In R.C.Marsh (ed.), *Logic and knowledge*. London: Macmillan, 41-56. (1956.)

Schachter, P.
1983 "Explaining auxiliary order". In F.Heny and B.Richards (eds.), 145-204.

Searle, J.R.
1969 *Speech acts*. New York: Cambridge UP.

Sperber, D. and D.Wilson
1986 *Relevance: Communication and cognition*. Oxford: Blackwell.

Vet, C.
1981 "Some arguments against the division of time into past, present and future". *Antwerp Papers in Linguistics* 23: 153-165.
1984 "Is there any hope for the 'futur'?" In H.Bennis and W.van Lessen Kloeke (eds.), *Linguistics in The Netherlands 1984*. Dordrecht: Foris, 189-196.
1986 *A pragmatic approach to tense in functional grammar*. Working Papers in Functional Grammar 16.

Vikner, S.
1985 "Reichenbach revisited: One, two or three temporal relations?" *Acta Linguistica Hafniensia* 19: 81-98.

Toward a Unified Analysis of Terms and Predications

Jan Rijkhoff
University of Amsterdam

0. Introduction[1]

Aristotle stated that movement or change "pertain[s] exclusively to quality, quantity, and locality, each of which embraces contrasts" (Physics, V. II; see also Rijksbaron 1989). I will argue that operators as well as satellites, both in the term phrase and in the predication, can be characterized by these three notions.

Additionally I will attempt to show, firstly, that operators in the term phrase do not all have the same scope; and secondly that these scope differences are formally reflected in the linguistic expression. In this respect this contribution can be regarded as an extension of Hengeveld (1989), which contains a proposal concerning the organization of operators in the predication and higher level domains. On the other hand, this article is also an amendment to his proposal, in that it argues that quantity operators have their own scope.

1. Terms and predications

I will argue that terms can be represented in the following way:

(1) $(\Omega \ x_i: \Omega \ \Phi_1 \ (x_i): \Phi_2 \ (x_i): \ ...: \Phi_n \ (x_i))^2$

(i) In (1) Ω stands for various term operators, which indicate, among other things, (in)definiteness and number. I use the phrase 'term operator' for any operator in the domain of the term phrase, including those operators that are supposed to have only the nominal predicate in their scope. Similarly, 'predication operator' (see below) is used for any kind of operator in the domain of the predication, including those operators that are supposed to have only the verbal predicate in their scope. Operators have a certain part (or 'layer') of some domain in their scope and may be expressed as grammatical (as opposed to lexical) elements; if expressed, term operators usually take the form of a determiner, a numeral/quantifier, or an inflectional element. This is discussed in more detail below.

(ii) x_i is the term variable symbolizing the intended referent.

(iii) Every $\Phi(x_i)$ is an open predication in x_i. Φ is a predicate, designating a property of the referent x_i, or a relation between x_i and one or maximally two other referents. These predicates are called restrictors: they progressively narrow down the set of potential referents of the term. Φ_1 is the first restrictor; this is usually the head noun (N), which designates the most characteristic property of a referent: its name (which may be a proper name like *Amsterdam* or a type name like *book*); Φ_2 is the second restrictor, e.g. an adjectival predicate (A) designating such properties as colour (*red*), size (*big*), propensity (*jealous*) etc. For instance (i = indefinite, d = definite):

(2) Two nice little houses in the country

(2') $(i2x_i: \text{house}_N (x_i): \text{little}_A (x_i): \text{nice}_A (x_i): \{(d1x_j: \text{country}_N (x_j))_{Loc}\} (x_i))$

Here the fourth restrictor is a term predicate with the semantic function Location (see Dik 1989: ch.8.5).

Predications can be represented as follows:

(3) $(\pi\ e_i: [\pi\ \Phi_V\ (T_1)\ (T_2)\ ...\ ]\ (e_i))$

(i) In (3) π stands for various predication operators, which indicate (among other things) aspect and tense. Predication operators too have a particular layer in their scope (Hengeveld 1989; Dik 1989). So far two layers are recognized in the predication, but I will contend below that three layers can be distinguished in this domain.

(i) e_i is the predication variable symbolizing the State of Affairs (SoA) (see Vet 1986 for the variable e).

(iii) Φ_V symbolizes the main (verbal) predicate.

(iv) (T_n) stands for term phrase.

For instance:

(4) The man gave the car to a friend

(4') $(\text{past } e_i: [\text{give}_V (d1x_i: \text{man}_N (x_i)_{AgSubj} (d1x_j: \text{car}_N (xj))_{GoObj} (i1x_k: \text{friend}_N (x_k))_{Rec}]\ (e_i))$

In sections 2. - 4. I will attempt to demonstrate that both in the term and in the predication operators can be characterized in terms of the notions 'quality', 'quantity', and 'locality'.

2. Quality operators

By definition 'quality' relates to the essential or characteristic properties of an entity; if there is a quality operator in the term or predication, this operator must, therefore, concern essential or characteristic properties of the referents of these domains. Since referents are most crucially defined by the lexical head of the domain (prototypically a noun or a verb), I will assume that a quality operator has only the head of the domain in its scope.

Qualitative operators should not affect the lexical meaning of a predicate, for then this predicate would designate a different property or relation. I assume that in addition to having a lexical meaning, predicates may be specified (overtly or covertly) for certain structural ('aspectual') characteristics of the designated property or relation which pertain to the spatial or temporal dimension. In other words, when a predicate is used in a referring expression (term or predication), it can also indicate something about a referent's representation in the dimension of time or space.

Referents of terms and predications are mental entities; in other words, they are not entities in the physical, external world (Dik 1989; Seiler 1986: ch.2). Furthermore, referents are mental constructs rather than mental copies of things as they occur in the external world. Because we construe and refer to mental constructs, the spatio-temporal characteristics of such a construct (the referent) need not necessarily coincide with those of its possible counterpart in the external world. What the referent 'looks like' mentally, partly depends on the spatio-temporal specifications coded on or in the predicate used in the linguistic expression. Thus, there can be certain discrepancies between referents and their real-world equivalents (if they exist) with respect to matters of time and space.

For instance, in some languages one and the same real-world situation may be referred to by a predication containing a verb in the perfective or in the imperfective form. The English sentence *I stood there for an hour* can be translated into Russian either with the verb in the imperfective form (*ja stojal tam cas*) or in the perfective form (*ja postojal tam cas*) (from Comrie 1976: 17).

That we refer to mental constructs can also be demonstrated by the fact that we can refer to things that cannot be perceived in the immediate linguistic or non-linguistic context (e.g. lost or invisible objects, *the Armada, oxygen*) or entities that do not exist in the real world (*Martians, unicorns*).

In short, nominal and verbal predicates may be marked for certain spatio-temporal specifications, i.e. for a particular verbal or nominal 'aspect'.

2.1. Verbal aspect

In the temporal dimension a relation or property X (*sleep, hit, go, arrive,* etc.) can be represented as unmarked; or it can be represented as having a beginning, an ending, or as having both:

(5) — — — — — — — —   = imperfective aspect (unmarked)
T_i> — — — — — —   = ingressive aspect (beginning)
— — — — — —<T_j = egressive aspect (ending)
T_i> — — — —<T_j = perfective aspect (beginning + ending)

Depending on the time interval between T_i and T_j, the relation or property designated by a perfective verb can be further characterized as 'punctual' or 'durative'. The four aspectual distinctions can also be represented as in diagram 1:

time	(unmarked)	beginning
(unm.)	imperfective	ingressive
ending	egressive	perfective

Diagram 1: **Verbal aspect**

Languages differ as to the extent to which they have grammaticalized aspectual distinctions. Cross-linguistically it seems that imperfective and perfective aspect are grammaticalized much more often than ingressive or egressive aspect. Furthermore, ingressive and egressive aspectual meaning can also be indicated by perfective verbal forms, and imperfective aspect can be further divided into e.g. progressive and non-progressive aspect (Comrie 1976: 19ff; Chung and Timberlake 1985; Dik 1989: ch.9).

Since verbal aspect is a much discussed phenomenon I will confine myself to these remarks. For an extensive discussion of aspect the reader is referred to Comrie (1976), Hopper ed. (1982) and Chung and Timberlake (1985). Nominal 'aspect', on the other hand, is probably a considerably less familiar notion, so this will receive some more attention below.[3]

2.2. Nominal aspect

Like relations and properties in time, relations and properties in the spatial dimension, too, can be characterized in terms of two parameters.[4] However, whereas verbal aspect is usually added to the predicate, I take it that nominal aspect is often coded in (rather than on) the noun.[5] If this is the case, nominal aspectual distinctions will be changed rather than specified by quality operators in the term phrase. One reason to suspect that aspectual distinctions are coded in nominal predicates is that nominal aspect markers are not attested very frequently. There is, however, other evidence to suggest that nominals are inherently coded for a particular aspect (see below for examples).

The two parameters along which nominal predicates can be classified with respect to aspectual distinctions are 'shape' and 'structure'. If something has shape it has an implied boundary in the spatial dimension. If something has structure it can be divided into smaller parts without losing its essential properties. This yields the basic nominal aspects indicated in diagram 2:

space	(unmarked)	structure
(unm.)	conceptual	mass
shape	individual	collective

Diagram 2: **Nominal aspect**

These nominal aspects are discussed below.

2.2.1. Conceptual aspect. A noun with 'conceptual aspect' (or: a concept noun) designates a property that is unmarked for the two aspectual parameters 'shape' and 'structure'. A term that is headed by a concept noun refers to a spatial entity with a certain property, say 'grapiness' (which is not an existing nominal predicate in English). However, the predicate as such gives no indication about shape or structure. Consequently, the real-world equivalent of the referent of a term that is headed by this concept noun may be anything essentially characterized by 'grapiness' (i.e. the concept), for instance: (i) one or more individual grapes; (ii) a mass characterized by 'grapiness' (for instance, the term may refer to the juice of grapes); or (iii) one or more collectives (bunches) of grapes.

In languages that employ numeral classifiers (see example below) most nominal predicates seem to be of this type (cf. Hundius and Kölver 1983: 166). Since a concept noun (but also a mass noun) designates a property of a referent that is not marked for a definite outline, such a referent cannot be counted (or measured). Not surprisingly, languages that presumably have many concept nouns in the lexicon (such as numeral classifier languages) make use of a special construction when the speaker wants to indicate explicitly that the referent has cardinality. In these instances we find a numeral classifier, which is in construction with the cardinal numeral. The following example is from Burmese (Wheatley 1987: 851):

(6)   θwà   lè-hcàun
      tooth   four-peg
      "Four teeth"

The numeral (lè- "four") and the classifier (hcàun "peg") cannot be separated (Greenberg 1975: 29; Allan 1977: 288); they form a special classifier phrase that seems to have an appositional relation with the rest of the term. According to Greenberg (1972: 28, 31) the combination of numeral-plus-classifier constitutes an anaphoric construction which can occur by itself in all numeral classifier languages (see also Payne 1986: 113; Downing 1986). This suggests that the numeral classifier functions as an anaphoric element, referring to the mental construct that was construed on the basis of a concept noun. This in turn points to the possibility that it is not space that is quantified in numeral classifier languages (which is impossible because there is no implied boundary), but rather the referent. Unbounded space as such cannot be quantified, but one can quantify a referent, even if it refers to unbounded space. Apparently referents are inherently bounded entities.

The numeral classifier itself nearly always arises from a noun and commonly has some lexical meaning. It is not a full noun anymore, since in that case it would require a classifier itself. However, many nouns that function as a numeral classifier can also appear as the head noun of a term phrase. This may indicate that synchronically, too, there is a relation between constituents that can appear as a head noun and as a numeral classifier. In that case this relation may be described in terms of a predicate formation rule that takes as its input certain nominals (notably hyperonyms or predicates relating to classifiable properties of first order - spatial - entities) and produces avalent nominal predicates that are used for anaphoric purposes. For this reason it might be more appropriate to speak of a predicate de-formation rule here (Nclf = classifier noun):

(7) **Numeral classifier formation**
   input: $\Phi_N(x_i)$
   output: Φ_{Nclf}

This rule changes a lexical element into a grammatical element. With these considerations in mind the Burmese example in (6) can be represented as follows:

(6') $(ix_i: \Theta wà_N (x_i): (i4\ hcàun_{Nclf}))$

In this representation the classifier phrase is an (appositive) anaphoric construction which functions as a restrictor of the same referent as that denoted by the term as a whole.

2.2.2. Mass aspect. A nominal predicate with 'mass aspect' (a mass noun) is not specified for a definite outline, just like a concept noun; hence it cannot be used in a direct construction with a cardinal numeral (*two gold(s)*). However, a mass noun is specified for the aspectual parameter 'structure', which means that the spatial entity can be divided without losing its typical properties: half a bar of gold is still gold.[6] This example already indicates that a mass can be measured. As opposed to the classifier phrase, the measure phrase (*three pounds* in (8)) does not seem to have an appositional relation with the rest of the term; hence it can be regarded as a special kind of operator. Following Dik (1987: 14-15, 1989: ch.7.5.3) this can be represented as in (8').

(8) Three pounds of tobacco

(8') $(i3\text{-}pound\ x_i: tobacco_N (x_i))$

2.2.3. Individual aspect. A nominal predicate with 'individual aspect' (an individual noun) designates a property that is specified as being spatially bounded. Therefore, such nouns (as well as other nouns that are specified for the parameter 'shape') can be used in a direct construction with a numeral. An individual noun is unmarked for the parameter 'structure'. Hence the space for which the designated property obtains cannot be divided, for then the property does not obtain any longer (half a grape is not a grape anymore; see also Greenberg 1972: 13). Nouns with individual aspect are typically found in the lexicons of, for instance, Dutch and English.

2.2.4. Collective aspect. Nominal predicates with 'collective aspect' designate a property that is specified as being spatially bounded and divisible: if the referent of a term headed by a collective noun were divided, the same property would still obtain. For example, a term headed by the nominal predicate *family* denotes a group of individuals (e.g. A & B & C & D) each of which is a member of the same family, and this does not change when the group is divided into smaller groups (for instance, A & B and C & D; A & B are still members of the same family, and so are e.g. A & C and A & D).

In summary, there are at least four basic ways in which a property can be defined in terms of its spatial characteristics. I assume that a nominal predicate is set for a certain aspect ('default aspect') which can sometimes be changed under the influence of a quality operator. But it may very well be that in some, perhaps even most cases the aspectual setting is invariable, or that it can only be changed by predicate formation (see note 6).

Apparently nominals that predicate something of non-spatial entities, such as abstract nouns (like *love*) and derived nouns (like *destruction*), are modeled after these basic types (or the plural form). Thus *sleep* is a mass noun (*much sleep*), *arrival* a count noun (*two arrivals*).

Note, finally, that number marking is only possible if the head noun carries the feature 'shape', so only terms containing a noun with individual or collective aspect can be marked for plurality (*grape - grapes, family - families*). Number, however, is a function of another kind of operator, which is to be discussed below.

2.3. *The representation of quality operators*

From the preceding sections it appears that there is sufficient reason to assume that in the domain of the term phrase and in the domain of the predication a similar kind of operator can be recognized that relates to qualitative properties of the referent.[7] Since this operator primarily affects the nominal or verbal predicate, we may give the variable symbolizing this operation a position next to the predicate in the underlying representation of the linguistic expression. For the domain of the predication this has already been recognized (Hengeveld 1989; Dik 1989). Thus the term and the predication can be represented as follows (Ω_1 and π_1 stand for quality operators):

(9) $\quad (\Omega_2 \, x_i \colon \Omega_1 \, \Phi_N \, (x_i) \colon ...)$ $\qquad\qquad\qquad$ term phrase

(10) $\quad (\pi_2 \, e_i \colon [\pi_1 \, \Phi_V \, (T_1) \, (T_2) \, ... \,] \, (e_i))$ $\qquad\qquad$ predication

The quality operator indicates how a property or relation is represented in time or space; the property or relation as such remains unaffected.

3. Quantity operators

3.1. Number and cardinality

Probably most languages have grammatical (i.e. non-lexical) ways to indicate number and/or cardinality in the term phrase, i.e. quantity operators. If number marking is absent, a term with a count noun refers to a singular entity: an individual (*a grape*) or a collective (*a family*). If there is some kind of plural marker, the term refers to more individuals or collectives (*grapes*, *families*). Most languages with count nouns have a singular/plural opposition, but in some languages finer distinctions are possible e.g. by means of a dual marker.

In addition to plural marking, which is not very precise, there is also the possibility of using a cardinal numeral (or a quantifier such as *many - few - some*, which is not very precise either). It is useful to distinguish between number marking and cardinality, because in certain languages (notably those of the Bantu group, such as Babungo; Schaub 1985: 197) number is expressed in the form of a class affix and numerals are expressed separately in a distinct phrase in the matrix term (Rijkhoff fc.). Consequently I will not be concerned with cardinal numerals and quantifiers in this context. Such elements do not seem to occur as an expression of a predication operator. At the level of the predication the nearest English equivalents of cardinals and quantifiers are adverbials (*often, sometimes, twice*) and expressions such as .. *times*.

Some languages, however, have at their disposal grammatical markers to indicate number in the domain of the predication. In the case of plurality this is called iterative (or: repetitive, frequentative) aspect. If there is an inflectional element indicating that a SoA obtains only once, this is called semelfactive aspect, although 'aspect' might not be the appropriate term if one prefers to reserve it for phenomena such as those discussed in 2.1.

Hengeveld (1989: 141) gives an example from Hidatsa, a Siouan language described in Matthews (1965), where the iterative marker (a quantitative predication operator) is less close to the predicate than the ingressive aspect marker (a qualitative predication operator):

(11) *Wío   i   hírawe   ki   ksa   c*
     woman she   sleep   INGR   ITER   MOOD
     "The woman fell asleep again and again"

Iterativity can be said to quantify the ingressive SoA as a whole (see also Chung and Timberlake 1985: 222).

Quantity is a property of a referent x_i or e_i as such. In other words, the scope of a quantity operator does not extend beyond the elements of the core domain (the core term or the core predication). The core domain maximally consists of a nominal or verbal predicate (plus arguments), a quality operator, and other (lexical) elements that further specify the spatial or temporal entity for its inherent, more or less characteristic properties. In the term phrase such elements are adjectives, and in the predication the so-called 'first-level satellites' (or: L1-satellites) with the semantic functions Manner, Speed or Instrument (cf. Dik et al. this vol.; Dik 1989).

If a referent can have its own quantity, this means, for instance, that number marking in matrix domains (*the child(ren)* in (12)) is independent of number marking in subordinate domains (*in front of the house(s)* in (12)), and vice versa. Since I would like to distinguish number marking from numerals and quanti-fiers, different symbols are used for 'singular' and 'plural' than those normally used in the representation of terms; instead of '1' and 'm' I use 's(ingular)' and 'p(lural)'.[8]

(12) a.   The child in front of the house   (s-s)
     a'. $(dsx_i: child_N (x_i): \{(dsx_j: house_N (x_j))_{Loc}\} (x_i))$
     b.   The children in front of the house   (p-s)
     b'. $(dpx_i: child_N (x_i): \{(dsx_j: house_N (x_j))_{Loc}\} (x_i))$
     c.   The child in front of the houses   (s-p)
     c'. $(dsx_i: child_N (x_i): \{(dpx_j: house_N (x_j))_{Loc}\} (x_i))$
     d.   The children in front of the houses   (p-p)
     d'. $(dpx_i: child_N (x_i): \{(dpx_j: house_N (x_j))_{Loc}\} (x_i))$

The only restriction is due to physical laws, as in *the chair in the rooms*; one individual cannot be in two places at the same time.

What has been said above about number in relation to the term phrase also seems to hold for predications; compare these paraphrases:

(13) **She called the police (repeatedly)** after he had threatened her
(once)   (p-s)

(14) **She called the police (once)** after he had threatened her
(repeatedly)   (s-p)

The number of instances of the SoA referred to by the matrix predication (in boldface) varies independently of the number of instances of the SoA referred to by the embedded predication.

3.2. The representation of quantity operators

Since quantity operators Ω_2 and π_2 have the core domain in their scope (see above), they are placed next to the variable symbolizing the referent. This indicates that the quantity operator has in its scope the particular space or time to which the relation or property designated by material of the core domain applies. In the case of spatial entities the quantity operator may also indicate cardinality or measure.

(15) $(\Omega_3\ \Omega_2\ x_i\colon \Omega_1\ N\ (x_i)\colon A\ (x_i))$ term phrase

(16) $(\pi_3\ \pi_2\ e_i\colon [\pi_1\ V\ (T_1)\ (T_2)\ \dots\ ]\ (e_i))$ predication

Note that in this representation π_2 symbolizes the quantity operator in the predication, whereas in Hengeveld (1989: 132) π_2 operators relate to tense, quantificational aspect and objective mood/polarity. Also, in Hengeveld (ibid.) π_3 operators relate to evidential and subjective mood, but here π_3 (to be discussed in the following section) stands for the locality operator in the domain of the predication.

4. The locality (or: deictic) operator

The third kind of operator in the term and in the predication should relate to
the notion 'locality'. In both domains there is an obvious candidate. In the
predication this is, of course, tense, which is defined as the "grammaticalised
expression of location in time" (Comrie 1985: 9). In the domain of the term
phrase the demonstrative is the direct manifestation of a locality operator. First
I will briefly consider tense and its correlate non-tense.

4.1. Temporal deixis: Tense

A SoA can precede, follow, or coincide with the speech situation.[9] If a SoA does
not coincide with the speech situation, it may be felt to have current relevance.
For future situations current relevance is indicated with the prospective, and for
past situations it is marked by the retrospective (or: perfect). Tense is a deictic
grammatical category in that it relates a SoA to a reference point.[10]

(17)

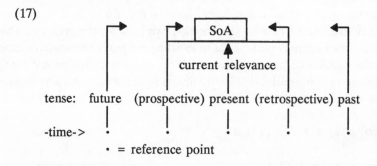

The notion 'location' is closely related to the notion 'existence': if an entity
exists it has a location, and vice versa (cf. Lyons 1977: 718-724; Bugenhagen
1986).[11] Tense indicates two things. Firstly, the mere fact that the predication
has tense (i.e. has been given a location in time) indicates that the SoA is
deemed to exist, that the SoA is regarded as real or actual. This is what can be
regarded as the modal element of tense. Although the realis/irrealis distinction
is often looked upon as a purely modal distinction, tense and mood are
inherently connected (as are tense and aspect). For an extensive discussion on
this matter I refer to Lyons (1977: ch.17.3), Comrie (1976: ch.4), Chung and
Timberlake (1985: 206ff), and Palmer (1986: ch.6). Secondly, the particular
tense used indicates where the SoA in question is located in time relative to the

speech situation (cf. Chung and Timberlake 1985: 203ff; Comrie 1985: 39ff).

Conversely, if the speaker refers to a SoA whose existence cannot be determined (because for some reason the SoA referred to does not have a location in time - as yet), the predication will not be marked for tense.[12] A SoA may be non-actual for several reasons, for instance because the predication referring to this SoA is expressed as a command (referring to a SoA to be brought about by the addressee) or because the potential existence of the SoA denoted by the predication is, for example, hoped, feared, or desired. Hence non-tensed (non-actual) predications are commonly under the scope of a modal or illocutionary operator. For instance, "in their strictly temporal sense [tense affixes] do not occur in the imperative/optative mood" in West Greenlandic (Fortescue 1984: 275). In Tamil "a good proportion" of the modal auxiliaries is not marked for tense (Asher 1982: 165), and in Kobon "the tense distinctions between simple past, remote past, present, and future are made only in the indicative mood" (Davies 1981: 168).[13]

4.2. Spatial deixis: (Attributive) demonstrative pronouns

Above we saw that tense indicates that a SoA has a location in time and that the relation between location and existence is a biconditional one: whatever *is* must *be* somewhere and whatever *is* somewhere must *be* (Bugenhagen 1986: 127). We also saw that on the one hand tense indicates that the SoA in question exists (the modal element of tense), and on the other that the particular tense used specifies the temporal location of this SoA relative to a reference point (the locality element of tense).

Generally speaking, (attributive) demonstrative pronouns indicate that the hearer is supposed to be able to identify the referent of the term phrase in the extra-linguistic context. Thus demonstratives also constitute a deictic category in that "their semantic values depend on the real-world context" (Anderson and Keenan 1985: 301). Pursuing the analogy between tense and demonstratives, one could say that a demonstrative on the one hand indicates that the referent of a term exists (the modal element of demonstratives), and on the other that it specifies the spatial location of the referent relative to a reference point (the locality element of demonstratives).[14]

Spatial reference often forms the basis for various metaphorical extensions (cf. Lakoff and Johnson 1980). Constituents indicating distance in space may be employed to indicate distance in time (temporal space) and distance in pragmatic, discourse, or psychological space (cf. Lyons 1977: ch.15.2; Greenberg

1983; Anderson and Keenan 1985: 277ff; Dik 1989: ch.2.4.2). Thus deictic elements may become anaphoric. In many languages there is a synchronic or diachronic relation between demonstratives on the one hand and definite articles (and third person pronouns) on the other.

Demonstratives are inherently definite constituents, and in a very general way definiteness can be said to mark identifiability (for an extensive study of definiteness and indefiniteness see Hawkins 1978). Conversely, indefiniteness generally indicates that the hearer is not expected to be able to identify the referent of a term, e.g. if the referent, or rather the existence/location of the referent, has not yet been established.

In other words, it appears that indefiniteness and non-tensedness are quite similar, in that in both cases it is indicated that we are dealing with an entity whose existence is undetermined (see Rijkhoff 1989).

The analogy between indefiniteness and non-tensedness is not as far-fetched as it may seem. Witness the examples below from Jacaltec, where both the exhortative mood and non-specificity (admittedly not indefiniteness) are expressed by the same suffix: *-oj*, "the general suffix of irrealis" (Craig 1977: 93):[15]

(18) *Way-oj   ab   naj*
      sleep-OJ   EXH   CL.he
      "Would that he sleep!"

(19) *X-Ø-'oc   heb   ix   say-a'   hun-uj   munlabel*
      ASP-A3-start PLUR   woman   look.for-FUT   a-OJ   pot
      "The women started looking for a pot"

(EXH = exhortative; CL = classifier; A3 = absolutive 3; ASP = aspect; FUT = future). In (18) *-oj* is suffixed to the intransitive verb in the exhortative mood, in (19) it marks the referent of the term phrase as non-specific.

4.3. The scope of locality operators

In view of the fact that by using (absolute) tense or an attributive demonstrative pronoun the speaker directly points out where the referent is located in time or space, it seems justified to assume that in the underlying representation a locality/deictic operator has in its scope all of the space or time taken up by the referent x_i or e_i at that particular location.

Whereas the quantity operator has in its scope the space or time designated by the nominal predicate (and adjectives, if present) or by the verbal predicate (plus its arguments and the so-called 'first-level satellites', if present; see above), the locality operator has in its scope the total amount of space or time occupied by the quantified referent x_i or e_i (Ω_3 and π_3 are locality operators in the domain of the term phrase and the predication, respectively):

(20) $(\Omega_3\ \Omega_2\ x_i:\ \Omega_1\ N\ (x_i):\ A\ (x_i))$ term phrase

(21) $(\pi_3\ \pi_2\ e_i:\ [\pi_1\ V\ (T_1)\ (T_2)\ ...\ ]\ (e_i))$ predication

The scope of these operators can also be represented as follows:

(22)

$(\Omega_3$ | Ω_2 | $x_i:$ | $\Omega_1\ N$ | $(x_i):\ A\ (x_i):\ ...\ A(x_i))$

(23)

$(\pi_3$ | π_2 | $e_i:$ | $[\pi_1\ V$ | $(T_1)\ (T_2)\ ...]\ (e_i))$

It may be useful to point out once again that this representation differs from Hengeveld's (Hengeveld 1989) in that here π_3 stands for a locality operator and π_2 for a quantity operator.[16]

It will be remembered that adjectives and level 1 (L1) satellites are within the scope of the quantity operator (see above); hence these elements must also be within the scope of the locality operator. Certain other material that is within the scope of the locality operator is not explicitly given in the representation above; this is discussed in 6.

5. Scope and the relative order of operators

With respect to the predication there is considerable evidence that the ordering
of operators in the underlying structure is directly reflected in the actual
linguistic expression (see also Hengeveld 1989). Bybee (1985) investigated the
ordering of inflectional morphemes relative to the verbal predicate in a
representative sample of fifty languages. She found that

> aspect occurs closest to the stem, followed by tense, and then by mood. The only exception
> to this ordering found in the 50-language sample is in Ojibwa, where the Dubitative suffix
> precedes the Preterite suffix. (Bybee 1985: 196)

Unfortunately Bybee does not give information concerning the relative position
of iterative aspect markers (but see example (11) from Hidatsa).

To my knowledge a large-scale study concerning the ordering of term
operators (or better: their formal manifestations) has never been undertaken,
but here Greenberg and Hawkins may shed some light. Greenberg investigated
a variety of ordering phenomena in thirty randomly selected languages, which
resulted in the formulation of a great number of universals of grammar
(Greenberg 1966). Hawkins (1983: 119-120) contains a revision of Greenberg's
Universal 20:

> Universal 20'. When any or all of the items (demonstrative, numeral, and descriptive adjective)
> precede the noun, they (i.e., those that do precede) are always found in that order. For those
> that follow, no predictions are made, though the most frequent order is the mirror-image of
> the order for preceding modifiers.

This universal indicates that the most frequently attested orderings reflect the
scope differences of the operators: demonstrative (Ω_3) # numeral (Ω_2) # noun;
or noun # numeral (Ω_2) # demonstrative (Ω_3).

Number, also an expression of Ω_2, is usually marked by inflection on the
noun. Nominal aspect (Ω_1) does not seem to be overtly expressed very often, at
least not grammatically, but apart from e.g. derivational means there are certain
other ways to signal nominal aspect. For instance, as noted in 2.1.1-2.1.2,
nominal aspect determines whether or not the noun can combine with a
numeral (if it can, the noun is a count noun or a collective noun) and which
quantifier is to be employed (e.g. in English *much* for mass nouns and *many* for
count nouns).

There are, however, languages (e.g. in the Afro-Asiatic and Nilo-Saharan
phyla; see e.g. Andrzejewski 1960; Hayward 1984; Stroomer 1987: 74-88; Unseth

1988) that have nouns which seem aspectually ambiguous with respect to the parameter 'structure'. Terms headed by such nouns may refer to an individual or a collective:

space	(unmarked)	structure
(unm.)	conceptual	mass
shape	set	

Diagram 3: **Ambiguous aspect - set**

When a 'set noun' is used in a term (without a cardinal) it is, strictly speaking, not clear whether the term refers to one or more individuals. Consider e.g. these examples from Oromo (Stroomer 1987: 74):

(24) *nama*   "man, men"   (Boraana dialect)
     simp'irree   "bird, birds"   (Orma dialect)
     anamaa   "man, person, people"   (Waata dialect)

However, the ambiguity may be resolved by certain affixes, which I presume change, or rather disambiguate nominal aspect. Such affixes turn a set noun either into an individual noun or a collective noun. Although these suffixes are often referred to as *singulative* or *plural* affixes, I think it is a mistake to regard them as number affixes, since number marking only applies to individual and collective nouns.[17]

The so-called plural marker on set nouns does not occur with cardinal numerals (Stroomer 1987: 76), so that in the case of a set noun cardinality seems to indicate the size of the set rather than the number of individuals or collectives. Perhaps one could say that in the case of a noun with individual or collective aspect the cardinal numeral must be viewed as a multiplier (n times an individual or a collective), whereas in the case of a set noun the cardinal functions as a divisor.

In any case, together these data suggest that in the term phrase, too, a general (iconic) ordering principle is functioning, which can be formulated as follows (see also Hengeveld 1989: 141; Dik 1989):

(25) **Principle of scope**
An operator is expressed in the periphery of the layer it has in its
scope.

Hawkins' Universal 20' suggests that there may be exceptions to this principle
when modifiers follow the noun. This happens, for instance, in Babungo. In the
Babungo term phrase the numeral follows the demonstrative, both following the
noun (i.e. noun # demonstrative # numeral; Schaub 1985: 77). However, within
the Babungo noun phrase the numeral is part of a larger structure which
constitutes a noun phrase by itself (ibid.: 187). For instance (example from
Schaub 1985: 187) (Babungo has fourteen noun classes; for the sake of
exposition I have glossed the class affixes separately. C = noun class; *gá*
"antelope" belongs to class 1/2, class 2 - C2 - being the plural of class 1):

(26) *və̀-ŋgá   njə̀-sə́   sə̀-bɔ̀ɔ   múu-mbɔ̀ɔ*
     C2-antelope digit-C10 C10-two   ten-two
     "twenty-two antelopes"

The numeral phrase (*njə̀sə́ sə̀bɔ̀ɔ múu-mbɔ̀ɔ* "twenty-two") constitutes a
complex noun phrase, involving the nominals *njə̀-* "digit" and *yìghúŋ* "ten". The
first instance of the numeral *-bɔ̀ɔ* "two" agrees in class with the noun *njə̀-*
"digit", which belongs to noun class 9/10 (class 10 is the plural of class 9), the
class for animals and many other things (such as abstracts). Together they form
the numeral phrase meaning "two". The internal structure of the numeral *múu-
mbɔ̀ɔ* "twenty" is less transparent: the plural of *yìghúŋ* "ten" is irregular and its
noun class membership unclear (i.e. class 5/?; Schaub 1985: 253-254).

From this it appears that Babungo (and presumably at least some other
Bantu languages as well) does not constitute a counterexample to the principle
of scope, because the Babungo numeral phrase is a lexical rather than a
grammatical expression of cardinality (Rijkhoff fc.).

6. Satellites in the term and in the predication

Similarities in the underlying structure of terms and predications go beyond
parallels between operators in these domains: they also seem to share the same
kind of satellites. In Hengeveld (1989), Dik (1989), and Dik et al. (this vol.)
the predication is considered to consist of two levels. At the lowest level we find
the verbal predicate and its arguments (or: nuclear predication). It is at this

level that the predicate (or: quality) operator applies and at which L1 satellites (indicating Manner, Speed, Instrument) may be added. This yields the core predication. At the second level we find tense operators (π_2 in the representation below but π_3 in my account), which apply to the core predication, and level 2 (L2) satellites, which constitute the lexical means to express locality in time or space, i.e. locality satellites (*last year* or *in the park*). Together these elements constitute the extended predication.

(27) level 2: π_2 - $\underline{\pi_1 - \text{V} + \text{arguments} \quad - \quad \text{L1 satellites}}$ - L2 satellites
core predication

level 1: π_1 - $\underline{\text{V} + \text{arguments}}$ - L1 satellites
nuclear predication

What is absent in this representation of Hengeveld's layers in (27) is the quantity operator, which also has its lexical counterpart in the form of quantity satellites such as *twice* or *often*. If we add another layer for quantity operators and quantity satellites we get the following picture (σ_n = level n predication satellites; σ_1 = quality satellites, σ_2 = quantity satellites, σ_3 = locality satellites; but cf. Dik et al. this vol.):

(28) π_3 - π_2 - π_1 - V + arguments - σ_1 - σ_2 - σ_3

full predication   (= extended pred.)

quantified predication

qualified predication   (= core pred.)

If we overtly mark the scopes of the various operators we get:

(29)

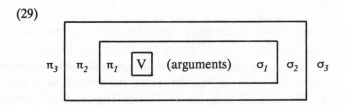

Elements in the term phrase, such as adjectives, term predicates and relative clauses (term satellites), can also be characterized in terms of quality-quantity-locality.[18] Adjectives can be regarded as level 1 term satellites (Θ_1) in that they further specify qualitative aspects of the entity in question.[19] Numeral phrases as they occur in e.g. Babungo function are level 2 term satellites (Θ_2) in that they lexically specify quantity, and attributive term phrases, i.e. term predicates with e.g. Locative or Possessor semantic function (*the book on the table*), and relative clauses are level 3 term satellites (Θ_3) in that they specify the existence/location of the referent of the matrix term.[20] Consider (Θ_n = level n term satellites):

(30) Ω_3 - Ω_2 - Ω_1 - N - Θ_1 - Θ_2 - Θ_3

      full term   (or: extended term)

      quantified term

      qualified term   (or: core term)

If we overtly indicate the scopes of the different kinds of term operators we get:

(31)

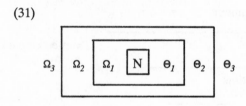

7. Conclusion

Both in the term and in the predication operators and satellites can be characterized in terms of three notions: quality, quantity, and locality. With respect to operators it appears that the scope differences of these operators are directly reflected in the positions that the formal manifestations of these operators occupy in the term or predication. This finding leads to greater conceptual and descriptive coherence in the representation of linguistic structures.

It remains to be seen if cross-linguistically the relative order of satellites conforms to an iconic ordering principle similar to the one that seems to hold for operators.

Notes

1. An earlier and rather different version of this article appeared in the Working Papers in Functional Grammar series (no. 29: "A typology of operators"). I am indebted to Richard Brown, Simon Dik, Casper de Groot, Kees Hengeveld, Lachlan Mackenzie, Hotze Mulder, the editors of WPFG, and the editors of this volume for their comments on earlier drafts. The usual disclaimers apply.

2. This representation differs from Dik's (Dik 1978, 1989) in that it has an operator position next to the head noun. This is accounted for below.

3. The only (implicit) references I know of are in Seuren (1974: 4) and Langacker (1987).

4. In the rest of this paper I will ignore derived and polyvalent nominal predicates. Basic nominal predicates such as *father* are supposed to designate a relation between entities: someone is always the father of someone else. I find it difficult to think of nominals as predicates that designate relations, especially because the so-called relation always seems to be of the same type (cf. Mackenzie 1983: 38). One could also say that such predicates designate a relational property, viz. the property of *being X's Y* or *the Y of X* (e.g. *X's father* or *the surface of X*).

5. De Groot (1985) argues, for example, that momentaneousness ($[\pm \text{Mom}]$) is an inherent feature of verbal predicates. If this is true, this could imply that the property or relation designated by a $[+\text{Mom}]$ verb, such as *reach* or *hit*, must be temporally bounded.

6. Aspectual distinctions can also be expressed by means of predicate formation (e.g. *child* vs. *childhood*). Sometimes a language has different predicates for different aspectual types, e.g. *pig* (= individual) vs. *pork* (= mass).

7. Similarities between nouns and verbs in terms of count versus mass and perfective versus imperfective have been discussed before (most recently in Langacker 1987; also Leech 1969; Greenberg 1972: 30; see for references Mourelatos 1981: note 27).

8. A similar distinction is made by Gerjan van Schaaik (p.c.) with respect to Turkish.

9. I will restrict myself to absolute tense here; see Comrie (1985) for the distinction between absolute and relative tense.

10. Recent contributions on deixis in general are Lyons (1977: ch.15), Levinson (1983: ch.2), Greenberg (1983), Anderson and Keenan (1985). Cf. also Post (1988), who attempts to relate temporal and non-temporal expressions.

11. By using the future tense the speaker predicts that a SoA will obtain. Interestingly Bybee (1985: 157) mentions a dialect of Yanomama as having an expected future and a desired future. The status of the future as a real tense has often been questioned. See e.g. Lyons (1977: 677, 816); Ultan (1978); Comrie (1985: 21); Chung and Timberlake (1985: 243); Palmer (1986: 216ff).

12. Or as Chung and Timberlake (1985: 241) put it: "Whereas there is basically one way for an event to be actual, there are numerous ways that an event can be less than completely actual."

13. There are some apparent counterexamples where finite forms are used in predications referring to non-actual SoAs, i.e. SoAs whose existence cannot be established. The fact that tense-like forms are used in predications that refer to non-actual SoAs is generally known, but remains unexplained (see e.g. Lyons 1977: 682; Palmer 1986: ch.6).

14. Analogies between demonstratives/definiteness and tense are observed also in e.g. Vet (1986) and Janssen (1989).

15. See also Guy (1974: 29-30), who states that in Sakao nouns are inflectable for the irrealis.

16. Apart form this, it would be better to use different symbols for operators in different domains (i.e. Ω for terms, π for predications only, and e.g. Σ for propositions etc.), just as different variables are employed for different kinds of entities.

17. One could hypothesize that, if in due course this assumed aspectual disambiguity of the noun were to disappear, the so-called plural marker (which I consider to be a collective aspect marker) might serve as a real plural marker in a language such as Oromo. Since in Oromo the singulative suffix (which I regard as an individual aspect marker) seems to be used productively only in the case of ethnonyms (Stroomer 1987: 83), one could expect this element to disappear altogether.

18. Term satellites were first introduced in Mackenzie (1983), who investigates parallels between terms and predications with respect to semantic-syntactic-pragmatic function assignment and the argument-satellite distinction.

19. In languages where the object follows the verb in the unmarked pattern there is an interesting correlation between the order of adverb and verb and the order of adjective and noun. Dryer (1988: 202) has evidence for the following, (almost) exceptionless, implicational universal: If VO and AdvV then AdjN.

20. Cognitively possessed items can be argued to be located 'at' the possessor. Similarities between possessive, locative and existential constructions have been noted by several authors (see e.g. Lyons 1967; Clark 1978; Bugenhagen 1986; see also Fox and Thompson 1989 on the function of relative clauses from a discourse perspective).

References

Allan, Keith
1977 "Classifiers". *Language* 53: 285-311.

Anderson, Stephen R. and Edward L.Keenan
1985 "Deixis". In T.Shopen (ed.), 259-308.

Andrzejewski, B.W.
1960 "The categories of number in noun forms in the Borana dialect of Galla". *Africa* 30: 62-75.

Asher, R.E.
1982 *Tamil*. Amsterdam: North-Holland.

Auwera, Johan van der and Louis Goossens (eds.)
1987 *Ins and outs of the predication*. Dordrecht: Foris.

Bolkestein, A.M., C.de Groot and J.L.Mackenzie (eds.)
1985 *Predicates and terms in functional grammar*. Dordrecht: Foris.

Bugenhagen, Robert D.
1986 "Possession in Mangap-Mbula: Its syntax and semantics". *Oceanic Linguistics* 25: 124-166.

Bybee, Joan L.
1985 *Morphology: A study of the relation between meaning and form*. Amsterdam: Benjamins.

Chung, Sandra and Alan Timberlake
1985 "Tense, aspect, and mood". In T.Shopen (ed.), 202-258.

Clark, Eve V.
1978 "Locationals: Existential, locative, and possessive constructions". In J.Greenberg et al. (eds.), vol.4, 85-126.

Comrie, Bernard
1976 *Aspect*. Cambridge: Cambridge UP.
1985 *Tense*. Cambridge: Cambridge UP.

Comrie, Bernard (ed.)
1987 *The world's major languages*. London: Croom Helm.

Connolly, John H. and Simon C.Dik (eds.)
1989 *Functional grammar and the computer*. Dordrecht: Foris.

Craig, Colette
1977 *The structure of Jacaltec*. Austin: University of Texas Press.

Craig, Colette (ed.)
    1986   *Noun classes and categorization*. Amsterdam: Benjamins.

Davies, John
    1981   *Kobon*. Amsterdam: North-Holland.

Dik, Simon C.
    1978   *Functional grammar*. Amsterdam: North-Holland. (Third revised edition: 1981,
           Dordrecht: Foris.)
    1987   "A typology of entities". In J.Van der Auwera and L.Goossens (eds.), 1-20.
    1989   *The theory of functional grammar, pt.1*. Dordrecht: Foris.

Dik, Simon C. (ed.)
    1983   *Advances in functional grammar*. Dordrecht: Foris.

Downing, Pamela
    1986   "The anaphoric use of classifiers in Japanese". In C.Craig (ed.), 345-375.

Dryer, Matthew S.
    1988   "Object-verb order and adjective-noun order: Dispelling a myth". *Lingua* 74: 185-217.

Foley, William A. and Robert D.Van Valin Jr.
    1984   *Functional syntax and universal grammar*. Cambridge: Cambridge UP.

Fortescue, Michael
    1984   *West Greenlandic*. London: Croom Helm.

Fox, Barbara and Sandra A.Thompson
    1989   *Relative clauses in English conversation*. L.A.U.D.-paper A-258.

Greenberg, Joseph H.
    1966   "Some universals of grammar with particular reference to the order of meaningful
           elements". In J.Greenberg (ed.), 73-113.
    1972   "Numeral classifiers and substantival number: Problems in the genesis of a linguistic
           type". *Working Papers on Language Universals* 9: 1-39.
    1975   "Dynamic aspects of word order in the numeral classifier". In C.Li (ed.), 27-45.
    1983   "Some iconic relationships among place, time, and discourse deixis". In J.Haiman (ed.),
           271-287.

Greenberg, Joseph H. (ed.)
    1966   *Universals of language*. (2nd ed.). Cambridge: MIT-Press.

Greenberg, J.H., C.A.Ferguson and E.A.Moravcsik (eds.)
    1978   *Universals of human language*. Stanford: Stanford UP.

Groot, Casper de
   1985   "Predicates and features". In A.M.Bolkestein et al. (eds.), 71-84.

Guy, J.B.M.
   1974   *A grammar of the northern dialect of Sakao*. Pacific Linguistics B-33.

Haiman, John (ed.)
   1983   *Iconicity in syntax*. Amsterdam: Benjamins.

Hawkins, John A.
   1978   *Definiteness and indefiniteness*. London: Croom Helm.
   1983   *Word order universals*. New York: Academic Press.

Hayward, Dick
   1984   *The Arbore language: A first investigation; including a vocabulary*. Hamburg: Buske.

Hengeveld, Kees
   1989   "Layers and operators in functional grammar". *Journal of Linguistics* 25: 127-157.

Hopper, Paul (ed.)
   1982   *Tense-aspect: Between semantics and pragmatics*. Amsterdam: Benjamins.

Hundius, Harald and Ulrike Kölver
   1983   "Syntax and semantics of numeral classifiers in Thai". *Studies in Language* 7: 164-214.

Janssen, Theo A.J.M.
   1989   *Present and past: Counterparts of 'this' and 'that'*. L.A.U.D.-paper A-269.

Lakoff, George and Mark Johnson
   1980   *Metaphors we live by*. Chicago: The University of Chicago Press.

Langacker, Ronald W.
   1987   "Nouns and verbs". *Language* 63: 53-94.

Leech, Geoffrey N.
   1969   *Towards a semantic description of English*. London: Longman.

Levinson, Stephen C.
   1983   *Pragmatics*. Cambridge: Cambridge UP.

Li, Charles N. (ed.)
   1975   *Word order and word order change*. Austin: University of Texas Press.

Lyons, John
   1967   "A note on possessive, existential and locative sentences". *Foundations of Language* 3:
          390-396.

1977   *Semantics*. Cambridge: Cambridge UP.

Mackenzie, J. Lachlan
1983   "Nominal predicates in a functional grammar of English". In S.C.Dik (ed.), 31-51.

Matthews, G.H.
1965   *Hidatsa syntax*. The Hague: Mouton.

Mourelatos, Alexander P.D.
1981   "Events, processes, and states". In P.J.Tedeschi and A.Zaenen (eds.), 191-212.

Palmer, Frank R.
1986   *Mood and modality*. Cambridge: Cambridge UP.

Payne, D.L.
1986   "Noun-classification in Yagua". In C.Craig (ed.), 113-131.

Post, Ans
1988   "Temporele predikatie en temporele kwantifikatie". *TTT* 8: 67-87.

Quirk, R., S.Greenbaum, G.Leech and J.Svartvik
1985   *A comprehensive grammar of the English language*. London: Longman.

Rijkhoff, Jan
1989   "The identification of referents". In J.Connolly and S.Dik (eds.), 229-246.
fc.   "Explaining word order in the noun phrase". *Linguistics*.

Rijksbaron, Albert
1989   *Aristotle, verb meaning and functional grammar*. Amsterdam: Gieben.

Schaub, Willi
1985   *Babungo*. London: Croom Helm.

Seiler, Hansjakob
1986   *Apprehension: Language, object and order, pt.3*. Tübingen: Narr.

Seuren, Pieter A.M.
1974   "Introduction". In P.Seuren (ed.), *Semantic syntax*. Oxford: Oxford UP, 1-27.

Shopen, Timothy (ed.)
1985   *Language typology and syntactic description, vol.3*. Cambridge: Cambridge UP.

Stroomer, Harry J.
1987   *A comparative study of three southern Oromo dialects in Kenya (phonology, morphology and vocabulary)*. Ph.D.-dissertation, University of Leiden.

Tedeschi, Philip J. and Annie Zaenen (eds.)
    1981   *Syntax and semantics, vol.14: Tense and aspect*. New York: Academic Press.

Ultan, Russell
    1978   "The nature of future tenses". In J.Greenberg et al. (eds.), vol.3, 83-123.

Unseth, Peter
    1988   "Majang nominal plurals, with comparative notes". *Studies in African Linguistics* 19: 75-91.

Vet, Co
    1986   *A pragmatic approach to tense in functional grammar*. Working Papers in Functional Grammar 16.

Wheatley, Julian K.
    1987   "Burmese". In B.Comrie (ed.), 834-854.

Layered Syntax in Role and Reference Grammar

Robert D. Van Valin, Jr.

University of California, Davis

0. Introduction[1]

All syntactic theories have, as one of their cornerstones, a particular conception of clause structure. For example, all generative theories save Relational Grammar assume a version of the X-bar theory of phrase structure. Role and Reference Grammar (RRG) posits a rather different concept of clause organization, *the layered structure of the clause* (LSC), which is concerned primarily with the representation of certain semantically motivated syntactic units rather than simple immediate constituency. The purpose of this paper is to present the RRG view of clause structure and to comment on the parallels and differences between it and the notion of layered syntactic structure that has developed within the Functional Grammar (FG) approach over the past few years.

The discussion will procede as follows. In section 1, the LSC in RRG will be sketched, and then in section 2 it will be compared with the FG version. In section 3 the crucial contrast between core and clause in the RRG model will be explored, while in section 4 the role of the LSC in complex sentence syntax will be discussed. Conclusions are presented in section 5.

1. The layered structure of the clause in RRG

Theories have different motivations for selecting a conception of clause structure. For example, immediate constituent representations are appropriate for theories of autonomous syntax, because the relevant hierarchical organization can be established by purely formal operations without reference to the meaning of the elements involved. RRG is greatly concerned with finding those aspects of clause structure which are common to languages of widely varying types: languages with rigid word order such as English, free-word-order languages such as Dyirbal and Warlpiri, flat-syntax languages like Malayalam, and head-marking languages (Nichols 1986) like Lakhota and Jacaltec. Immediate constituent structure is problematic in general for some of these languages, for a variety of reasons, and the postulation of a VP node in particular in their clausal organization is highly questionable for some of them as well (cf. Van Valin 1987a). What is common to clause structure in all languages is two basic contrasts: one between the predicate and its arguments, and one between those argument-like elements in a clause which are arguments of the predicate and those that are not.

While the idea of dividing clauses up into distinct subunits based on whether the elements in each section bear a direct relation to the verb or not is not unique to RRG (cf. e.g. Dixon 1977; Dik 1978; Pike and Pike 1982; Andrews 1985), the particular formulation assumed in RRG derives from Olson's (1981) analysis of Barai (Papua-New Guinea) clause structure. Olson proposed that clauses are constituted by three layers, each enclosing the lower ones rather like the layers of an onion: the innermost layer is the *nucleus*, containing the predicate; the nucleus plus the non-oblique arguments of its predicate constitute the *core*; the outermost layer is the *periphery*, which includes the core, the oblique arguments of the predicate and non-arguments, especially setting and temporal adverbials (cf. figure 1 below). Each of these layers is modified by one or more operators such as aspect, modality, tense or illocutionary force. The operators are given in (1).

(1) a. nuclear operators: aspect
                            directionals (only those modifying orientation of action or event without reference to participants)
     b. core operators: directionals (only those expressing the orientation or motion of one participant with reference to another participant or to the speaker)
                            modality (root modals, e.g. ability, permission, obligation)
                            internal (narrow scope) negation
     c. clausal operators: status (epistemic modality, external negation)
                            tense
                            evidentials
                            illocutionary force (IF)

This schema was modified slightly in Foley and Van Valin (1984) (FVV); a distinction was introduced in the periphery between the inner periphery (the oblique arguments of the predicate) and the outer periphery (non-arguments). No formal representation of these distinctions aside from rather inexact labelled bracketings like the one in figure 1 was employed at that time; they were intended as representations of the actual structure of sentences. They obviously were far from adequate, leaving many important questions open. For example, there was no discussion of important issues such as the position of topicalized elements, question words, or complementizers.

(IF (evid (tense (status [PP/ADV... (modality [NP (NP) (dir (asp [predicate]))])])))))
            periphery   core   nucleus

Figure 1

Research subsequent to the publication of FVV revealed two major problems with aspects of the LSC. The first concerns the contrast between core and inner peripheral arguments. There are three types of nominal elements in a clause: (a) those that are arguments of the predicate (i.e. are represented in the logical structure (LS) of the verb) and are in morphosyntactically privileged positions (i.e. in a 'direct' case, as in German, morphologically unmarked, as in English, or cross-referenced on the verb, as in Lakhota); (b) those that are arguments of the predicate but are obliquely marked, e.g. the to-argument with give and other ditransitive verbs; and (c) those that are not arguments of the predicate and are obliquely marked, e.g.setting temporal and locative elements. In Olson (1981) and FVV, the division among these three types was made on the basis of direct vs. oblique morphosyntactic coding, and accordingly (b) and (c) were grouped together as peripheral in opposition to (a). This split leads to a number of incorrect predictions regarding complex sentences (see Van Valin 1987b for discussion), and moreover, attempts at formalization of it also revealed a number of serious problems. The alternate way of grouping the elements in (a), (b) and (c) is to group together (a) and (b), the arguments of the predicate, in contrast to (c); this puts all of the arguments of the predicate into the core, regardless of their morphosyntactic coding. This conception of the core-periphery contrast was put forth in Foley and Van Valin (1985), and it is the one to be presented herein. Thus, an argument which is represented in the LS of the predicate in a clause will appear in the core, unless it is assigned peripheral status by virtue of occurring in a passive or antipassive construction. The converse, however, is not always true; in a 'raising' construction (cf. FVV: 6.5), an argument may appear as a core argument in a core in which it is not an argument of the nucleus of that core but rather of the nucleus of a linked, dependent core.

The second issue concerns the relation of the periphery to the core and nucleus. In the schema assumed in FVV, the periphery encloses the core, which in turn encloses the nucleus; this is represented in the left diagram in figure 2. Watters (1987) showed that this model makes incorrect predictions regarding the possibilities of peripheral adverbials in Turkish core junctures (cf. also FVV: 5.5) and proposed an alternative in which the periphery no longer subsumes the core but rather is a 'sister' to it in the clause. This may be informally represented as in the right diagram in figure 2.

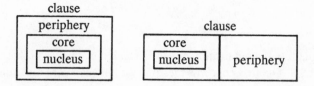

Figure 2

It must be emphasized that this change affects only constituents and not operators; the latter are in a relation of inclusion, with the outer ones (now called 'clausal operators' instead of 'peripheral operators') enclosing and having scope over the more inner ones. There is thus an interesting asymmetry between constituents and operators, with operators being in a 'pure' layered structure and with constituents being in this modified arrangement.

A major extension of the LSC since FVV is the treatment of topicalized and dislocated elements. In addition to the core and the periphery, the clause also includes the *precore slot* (PCS), the position in which WH-words appear in languages in which WH-words do not occur in situ and in which the fronted element in sentences like *John I can't stand* occurs. RRG distinguishes between sentences and clauses in much the traditional sense, i.e. a sentence may be composed of multiple clauses. In addition to a clause, a sentence may also contain a *left-detached position* (LDP)[2]; it is the location of some sentence-initial adverbials (those that are set off by a pause) and the 'displaced' element in a left-dislocation construction, e.g. *As for John, I haven't seen him in two weeks*. The LDP, like the periphery, is never obligatory.

The final major development since FVV is the projection grammar formalization of the LSC proposed in Johnson (1987). A particularly important problem in representing predicates and arguments, on the one hand, and operators, on the other, is separating out the universal from the language-specific restrictions on them. Predicates and arguments can occur in any possible order, but this is not true of operators; rather, as argued in FVV, their ordering vis-a-vis each other and the nucleus is subject to strong universal constraints. The main language-specific factor influencing their realization is the basic word-order type of the language, which affects whether the operators are predominantly prefixes or suffixes, if they are bound morphemes, or whether they occur before or after the nucleus, if they are free morphemes. Johnson (1987) proposed that operators be presented in a distinct representation of the clause from the predicate and its arguments, and this formalism he labelled a *projection grammar.* The general schema for the projection grammar representation of the LSC is given in the left part of figure 3; the top part of the representation is called the 'constituent projection' and the bottom the 'operator projection'. The ordering of the core and periphery and of the elements within the core is not fixed. The right part of the figure gives a schematic representation of how semantic representations (based on the logical structure of the predicate) are related to syntactic representations; the syntactic functions are mapped into the appropriate positions in the core and in the clause.[3]

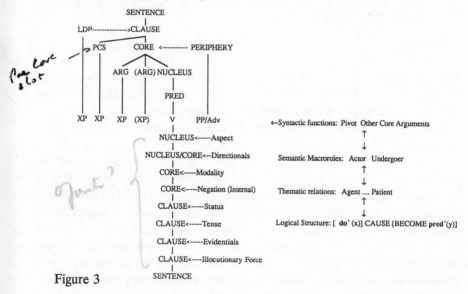

Figure 3

The '--->' relating the LDP to the clause and the periphery to the core indicates that they are optional adjuncts. Despite the distinct projections, the scopes of operators are clearly indicated; everything dominated by the 'clause' node in the constituent projection is in the scope of the operators modifying the 'clause' node(s) in the operator projection, and the same holds for the 'core' and 'nucleus' nodes in the two projections. The LDP phrase, for instance, is not part of the 'clause' and therefore is not within the scope of the IF operator over the clause; it therefore cannot be questioned or asserted, unlike the phrase in the PCS, which is clause-internal and hence in the scope of the IF operator. Some examples from English are given in figure 4.

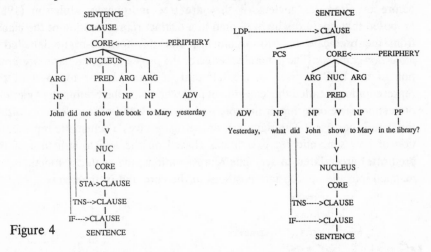

Figure 4

These projection grammar representations are vastly superior to the labelled bracketing used in FVV (cf. figure 1), both in terms of explicitness and in the amount of information about a sentence that they impart.

In these representations, the internal structure of NPs and PPs has not been given. Prepositions (and adpositions in general) are of two basic types, predicative and non-predicative. Predicative adpositions are treated as predicates and their object as an argument; they contribute substantive semantic information to the clause, both with regard to their own meaning and that of the argument they introduce into the clause. An example of a predicative preposition in English would be a peripheral locative (setting) prepositional phrase. Non-predicative prepositions, on the other hand, do not add any substantive semantic information to the clause and do not introduce a new argument into the clause; rather, their argument is licensed by the predicate in the nucleus, and they are in essence case markers assigned by the predicate to one of its arguments.

These two types of adposition would be represented differently in the projection grammar representations of clause structure. Since non-predicative adpositions mark core arguments, the phrases in which they occur would be NPs under the 'arg' node in the core; the adposition would be treated the same as a case marker, and in particular it would not be considered the head of the phrase. Hence the *to Mary* phrase in figure 4 is an NP, not a PP. Predicative adpositions, on the other hand, are the head and nucleus of the phrase in which they occur, and their object is in fact their single argument. The peripheral setting phrase *in the library* in figure 4 is labeled a PP, since *in* is not assigned by the predicate *show* and is therefore predicative; it licenses the occurrence of the NP *the library*.

NPs have a layered structure analogous to but not identical to that of the clause; they have a nominal rather than a predicative nucleus. Noun modifiers like definiteness, negation and quantification are treated as operators and would be represented in a distinct projection from the nominal head and its complements. Nunes (1989) has explored argument linking in complex derived nominals, e.g. *the destruction of the city by the enemy*, and found that the linking rule is very close to that for clauses but differs from it in subtle but crucial ways. The internal structure of NPs has not received nearly as much attention as that of clauses and sentences in RRG, and it is an area where a great deal more work is necessary.

2. Layered clause structure and operators in FG

It was noted in 1. that some of the basic ideas behind the LSC in RRG can be found in Dik (1978), but serious explorations of layered clause structure and operators in FG began with Hengeveld (1987, 1988), who refers to the original LSC model in FVV. While we seem to have come full circle, the model proposed by Hengeveld is in fact very different from the one proposed in FVV and the one presented herein. Before any critical comparison of the two models can be made, it is necessary to establish just exactly how they are alike and how they differ. This will be the focus of this section, and a number of questions about the FG model will be raised from an RRG perspective.

While Hengeveld (1987, 1988) and Dik et al. (this vol.) talk about hierarchical layers in the structure of the clause, it appears that they are operating with a *semantic* conception of the clause, not a syntactic one. The representation of clause layers and operators (indicated as 'π_n') proposed in Hengeveld (1988) is given in figure 5.

clause

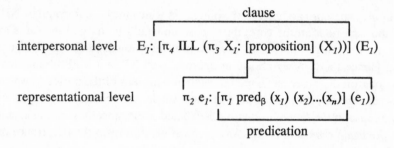

interpersonal level E_i: $[\pi_4$ ILL $(\pi_3\ X_i$: [proposition] $(X_i))]$ (E_i)

representational level $\pi_2\ e_i$: $[\pi_1\ pred_\beta\ (x_1)\ (x_2)...(x_n)]$ $(e_i))$

predication

Figure 5

The clause consists of a proposition embedded in an illocutionary frame (ILL) together with operators modifying the proposition (π_3) and the illocutionary frame (π_4). This is the interpersonal level of representation; that is, it refers to the presentation of the propositional content "in such a way that the addressee is able to recognize the communicative intention of the speaker" (Hengeveld 1988: 2). A proposition is composed of a predication together with a variable representing its spatio-temporal locus (e_i) and predication operators (π_2). A predication consists of a predicate, its arguments, and predicate operators (π_1). This is the representational level; here "a State of Affairs (SoA) is described in such a way that the addressee is able to understand what real or hypothesized situation is referred to" (ibid.). Each of these will be discussed with reference to possible RRG LSC counterparts below.

All of these units are semantic or pragmatic, and none appear to be syntactic in nature, although they presumably underlie syntactic units. This is the essence of the distinction between predicate and nucleus in the LSC, for example: the predicate is semantic in nature and is represented semantically by its logical structure, while the nucleus is the syntactic unit which contains one or more predicating elements. In the two papers cited above, as well as in Bolkestein (this vol.), no representations of the syntactic structure of any example sentence are given; rather, semantic representations like the following are given (from Hengeveld).

(2)   a.   I knew you would come
      b.   (Past e_i: know$_V$ $(x_i$: p1 $(x_i))_{\theta Exp}$ (Cert X_i: [(Fut e_j: [come$_V$ $(x_j$: p2 $(x_j))]$ $(e_j))]$ $(X_i)_{Go}]$ $(e_i))$

This is a representation of aspects of the semantic structure of (2a), not its syntactic structure. Nevertheless, this representation does bear some resemblance to the representation in figure 1, in that predicates, arguments and operators are presented together.

Representations like (2a) are not equivalent to syntactic representations, and this becomes particularly clear when the same meaning is expressed in languages with radically different syntactic structures. Dik (1978) includes typological adequacy among the types of adequacy that a linguistic theory should meet: a theory of language "should be capable of providing grammars for typologically quite different languages, while at the same time accounting for the similarities and differences between these languages" (ibid.: 8). The problem with providing only semantic representations is that crucial syntactic differences between languages are not captured; this will be discussed in more detail in 4.4.

Given that the FG hierarchical clause model is semantic, not syntactic, in nature, direct comparison with the LSC in RRG is difficult. Also, the FG layers include in some cases notions that are treated as operators in RRG. For example, the clause layer as proposed by Hengeveld consists of a proposition embedded in an illocutionary frame, as noted above, and the illocutionary frame corresponds to the IF operator in RRG. Moreover, the illocutionary operators, π_4 in figure 5, are adverbial and other elements which modify the illocutionary frame; these correspond to operator modifiers in RRG, not a distinct type of operator (cf. FVV: 222-223).

The next layer, the predication, would appear to be a direct equivalent of the core in the LSC, but in fact there are important differences. Like the core in RRG, the predication has internal complexity. It is illustrated in figure 6, from Dik (1978: 26).

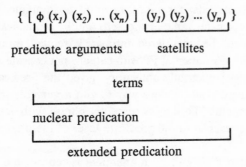

Figure 6

(Satellites are defined in note 17.) These may be compared with their RRG counterparts in the following table (LS = logical structure of predicate).

FG	RRG: semantic	RRG: syntactic
predicate	predicate	nucleus
argument	syntactically obligatory argument in LS of predicate	core argument$_1$
satellite	syntactically optional argument in LS, non-arguments	core argument$_2$, peripheral element
nuclear predication	predicate + syntactically obligatory arguments	core (only core arguments$_1$)
extended predication	predicate + arguments + non-arguments	clause (= core + periphery)

Table 1

The primary difference between the contents of a nuclear predication and a core follows from the contrasting conceptions of what an argument is and the different lexical representations that the two theories adopt. FG assigns predicate frames to each predicate, e.g. 'kill$_V$ (x$_1$)$_{Ag/Fo}$ (x$_2$: animate (x$_2$))$_{Go}$' (Dik 1978: 49), in which the arguments and their semantic role functions are represented, among other things. In order for a term to count as an argument, it must be represented in the predicate frame of the verb and be syntactically obligatory. Elements which might be considered intimately related to the meaning of the predicate, e.g. the instrumental PP with *cut*, are not considered arguments because they are not syntactically obligatory; given the predicate frame representations in FG, there is no obvious way to add arguments in a non-ad hoc manner. Hence elements like the instrumental phrase with verbs like *cut* are treated as satellites attached to the predicate layer of the predication.

The situation in RRG is rather different. If an argument is represented in the LS of a predicate, it will be a core argument in the clause, unless it is linked to a peripheral position by virtue of occurring in a marked construction like passive. Because the LS is a decompositional representation and not just a lexical form with a list of roles, it can be expanded in certain limited ways to allow the expression of more arguments than the syntactically obligatory bare minimum. Examples of two LSs are given in (3).

(3) a. [do' (x)] cause [become **dead'** (y)]
         "x kill y"
     b. [run' (x)] cause [become be-at' (y,x)]
         "x run to y"

These lexical representations are central to the RRG theory of semantic roles, and they provide the basis for the independently motivated assignment of thematic relations to verbs (cf. note 3). In the context of this discussion they are significant in terms of the restrictions on additional arguments that are inherent in them. Jolly (1987) shows that LSs may be expanded only three ways to permit additional core arguments: (i) the causal chain may be further specified, and this involves the elaboration of the first argument of 'cause' in LSs like (3a); (ii) with verbs of motion or transfer, the LS may be expanded to include the full range of the motion or transfer, i.e. to include the source, the path and the goal, and this involves the elaboration of the second argument of 'cause' in LSs like (3b); and (iii) a benefactive LS may be joined to the basic LS, yielding an additional benefactive argument. Jolly demonstrates that there are intrinsic restrictions on these expansions. For example, argument instrumentals are only possible with accomplishment verbs like *kill* and *cut*, because they are part of the 'causal chain' inherent in the bringing about of the result, e.g. the agent manipulates the knife which does the actual cutting. This causal chain is expressed through the first argument of 'cause' (cf. FVV: 54-56), and therefore only verbs with a 'cause' in their LS can take an argument instrumental. This rules them out with state, activity and achievement verbs and makes the correct prediction that when an instrumental phrase appears with a verb from one of these classes, e.g. *he watched the parade through binoculars*, the phrase is an adjunct. Dik et al. (this vol.) note that predicate-level satellites like instrumentals share many properties with arguments, and the reason for this is that they are in fact arguments in the expanded LS of the predicate.

Thus because phrases of this type are considered core arguments in RRG but satellites in FG, a nuclear predication is not composed of the same elements as a core in RRG.[4] The closest equivalence in table 1 is FG extended predication with RRG clause; the difference between them is that the FG unit is semantic in nature and presumably underlies a syntactic unit, whereas the RRG unit is syntactic and contains the semantic material that constitutes an extended predication. Thus the RRG clause corresponds to the representational level in figure 5, and in order to reach the interpersonal level, all of the clausal operators must be added.

3. The syntactic constrast between core and clause: The need for explicit syntactic representations

The distinction between core and clause is vital for the RRG theory of complex sentences (to be discussed in 4.), and it also allows a straightforward statement of certain kinds of word order restrictions and a means for capturing fundamental typological differences in clause structure across languages.

3.1. The V/2 constraint in Icelandic

In Icelandic, as in some other Germanic languages, there is a rigid constraint to the effect that in all utterances except yes-no questions the finite verb must be in second position in the clause (the 'V/2' constraint). This is illustrated in (4) and (5), from Maling and Zaenen (1981); in (4) the dative NP *henni* "her" is the syntactic subject of the clause (cf. Thráinsson 1979; Van Valin 1989b). The finite verb is in boldface, and the subject is underlined. The LSCs for (5a) and (5b) are given in figure 7.

(4) a. <u>*Henni*</u> **hefur** *alltaf þótt Ólafur leidinlegur*
her.DAT has always thought Olaf.NOM boring.NSG
"She has always considered Olaf boring"

b. *Ólafur* **hefur** <u>*henni*</u> *alltaf þótt leidinlegur*
Olaf.NOM has her.DAT allways thought boring.NSG
"Olaf she has always considered boring"

c. **Ólafur <u>henni</u> **hefur** alltaf þótt leidinlegur*

d. **Ólafur **hefur** alltaf þótt <u>henni</u> leidinlegur*

(5) a. <u>*Hún*</u> **hafdi** *unnid ad brúarsmídi í sumar*
she.NOM had worked at bridge-building in summer
"She worked at bridge-building in the summer"

b. *Í sumar* **hafdi** <u>*hún*</u> *unnid ad brúarsmídi*
in summer had she.NOM worked at bridge-building
"In the summer she worked at bridge-building"

c. **Í sumar <u>hún</u> **hafdi** unnid ad brúarsmidi*

d. *Í sumar hafði unnið hún að brúarsmiði
e. Hvenær hafði hún   unnið   að   brúarsmiði?
    when had she.NOM worked at   bridge-building
    "When did she work at bridge-building?"
f. *Hvenær hún hafði unnið að brúarsmiði?

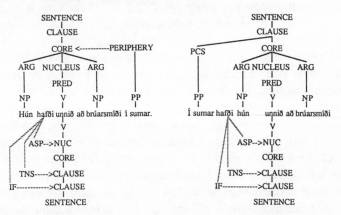

Figure 7

Subject-finite verb inversion is obligatory when there is a topicalized NP, as in
(4b), or a preposed adverbial, as in (5b), or a WH-word in a question, as in
(5e). It is not triggered, however, by a LDP phrase or a complementizer, as in
(6a), which would be represented as in figure 8.[5]

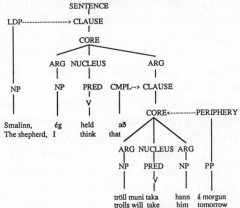

Figure 8

(6) a. *Smalinn,*   *ég*   **held**   *ad*   <u>tröll</u>
        the.shepherd.NOM I.NOM think.1SG CMPL trolls.NOM
        muni *taka hann*   *á morgun*
        will   take   him.ACC tomorrow
        "The shepherd, I think that trolls will take him tomorrow"
    b. **Smalinn,* **held** *ég ad* <u>tröll</u> ***muni*** *taka hann á morgun*
    c. **Smalinn,* *ég* **held** *ad* ***muni*** <u>tröll</u> *taka hann á morgun*

These word-order restrictions can be stated as follows in terms of the LSC:
the finite verb in Icelandic must be in second position in the *clause* (except in
yes-no questions), and the subject, which is always adjacent to the finite verb,
must be the initial non-verbal element in the *core*.[6] In a simple clause like (4a)
or (5a), the subject is the first element in the core and also the clause, and the
finite verb is in second position in the clause. When an element occupies the
PCS, be it an adverbial as in (5b), a topicalized NP as in (4b), or a WH-word
as in (5c), it is the clause-initial element, and the finite verb immediately follows
it. Note that although the subject follows the finite verb, its position within the
core is unchanged; it is still the first non-verbal element in the core, as figure
7 clearly shows. If it is not, the result is ungrammatical, as in (4d) and (5d).
Since both the LDP phrase and complementizer are outside of the clause in (6),
neither can trigger inversion. When the subject is missing or postposed and
nothing fills the PCS, then the dummy filler *þad* "it" must appear in clause-initial
position to satisfy the V/2 condition.[7] The structure of (7a) is given in figure 9;
the subject is still the first non-verbal element in the core.

(7) a. *Þad*   *var*   *mikill*   *snjór*   *á jördinni*
        it.NOM was   much   snow.NOM   on the.ground.DAT
        "There was much snow on the ground"
    b. *Í gær*   *var*   *(*þad)*   *mikill*   *snjór á jördinni*
        yesterday was   (it.NOM) much   snow on the.ground.DAT
        "Yesterday (there) was much snow on the ground"
    c. *Var* *(*þad)*   *mikill*   *snjór á jördinni?*
        was   (it.NOM) much   snow on the.ground.DAT
        "Was (there) much snow on the ground?"
    d. *Hvad*   *var*   *(*þad)*   *á jördinni?*
        what   was   (it.NOM)   on the.ground.DAT
        "What was on the ground?"

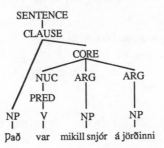

Figure 9

Thus the distinction between core and clause affords a simple formulation of the V/2 constraint on Icelandic word order.

3.2. Clause structure in head-marking and dependent-marking languages

In English and Icelandic, as in most of the languages which are examined in theoretical discussions, the arguments of the nucleus are instantiated in independent NPs, which may be headed by a lexical NP or a pronoun and which may carry case or some other indicator of their relationship to their governing verb or preposition. Nichols (1986) proposes a typological contrast between languages like English and Icelandic, in which the morphosyntactic indicators of the relationship between a head and its dependents are indicated on the dependents, and languages like Lakhota (Siouan; North America), Jacaltec (Mayan) and Abkhaz (Caucasian; USSR), in which that relationship is indicated on the head. The former she labels *dependent-marking* languages and the latter *head-marking* languages. The following examples illustrate this contrast.

(8) **Adpositional phrases: Dependent marking**
   a. *zu dem   Mann*
      to the.DAT man
      "to the man"   (German)
   b. *s   Ivan-om*
      with Ivan-INST
      "with Ivan"   (Russian)

(9) Adpositional phrases: Head marking

    a.   *a-jəyas   a-q'nə*
        the-river 3SG-at (lit.: the river$_i$ at-it$_i$)
        "at the river"   (Abkhaz)

    b.   *y-ul   te'   ŋah*
        3ERG-in CL.the house (lit.: in-it$_i$ the house$_i$)
        "in the house"   (Jacaltec)

(10) Possessive phrases: Dependent marking

    a.   *das Haus des   Mann-es*
        the house the.GEN man-GEN
        "the man's house"   (German)

    b.   *bayi   waŋal   ba-ŋu-l   yaɽa-ŋu*
        NM.ABS boom.ABS NM-GEN man-GEN
        "the man's boomerang"   (Dyirbal)

(11) Possessive phrases: Head marking

    a.   *a-č̓k̓'ən   yə-ŷnə*
        the-boy   3GEN-house (lit.: the boy$_i$ his$_i$-house)
        "the boy's house"   (Abkhaz)

    b.   *s-mam   naj   winaj*
        3ERG-father CL.the man (lit.: his$_i$-father the man$_i$)
        "the man's father"   (Jacaltec)

(12) Clauses: Dependent marking

    a.   *Die   Frau sah den   Mann*
        the.NOM woman saw the.ACC man
        "The woman saw the man"   (German)

    b.   *Kʷixʔid-ida bəgʷanəma-x̲-a q'asa-s-is   t̓əlwagʷayu*
        clubbed-the man-ACC-the otter-INST-his club
        "The man clubbed the sea-otter with his club"   (Kwakwala)

(13) Clauses: Head marking

    a.   *Ma Ø-tzaj   ky-tzyu-'n   kab' xiinaq Luuch*
        REC 3SG.ABS-DRC 3PL.ERG-grab-DRC two man   Pedro
        (lit.: they$_i$-grabbed-him$_j$ two men$_i$ Pedro$_j$)
        "Two men grabbed Pedro"   (Mam)

b. *Wašíču ki hená mathó óta wičhá-Ø-kte-pi*
   whiteman the those bear many 3PL.OBJ-3SUBJ-kill-PL
   (lit.: those whitemen$_i$ many bears$_j$ they$_i$-killed-them$_j$)
   "Those whitemen killed many bears" (Lakhota)

In the German and Russian examples in (8) the dependence of the NP on the preposition is signalled by the case that it bears, while in the examples from Jacaltec (Craig 1977) and Abkhaz (Hewitt 1979) in (9) the relationship is coded by a morpheme on the adposition itself. The same contrast is found in the possessive phrases in (10) and (11): in German and Dyirbal (Dixon 1972) the possessive relation is signalled on the dependent, the possessor, whereas in Jacaltec and Abkhaz it is indicated on the head, the possessed NP. Finally, in (12) and (13) head-marking vs. dependent-marking clause structure is contrasted; in German and Kwakwala (Anderson 1984) the relation between a predicate and its arguments is marked on the argument NPs, while in Mam (England 1983) and Lakhota pronominal affixes on the verb execute this function. This apparently minor difference in where the marker indicating a relationship is placed has a major syntactic consequence: all of the head-marking constructions are *endo*centric, while the dependent-marking ones are *exo*centric, in the sense of Bloomfield (1933). If the dependents are omitted in (8), (10) and (12), the result is either ungrammatical ((8) and (12)) or no longer a phrase of the same type ((10)). In contrast, if the dependents are omitted in (9), (11) and (13), there is no change in the status of these constructions: *yul* "in it" and *aq'nə* "at it" in (9) are still grammatical adpositional phrases, *yəÿnə* "his house" and *smam* "his father" in (11) are still grammatical possessive phrases, and *ma tzaj kytzyu'n* "they grabbed him" and *wičháktepi* "they killed them" in (13) are still full clauses.

This contrast has important implications for syntactic theories based primarily, if not exclusively, on the analysis of dependent-marking languages; see Van Valin (1985, 1987a) for detailed discussion. Given that it underlies significant differences in what can count as a possible phrase or clause in the two types of language, any descriptively adequate theory of clause structure must be able to capture them. In RRG this is straightforward; as argued in Van Valin (1985, 1987a), the pronominal affixes on the verb are the core arguments in the clause, not the optional independent lexical NPs and pronouns. This is represented in figure 10 with an example from Lakhota;[8] the operator projections are omitted.

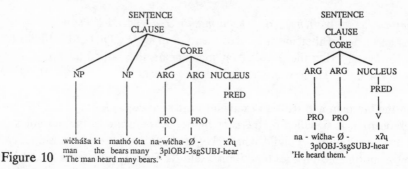

Figure 10

The independent NPs are in clause-internal but core-external positions. That they must be clause-internal can be seen from the fact that an NP in either position can be questioned, as shown in (14).

(14) a. *Wičháša ki   igmú ki   na-Ø-Ø-xʔú*
         man   the   cat the   3SG.OBJ-3SG.SUBJ-hear
         "The man heard the cat"

     b. *Wičháša ki   igmú ki   na-Ø-Ø-xʔú*   *he*
         man   the   cat the   3SG.OBJ-3SG.SUBJ-hear   Q
         "Did the man hear the cat?"

     c. *Wičháša ki   táku   na-Ø-Ø-xʔú*
         man   the   something 3SG.OBJ-3SG.SUBJ-hear
         "The man heard something"

     d. *Tuwá   igmú ki   na-Ø-Ø-xʔú*
         someone cat the   3SG.OBJ-3SG.SUBJ-hear
         "Someone heard the cat"

     e. *Wičháša ki   táku na-Ø-Ø-xʔú*   *he*
         man   the   what 3SG.OBJ-3SG.SUBJ-hear   Q
         "What did the man hear?"

     f. *Tuwá igmú ki   na-Ø-Ø-xʔú*   kte   *he*
         who   cat the   3SG.OBJ-3SG.SUBJ-hear   FUT   Q
         "Who will hear the cat?"

Question words in Lakhota do not move to clause-initial position, as (14e) shows, and a question word can occur in any position before the nucleus other than in initial position set off by a pause from the remainder of the sentence, i.e. in the LDP. Since question words must be clause-internal in order to be within the scope of the interrogative IF operator (instantiated by the sentence-final particle *he* in Lakhota), any position which one can occupy must be clause-internal. While this argues for these NPs being inside the clause, it also argues against postulating a PCS for Lakhota, since there is no special position for question words. Also, there is nothing comparable to *John I can't stand* involving preposing in this language; this would be handled either by a focus particle or a cleft construction. The structure of a sentence like (14f) (but with a plural direct object instead of singular, hence the different cross-reference morpheme on the verb) is given in figure 11.

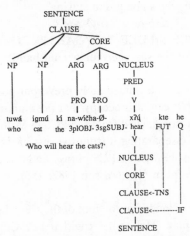

Figure 11

There are head-marking languages in which the LDP, PCS and core-external/clause-internal positions are clearly distinguished, for example Tzotzil (Mayan; Aissen 1987). Tzotzil is verb-initial, unlike Lakhota, and consequently the verb forms a natural demarcation between the unmarked and marked positions for NPs to appear in. Tzotzil is VOS, with the unmarked position for independent lexical NPs or pronouns being after the nucleus, as illustrated in (15a), and the verb alone constitutes a complete clause, as in (15b).

(15) a. *?i-Ø-s-pet*   *lokel ?antz   ti   íul-e*
ASP-3ABS-3ERG-carry away woman DEF rabbit-DEF
"The rabbit carried away the woman"

   b. *L-i-s-pet-otik*
ASP-1ABS-3ERG-carry-1PL.INCL
"He carried us (inclusive)"

   c. *Buch'u   Ø-s-tam?*
who   3ABS-3ERG-take
"Who took it?"

    d.   *Kusi ch-Ø-a-kan?*
        what ASP-3ABS-2ERG-want
        "What do you want?"

    e.   *Vo?ot   la   ch-a-bat   ?un, vo?on la   ch-i-kom*
        you   CL ASP-2ABS-go CL I   CL   ASP-1ABS-stay
        ?un
        CL
        "It's you who's going, I'm staying"

    f.   *?a   ti   tzeb-e,   ?i-Ø-s-sa?*   *s-malal*
        TOP DEF girl-DEF ASP-3ABS-3ERG-search 3ERG-husband
        "The girl, she searched for her husband"

Question words occur in the immediately preverbal position, as in (15c) and
(15d), and a fronted NP can also occupy that position, as in (15e) shows. This is
the PCS. The LDP is distinguished from the PCS by virtue of the topic-marking
particle *?a* and a pause separating it from the rest of the sentence, as in (15f).
The contextual contrast between a PCS phrase and a LDP phrase can be seen
clearly in the text excerpt in (16) (Aissen 1987: 158).

    (16) (Something had landed at the foot of the tree, they went to look. There
          was a straw mat. "Hell, what could it be? Come on, let's untie the
          straw mat!" the two men said to each other. They untied it. You know
          what?--

        a.   *Tzeb san-andrex   la   te   Ø-s-ta-ik*   *?un*
            girl San Andreas CL   there 3ABS-3ERG-find-PL CL
            "A San Andreas girl they found there"

        b.   *?a   ti   tzeb san-antrex   ?un-e,*
            TOP DEF girl San Andreas CL-DEF
            ?i-Ø-y-ik-ik   *la ech'el ?un*
            ASP-3ABS-3ERG-take-PL CL away   CL
            "The San Andreas girl, they took her with them"

In (a) *tzeb san-andrex* "a San Andreas girl" is a piece of surprising new
information and is the major focus of the assertion, and accordingly it must be
in a clause-internal position in order to be within the scope of the IF operator.
It is preverbal but not marked by the topic marker *?a* and is not set off by a
pause, and therefore it is in the PCS. By contrast, in (16b) it is marked by *?a*
and set off by a pause, and moreover, it has already been established as an
important participant in the context. Hence here it is in the LDP. Thus in

Tzotzil, unlike Lakhota, there is clear evidence for a PCS in the clause, and it is distinguished from the unmarked position for independent NPs by its preverbal position and from the LDP by the lack of ?a and of a pause after it. The LSC in Tzotzil may be represented as in figure 12.

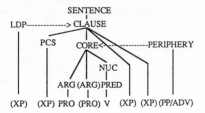

Figure 12

Thus capturing the contrast in clause structure between head-marking and dependent-marking languages requires the distinction between core and clause in the LSC. In both types non-peripheral independent lexical NPs and pronouns are within the clause, but, crucially, in head-marking languages they are not in the core, while in dependent-marking languages they are.

4. Complex sentences

The RRG theory of the syntax of complex sentences has two components, the theory of juncture (the units in the complex constructions) and the theory of nexus (the relations between the units).

4.1. Juncture

The theory of juncture is based on the LSC: the units that combine to form complex sentences are the nucleus, core and clause. In the unmarked case, nuclei combine with nuclei, cores with cores, and clauses with clauses.[9] The joining of nuclei yields a *nuclear juncture*, of cores a *core juncture* and of clauses a *clausal juncture*. This is schematically represented in figure 13.

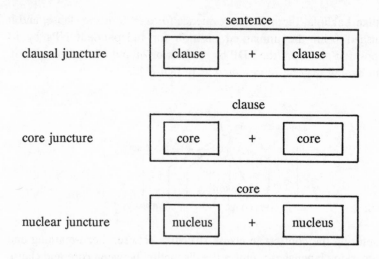

Figure 13

Examples of nuclear junctures from a variety of languages are given in (17) ((17c) is from Hansell 1987); in each instance the predicates form a complex nucleus, e.g. *paint red* in English and *faire manger* in French, within a single core in a single clause. The structure of the French example is given in figure 14; the operator projection is omitted.

(17) **Nuclear junctures**
    a.   John painted the table red.   (English)
    b.   *Je   ferai   manger les   gâteaux à Jean*
        1SG make.FUT eat   the   cakes   to John
        "I will make John eat the cakes"   (French)
    c.   *Tā qiāo pò   le   yí   ge   fànwǎn*
        3SG hit   break PFV one CL   ricebowl
        "He broke (by hitting) a ricebowl"   (Mandarin Chinese)
    d.   *Fu fase fi isoe*
        3SG letter sit write
        "He sat writing a letter"   (Barai)
    e.   *X-in-y-a'*   *mak-a' naj t-aw-et*
        PAST-1SG.ABS-3ERG-cause hit-INF 3SG AUG-2SG.ERG-to
        "He made you hit me"   (Jacaltec)

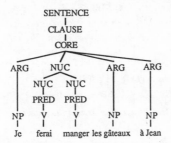

Figure 14

Examples of core junctures are given in (18). In a core juncture there are two nuclei, each with its own set of core arguments, constituting two distinct but overlapping cores; they overlap in that in all of the examples in (18) the linked core shares one core argument with the matrix core. By 'sharing a core argument' is meant that one of the core arguments is an argument of both nuclei. In (18a), *Bill* is semantically an argument of both verbs, as is *Jean* in (18b), *wǒ* "I" in (18c), *fu* in (18d), and the first person argument in (18e). This notion is given a formal definition in terms of the RRG linking algorithm which links semantic representations to syntactic representations.[10] The structure of (18b) is given in figure 15; the operator projection is omitted.

(18) **Core junctures**

    a.   John forced Bill to leave the party.   (English)

    b.   *Je   laisserai   Jean manger les   gâteaux*
        1SG let.FUT   John eat   the cakes
        "I'll let John eat the cakes"   (French)

    c.   *Tā jiāo wǒ xiě zì*
        3SG teach 1SG write characters
        "He teaches me to write"   (Mandarin Chinese)

    d.   *Fu fi fase isoe*
        3SG sit letter write
        "He sat (down) and wrote a letter"   (Barai)

    e.   *X-Ø-w-ilwe*   *hin-watx'e-n*   *kap camïxe*
        PAST-3ABS-1SG.ERG 1SG.ERG-make-SUFF CL shirt
        (lit.: I tried it, I make the shirt)
        "I tried to make the shirt"   (Jacaltec)

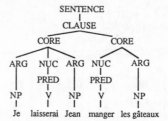

Figure 15

A major difference between nuclear and core junctures concerns how arguments are coded. In a nuclear juncture, as in figure 14, all of the arguments of both verbs are treated as arguments of a single complex nucleus in a single core; there is nothing in the coding indicating directly which argument is associated with which verb. In a core juncture, on the other hand, the non-shared arguments are coded as arguments of distinct nuclei in distinct cores.

4.2. Nexus

In figure 14, the relationship of the nuclei to the dominating core node is not the same as that between the core nodes and the dominating clause node in figure 15. This is because the two constructions differ not simply in the units joined, i.e. the level of juncture; they also differ in the relationship between the units. Traditionally, two relations between units in a complex construction have been recognized, coordination and subordination. Based on Olson's (1981) analysis of Barai clause linkage, RRG distinguishes *three* linkage or *nexus* relations between units in a juncture: subordination, which is characterized primarily by embedding, and two non-subordinate relations, coordination and *cosubordination*, in which there is no embedding (cf. FVV: ch. 6; Van Valin 1984). Cosubordination is 'dependent coordination': while the linked unit is not embedded as an argument or modifier of the matrix unit, it is dependent on it for the expression of at least one of the operators over the level of the juncture. Thus in a clausal juncture, for example, each unit may be a full clause, but the dependent clause lacks the coding of a clausal operator and is therefore dependent upon the matrix clause for its expression. The contrast between coordination (no embedding, no operator dependence at the level of juncture) and cosubordination (no embedding, operator dependence at the level of juncture) can be seen clearly in the following minimal pair from Tonkawa (Hoijer 1949).

(19) a.   *Tekekeʔe:k   šʔa:pa-w   ʔe:-ta   ke-yaše-w*
           in.that.bush   hide-IMP   and-SS   1SG.OBJ-watch-IMP
           "Hide in that bush and watch me!"
     b.   *Tekekeʔe:k   šʔa:pa-ta   ke-yaše-w*
           in.that.bush   hide-SS   1SG.OBJ-watch-IMP
           "Hide in that bush and watch me!"

In (19a) each clause is in fully independent form (both carry the imperative suffix *-w*) and could stand on its own as a complete utterance; they are linked by the conjunction *ʔe:-ta* "and-same subject". This is an example of coordination at the clause level. In (19b), however, only the final clause could stand on its own as an independent utterance; the first clause lacks a morpheme coding IF, its place taken by the switch-reference suffix *-ta* "same", and therefore it is dependent upon the second clause for the expression of its IF. This is, therefore, an example of cosubordination at the clause level. The three nexus types may be represented as in figure 16.

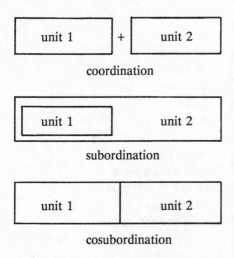

Figure 16

All of the examples in (17) and (18) involve non-subordinate nexus types. All of the nuclear junctures in (17) are cosubordination, the overwhelming most frequent type of nuclear juncture. In (18), (a)-(c) are examples of coordination, while (d)-(e) exemplify cosubordination.[11] Examples of subordination at the core level are given in (20).

(20) a.   That Mary won the award shocked everyone
     b.   Mary's winning the award shocked everyone
     c.   For Mary to win the award would be the shock of the year

In all of these sentences the dependent unit functions as a core argument of the matrix nucleus. Note that even though there are three formally distinct construction types, they all instantiate the same abstract clause linkage (juncture-nexus) relation. An example of a clause used as a core argument is given in figure 8.[12]

The three levels of juncture and the three nexus relations combine to yield a universal typology of possible clause linkage relations.

syntactic relations   **semantic relations**

    strongest   closest

nuclear cosubordination

                     causative
nuclear subordination   aspectual
                     psych-action
nuclear coordination   purposive
                     jussive
core cosubordination   direct perception
                     propositional attitude
core subordination   cognition
                     indirect discourse
core coordination   temporal adverbial
                     conditionals
clausal cosubordination   simultaneous actions
                     sequential actions: overlapping
clausal subordination   sequential actions: non-overlapping
                     action-action: unspecified
clausal coordination

    weakest   loosest

Figure 17

There are three levels of juncture and three nexus relations, resulting in nine abstract linkage relations. As shown in the left part of figure 17, these may be ranked in terms of the strength of the syntactic bond between the units, with nuclear cosubordination being the strongest and clausal coordination being the weakest (cf. FVV: 6.3). Each of these syntactic linkage relations can express one or more semantic relations holding between the units, e.g. causation, purpose, or temporal sequence. The relationship between the syntactic and semantic relations in clause linkage is very complex, i.e. it is not one-to-one, but there are some striking regularities cross-linguistically. While the syntactic linkage relations are ranked hierarchically in terms of the strength of the syntactic bond between the units, the semantic relations may likewise be ranked in terms of how closely related the propositions in the linkage are, i.e. to what extent they are coded as aspects of a single action or event or as discrete events. The primary principle governing the interaction of the two hierarchies is: the closer the semantic relation between two propositions is, the stronger the syntactic link joining them. This is captured in the Interclausal Relations Hierarchy (IRH) in figure 17.[13]

4.3. The role of operators in complex sentences

The operator projection is crucial for differentiating coordinate from cosub-ordinate nexus, since it is operator dependence that distinguishes the two. This can be seen most clearly in the following sentences from Turkish (Watters 1987).

(21) a.   *Gid-ip   gör-meli-yiz*
           go-CMPL   see-MOD-1PL
           "We ought to go and see"

     b.   *Müzik   dinle-yebil-erek   uy-ur-um*
           music   listen-MOD-CMPL   sleep-AOR-1SG
           (lit.: being able to listen to music, I sleep)
           "I can listen to music while sleeping"

     b'. *Müzik   dinle-yerek   uyu-yabil-ir-im*
           music   listen-CMPL   sleep-MOD-AOR-1SG
           "I can sleep (while) listening to music"

In (21a) both cores are under the scope of the modality operator *-meli-* "ought", and there is a shared argument, the first-person plural actor coded by *-yiz*;

accordingly, this is an example of core cosubordination. In (21b) and (21b'), on the other hand, one core is modified by a single modality operator, -ebil- "able", while the other is outside its scope; again there is a shared argument, the first-person singular subject, and therefore these construction are examples of core coordination. The structure of (21a) and (21b') is given in figure 18.

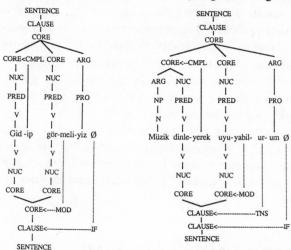

Figure 18

In the constituent projections the two linked cores are dominated by a superordinate core node which also dominates the shared argument; the crucial difference between them lies in the operator projections. Complementizers are treated as functioning on the level of the juncture; thus in figure 18 the dependent unit markers, -erek/-ip in Turkish, are core complementizers, as is to in English. When the dependent unit is a clause, as in a typical object complement, the marker, e.g. that in English or að in Icelandic (cf. (6), figure 8, note 5), is a clausal complementizer. In the operator projection of (21a), the modality operator modifies a superordinate core node, indicating that it has scope over both of these cores; this is the defining feature of cosubordinate nexus in a core juncture. In the representation of (21b'), on the other hand, the modality operator has only a single core in its scope, and the two cores are treated as independent units of the clause; this is coordination at the core level. Naturally, all clausal operators have both cores in their scope, and this highlights the fact that it is operator (in)dependence *at the level of the juncture only* which is diagnostic for coordination vs. cosubordination in non-subordinate core junctures.

Little has been said about clausal juncture, since that is the one level of

juncture that RRG shares with all other theories. One point that should be
made is that adverbial subordinate clauses are treated like peripheral
propositional phrases of time or place, in that the subordinating conjunction is
assumed to be a preposition which takes a NP argument in the one case and a
clausal argument in the other. An example of a temporal adverbial subordinate
clause is given in figure 19.

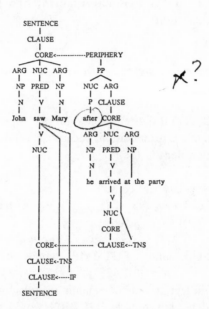

Figure 19

Thus the RRG theory of layered clause structure with operators is the
foundation of the theory of complex sentence structure. The clause layers define
the units which are linked in complex constructions, and the operators are
essential for distinguishing between the two non-subordinate nexus relations.
The projection grammar representational schema is particularly useful with
respect to complex sentences, as the separation of constituents from operators
allows perspicuous representation of the different contributions that each makes
to the juncture and nexus of the construction.

   Hengeveld (1988) discusses the implications of the FG model of clause
structure for the analysis of complex sentences, and he discusses the combining
and embedding of predications, propositions and clauses. As noted with respect
to (2), only semantic representations of the complex constructions are given, and
consequently the analyses proposed do not map directly onto the juncture-nexus
combinations proposed in RRG. Thus discussions of interclausal relations in

FG seem to focus more on what is captured in the right side of the IRH in figure 17 than what is on the left. However, because the FG layers contain operators, Hengeveld makes claims analogous to those in RRG regarding their distribution in certain complex sentence forms, and he is able to show how the operator dependence underlying cosubordination can be handled in FG. A detailed comparison of the RRG and FG theories of complex sentences awaits the development of an explicit FG representation of the syntactic structure of the constructions in question.

4.4. The representation of complex sentences in head-marking and dependent-marking languages

It was pointed out in 1. that the representation in (2b), repeated below, is not equivalent to a syntactic representation, because it could apply equally to (2a) or to its Lakhota equivalent in (2c).

(2) a. I knew you would come

b. (Past e_i: know$_V$ (x_i: p1 (x_i))$_{\phi Exp}$ (Cert X_i: [(Fut e_j: [come$_V$ (x_j: p2 (x_j))] (e_j))] (X_i))$_{Go}$] (e_i))

c. *Ya-hí*   *kte ki*   *slol-wá-ye*
2SG.SUBJ-come   FUT CMPL know-1SG

RRG, like FG, would give the same semantic representation to both (2a) and its Lakhota equivalent, but unlike FG, RRG would assign very different syntactic structures to the two sentences. This is shown in (22) and figure 20; (2a) has been changed to include third-person NP arguments, in order to highlight the contrast between the two languages, and (22e) represents an English-like analysis of the (22c).

(22) a. **know'** (the boy, [**come'** (the women)])^{14}

b. The boy knew that the women would come

c. *Hokšíla ki*   *wíyą ki*   *hená*   *hí-pi*   *kte ki*
boy   the   woman the   those come-3PL FUT CMPL
slol-Ø-yé
know-3SG

c'. **Wįyą   ki   hená hokšíla ki   hípi   kte   ki**
   woman the   those boy   the   come   FUT   CMPL
   slolyé   (= 22b-c)
   know

d. **Hí-pi   kte   ki   slol-Ø-yé**
   come-3PL FUT CMPL know-3SG
   "He knew that they would come"

e. [$_{S1}$ Hokšíla ki [$_{S2}$ *wįyą* ki hená hí-pi kte ki] slol-Ø-yé](= 22c)

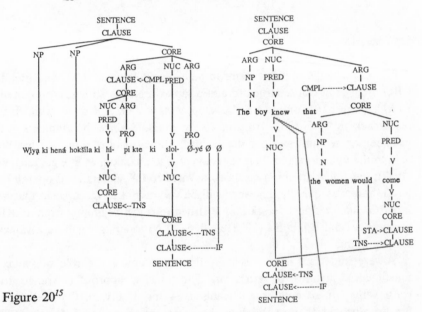

Figure 20[15]

While both of these sentences have the same semantic representation, (22a),
and the operator projections for both are comparable, their syntactic structures
are quite distinct,[16] and this is a function of the fact that English is a dependent-
marking language and Lakhota is head-marking. The full NPs in the Lakhota
are both in the matrix clause, and if they were omitted, the result would be the
fully grammatical sentence (22d).[17] Moreover, the fact that when the NPs are
present, their order is irrelevant, as (22c-c') show, is very significant. If the full
NPs were the arguments and the affixes on the verbs only agreement markers,
as (22c) is represented in (22e), then (21c') would have to be analyzed as a
construction with a LDP, since *wįyą ki hená* "the women" would not be in the
same clause as its verb in this analysis. But there is no evidence to support the
claim that this NP is in a clause-external position, and Van Valin (1985)

presents additional arguments against an analysis of Lakhota in which independent NPs are considered core arguments. The situation in English is very different, since the full NPs are members of distinct cores and cannot be omitted under any circumstances in this construction. Thus one of the problems which must be dealt with in the development of the FG theory of clausal syntax is how semantic representations like (2b) map into the different types of clause structures found in the world's languages; this is essential if the goal of typological adequacy is to be reached.

5. Conclusion

A fruitful exchange of ideas seems to be evolving between RRG and FG. The RRG theories of clause structure and complex sentence structure presented in FVV have in part inspired new developments in FG, and there is much that researchers in RRG can learn from it. For example, since the emphasis in FG has been on semantics rather than syntax, a great deal of attention has been paid to the operators and their semantic characterization, as in e.g. Hengeveld (1987); much less attention has been devoted to the semantics of operators in RRG, and consequently this work will be very useful to research in that area in RRG. As noted in 1., work on NP structure is just beginning from an RRG perspective, and Rijkhoff's (1988) analysis of NP operators will be a valuable starting point.

A very important issue raised by this discussion is the role of syntax in functionalist theories of grammar. Functionalist approaches range from conservative to extreme (see Nichols 1984 for a survey). On the extreme functionalist end, as exemplified by the 'emergent grammar' of Hopper (1987), the validity of syntax in particular and grammar in general is denied and the attempt is made to reduce all grammatical phenomena to discourse phenomena of some kind. Neither FG nor RRG advocates such a view, and they are both what Nichols called 'moderate functionalist' theories.

Dik (1978: 5) lays out the FG view as follows:

> (P)ragmatics is the all-encompassing framework within which semantics and syntax must be studied; semantics is subservient to pragmatics and syntax to semantics; the priorities run from pragmatics via semantics to syntax.

The discussion of syntax in Dik (1978) concerns the syntactic relations of Subject and Object, their morphosyntactic expression, and their role in the grammar; there is no discussion of non-relational syntactic structure per se, and this raises a question with respect to the status of non-relational syntactic structure in FG. This is the point that was brought up with respect to (2) and (22). There are aspects of clause structure which are not reducible to either semantics or to syntactic relations like Subject and Object; the contrast between the structure of clauses in head-marking vs. dependent-marking languages is a prime example (cf. figure 20). The apparent lack of a theory of non-relational syntactic structure is perhaps a reflection of the priorities given above, but the development of such a theory and an explicit means of representing syntactic structure is essential.

RRG maintains that syntax cannot be understood without reference to semantics and pragmatics, but it does not attempt to reduce genuine syntactic phenomena to anything else. While the units in the LSC are syntactic, they are semantically motivated, and one of RRGs major goals is to show how syntactic structure and syntactic phenomena are not radically arbitrary, as in Generative Grammar, but are *relatively* motivated (in Saussure's sense) by semantics and pragmatics. The recognition of syntactic structure as distinct from semantic structure and information/interpersonal structure (pragmatics) is crucial if we are to understand how semantics and pragmatics interact in languages with different systems of syntactic organization.

Notes

1.   I would like to thank Jan Nuyts and David Wilkins for comments on an earlier draft. This work was supported in part by a UC Davis Faculty Research Grant. Abbreviations: AOR = 'aorist', AUG = 'stem augment', CL = 'classifier', CMPL = 'complementizer', DRC = 'directional', IMP = 'imperative', MOD = 'modality', NM = 'noun marker', PFV = 'perfective', REC = 'recent past', SS = 'same subject'.

2.   This term is taken from Lambrecht (1986). In FG terms, the PCS = P1 and the LDP = P2. There is also a right-detached position (P3 in FG), as in sentences like *I know them, those boys*. Since it does not play as important a role as the LDP, it will not be discussed further.

3.   See FVV (4.6, 6.5), Van Valin (1989a) for detailed discussion of the linking scheme in RRG. The logical structure is a decomposed semantic representation of the predicating element, based on the decomposition scheme in Dowty (1979), which is in turn founded on the verb classifications proposed in Vendler (1967). The generic example given in figure 3 is an accomplishment logical structure. These representations are crucial to the RRG theory of semantic roles, for the thematic relations that the theory uses are defined in terms of argument positions in these representations. See FVV (ch.2), Van Valin (1989a).

4. It is more similar to the original notion of core presented in Olson (1981) and FVV, which, as mentioned in 1., was rejected as inadequate on a number of grounds.

5. Complementizers are treated as adjuncts to the linked unit in the complex construction, and in a construction like this they occupy the same position as the LDP, thereby ruling out the possibility of an LDP phrase in an embedded clause.

6. There is a special indefinite subject postposing construction, illustrated in (7a). In this example the generalization still holds, but there are cases in which the subject may be put at the end of the core, as in *þad munu kaupa þessa bók margir stúdentar* "there will buy this book many students". See Maling (1980), Thráinsson (1986). Hence this generalization does not apply to this marked construction.

7. *Þad* is not a dummy subject like English *it* or *there* but is simply a filler satisfying the V/2 constraint; it does not occur in the core but rather in clause-initial position outside the core. See Van Valin (1989b) for discussion.

8. The Lakhota verb for "hear" is *naxʔú*, and it takes the subject and object affixes as infixes. Also, the terms 'subject' and 'object' are used in glossing, even though they have no status in RRG. Since the nature of grammatical relations is not an issue in this paper, the traditional labels will be used.

9. Hengeveld (1988: 30) misinterprets this markedness statement as an absolute restriction on junctures, but it is simply a statement about markedness relations, not an absolute prohibition again asymmetric linkages. He also says that it "runs into trouble where it has to deal with complementation", referring to the analysis of complementation in FVV (251-256), but in fact considering clauses functioning as core arguments to be highly marked is in accord with a range of facts. First, there are languages, e.g. Dyirbal, which lack them altogether. Second, in languages which have clausal arguments, there are inevitably grammatical strategies which put the clausal arguments outside of the core, e.g. extraposition. This is certainly the case in English, for example, in which peripheral elements freely occur between the nucleus (and a direct core argument, if present) and the clausal argument, e.g. *John told Mary at the party that he was leaving town*, and in which the unmarked status for a clausal argument interpreted as the subject of a verb is for it to appear in a core-external extraposed position at the end of the clause. Third, there are languages like Jacaltec which have clausal arguments, but such arguments never occur within the core (cf. FVV: 283-285).

10. Cf. FVV (6.5), Van Valin (1989a) for detailed discussion.

11. See FVV (6.2, 6.5), for detailed justification of this claim. There is considerable syntactic evidence that the infinitive in sentences like (16a) is not an instance of subordination; that is, they are not complements akin to *that*-clauses and gerunds, e.g. they do not cleft like *that*-clauses and gerunds, as shown in (a)-(b) below, and if they occur with a verb which can passivize, gerunds and *that*-clauses can occur as subject of the passive but the infinitive cannot. (See FVV: 247-248.) The contrast between true subordination on the core level and coordination may be represented as follows:

coordination   subordination

John told Bill to open the door John deplored Bill's stealing the car
-----------------   _____   ----------------------------
    core1   core2   core2
------------------------------------   ---
          clause   core1
                                       ----
                                                          clause

(a) *It was to open the door that John forced Bill
    It was Bill's stealing the car that John deplored

(b) *What John forced Bill was to open the door
    What John deplored was Bill's stealing the car

12.   The use of a clause as a core argument in (6a) and (20a) is a marked, asymmetrical
      linkage; see note 9.

13.   For detailed discussion of these points, see FVV (ch.5-6), Van Valin (1984), Van Valin and
      Wilkins (1989), Silverstein (1976), Givón (1980).

14.   This RRG logical structure differs from the FG semantic representation in (2b) in that it
      involves only predicates and their arguments; operators are not included. There is no RRG
      equivalent to (2b), in the sense of a logical structure and operators represented together.
      Rather, the operators are presented only in the operator projection of the sentence, and
      the whole representation in figure 3 forms the basis of the complete semantic interpretation
      of the sentence.

15.   In both examples the complement clause has been treated as a core argument, in spite of
      the caveat of note 7 and the discussion in FVV referred to there; this facilitates comparison
      of the syntactic contrasts between English and Lakhota. In the English example, *would* is
      treated as *will*, a status operator, plus tense (cf. FVV: 232). A couple of points need to be
      made about the Lakhota example. First, this is the structure of (22c'); the order of NPs
      is irrelevant to the interpretation. Second, *slolyá* "know", like *naxʔú* in figures 10 and 11,
      takes its argument affixes as infixes. Third, only animate arguments are realized by verbal
      affixes, and since the complement clause is not animate, there is no affix on the verb to
      indicate its argument status. Since it is a core argument of *slolyá*, it must be considered to
      be core-internal, unlike the full NPs.

16.   It is only by virtue of this factoring out of operators from constituents (i.e. predicates, their
      arguments, and peripheral elements) that what is common to both languages and what is
      different can be clearly seen.

17. See Van Valin (1985) for arguments that full NPs in Lakhota constructions like this are not directly involved in the embedding. The optionality of all full NPs in Lakhota raises the issue of their treatment in FG, where they would appear to be satellites. Dik et al. (this vol.) define 'satellite' as follows.

We consider satellites to be optional lexical means conveying additional information on one of the layers in the hierarchical clause model. *Optional* since they can be left out without affecting the grammaticality of the sentence. *Lexical* in opposition to grammatical categories such as tense, mood and aspect. *Conveying additional information* since the main information pertaining to a particular layer is carried by the kernel structure to which the satellite is added.

This would seem to fit the full NPs in e.g. (22c) perfectly, and yet it seems very odd to equate these NPs with optional adverbial elements, like (in RRG terms) peripheral prepositional phrases, since the two kinds of optional element (all of which would be considered predicate satellites in FG terms) have very different properties in the language.

References

Aissen, Judith
1987   *Tzotzil clause structure*. Dordrecht: Reidel.

Anderson, Stephen
1984   "Kwakwala syntax and the government-binding theory". In E.-D.Cook and D.Gerdts (eds.), *Syntax and semantics 16: The syntax of native American languages*. New York: Academic Press, 21-75.

Andrews, Avery
1985   "The major functions of the noun phrase". In Timothy Shopen (ed.), *Language typology and syntactic description, vol.1: Clause structure*. Cambridge: Cambridge UP, 62-154.

Bloomfield, Leonard
1933   *Language*. New York: Holt.

Craig, Colette
1977   *The structure of Jacaltec*. Austin: Univ. of Texas Press.

Dik, Simon
1978   *Functional grammar*. Amsterdam: North-Holland.

Dixon, R.M.W.
1972   *The Dyirbal language of North Queensland*. Cambridge: Cambridge UP.
1977   *A Grammar of Yidin*. Cambridge: Cambridge UP.

Dowty, David
1979   *Word meaning and montague grammar*. Dordrecht: Reidel.

England, Nora
1983   *A grammar of Mam*. Austin: Texas Press.

Foley, William A. and Robert D.Van Valin, Jr.
1984   *Functional syntax and universal grammar*. Cambridge: Cambridge UP.
1985   "Information packaging in the clause". In Timothy Shopen (ed.), *Language typology and syntactic description, vol.1: Clause structure*. Cambridge: Cambridge UP, 282-364.

Givón, Talmy
1980   "The binding hierarchy and the typology of complements". *Studies in Language* 4: 333-77.

Hansell, Mark
1987   "Serial verbs and complement constructions in Mandarin: A clause linkage analysis". *Davis Working Papers in Linguistics* 2: 38-54.

Hengeveld, Kees
1987   "Clause structure and modality in functional grammar". In J.van der Auwera and L.Goossens (eds.), *Ins and outs of the predication*. Dordrecht: Foris, 53-66.
1988   *Layers and operators*. Working Papers in Functional Grammar 27. (Revised version reprinted as: "Layers and operators in functional grammar". *Journal of Linguistics* 25: 127-157. 1989.)

Hewitt, B.G.
1979   *Abkhaz*. Amsterdam: North-Holland.

Hoijer, Harry
1949   "Tonkawa syntactic suffixes and anaphoric particles". *Southwestern Journal of Anthropology* 5: 37-55.

Hopper, Paul
1987   "Emergent grammar". *Proceedings of the Annual Meeting of the Berkeley Linguistic Society* 13: 139-157.

Johnson, Mark
1987   "A new approach to clause structure in role and reference grammar". *Davis Working Papers in Linguistics* 2: 55-59.

Jolly, Julia
1987   "An analysis of selected English prepositions within the framework of role and reference grammar". *Davis Working Papers in Linguistics* 2: 60-114.

Lambrecht, Knud
1986   *Topic, focus and the grammar of spoken French*. Ph.D.-thesis, University of California, Berkeley.

Maling, Joan
1980   "Inversion in embedded clauses in Modern Icelandic". *Íslenskt mál* 2: 175-193.

Maling, Joan and Annie Zaenen
1981   "Germanic word order and the format of surface filters". In F.Heny (ed.), *Binding and filtering*. Cambridge: MIT-Press, 255-278.

Nichols, Johanna
1984   "Functional theories of grammar". *Annual Review of Anthropology* 13: 97-117.
1986   "Head-marking and dependent-marking grammar". *Language* 62: 56-119.

Nunes, Mary L.
1989   *Aspects of the syntax and semantics of the English noun phrase*. M.A.-thesis, University of California, Davis.

Olson, Michael L.
1981   *Barai clause junctures: Toward a functional theory of interclausal relations*. Ph.D.-thesis, Australian National University.

Pike, Kenneth L. and Evelyn G.Pike
1982   *Grammatical analysis*. (2nd ed.) Arlington: Summer Institute of Linguistics.

Rijkhoff, Jan
1988   *A typology of operators: Towards a unified analysis of terms and predications*. Working Papers in Functional Grammar 29.

Silverstein, Michael
1976   "Hierarchy of features and ergativity". In R.M.W.Dixon (ed.), *Grammatical categories in Australian languages*. Canberra: Australian Institute of Aboriginal Studies, 112-71.

Thráinsson, Höskuldur
1979   *On complementation in Icelandic*. New York: Garland.
1986   "On auxiliaries, AUX and VPs in Icelandic". In Lars Hellan and Kirsti Koch Christensen (eds.), *Topics in Scandinavian syntax*. Dordrecht: Reidel, 235-265.

Van Valin, Robert D., Jr.
1984   "A typology of syntactic relations in clause linkage". *Proceedings of the Annual Meeting of the Berkeley Linguistic Society* 10: 542-558.
1985   "Case marking and the structure of the Lakhota clause". In Johanna Nichols and Anthony Woodbury (eds.), *Grammar inside and outside the clause*. Cambridge: Cambridge UP, 363-413.
1987a "The role of government in the grammar of head-marking languages". *IJAL* 53: 371-397.
1987b "Recent developments in role and reference grammar: The layered structure of the clause and juncture". *Davis Working Papers in Linguistics* 2: 1-5.
1989a "A synopsis of role and reference grammar". In R.D.Van Valin, Jr. (ed.), *Advances in role and reference grammar*. Amsterdam: John Benjamins. To appear.

1989b "Another look at Icelandic case marking and grammatical relations". Unpublished ms.

Van Valin, Robert D., Jr. and David P.Wilkins
1989 "Predicting syntactic structure from semantic representations: Remember in English and Mparntwe Arrernte". In Robert D.Van Valin, Jr. (ed.), *Advances in role and reference grammar*. Amsterdam: John Benjamins. To appear.

Vendler, Zeno
1967 *Linguistics in philosophy*. Ithaca: Cornell UP.

Watters, James K.
1987 "An investigation of Turkish clause linkage". *Davis Working Papers in Linguistics* 2: 130-141.

On the Semantics of Conditionals

Simon C. Dik
University of Amsterdam

0. Introduction[1]

Conditional constructions pose notorious problems for both linguistic and logical analysis. In this paper, I approach some of these problems from the point of view of the framework of Functional Grammar (FG) and Functional Logic (FL). I first sketch some general principles for a functional approach to conditionals (1.); then I outline the basic principles of FL (2.), both as regards its syntactic (2.1) and its semantic aspects (2.2). Within this framework, I give a general interpretation of conditionals, and point to some linguistic features which can be explained in terms of this interpretation (3.). Then, I discuss a number of different types of conditionals, specifying for each type its formal, semantic and pragmatic properties (4.).

1. General framework

A functional grammar is a model of a natural language M[NL] which strives to attain psychological and pragmatic adequacy. The theory of FG tries to define M[NL]s which are typologically adequate (i.e. formulated in terms of general principles underlying natural languages).

A more ambitious aim for functional linguistics is to try and develop a model of the natural language user M[NLU] which describes and explains how NLUs go about in communicating with each other through linguistic means. The best M[NLU] is that model which most closely and 'naturalistically' approaches the communicative performance of 'real' NLUs. The best M[NL] is that model of the grammar of a language which fits in most easily with an adequate M[NLU].

M[NLU] will have to capture much more than the grammatical competence of an NLU. At least the following capacities are involved in successful linguistic communication:

(i) A *linguistic* capacity: the capacity of correctly producing and interpreting linguistic expressions.

(ii) An *epistemic* capacity: the capacity to build up, maintain, and utilize an organized knowledge base.

(iii) A *logical* capacity: the capacity to validly infer new pieces of knowledge from given pieces of knowledge.

(iv) A *perceptual* capacity: the capacity to perceive the outside world, derive knowledge from these perceptions, and utilize this knowledge in producing and interpreting linguistic expressions.

(v) A *social* capacity: the capacity of determining what to say how and when and where to whom, in order to achieve one's communicative goals.

In this paper I will restrict my attention to the first three capacities. Concerning the interplay between these three capacities I have elsewhere (Dik 1987, 1988) argued for the following hypotheses:

(H1) Underlying linguistic structures, pieces of non-perceptual knowledge, and logical forms[2] can be expressed in one and the same unified cognitive representation language.

(H2) The representation language used for underlying predications in FG is a good approximation to this cognitive representation language.

The claims embodied in these hypotheses can be illustrated by means of the following example:

(1) a.   All humans are mortal
     b.   Gen e_i: [mortal$_A$ (all x_i: human$_A$ (x_i))$_\emptyset$] (e_i)

In (1b) the predicate 'mortal' is applied to a universally quantified term 'all humans'; the predication specifies a State of Affairs (SoA) e_i for which generic (Gen) validity is claimed.[3] According to (H1)-(H2), (1b) not only provides a representation for the grammatical structure underlying (1a), but also the format in which the piece of knowledge 'all humans are mortal' is stored, as well as the logical form of sentence (1a), which can thus figure in patterns of logical reasoning.

2. Functional Logic

Within the over-all model of M[NLU] we need a logic which can easily communicate with both the linguistic and the epistemic component. A logic (= a system through which valid patterns of reasoning can be described) can be defined in terms of (i) the *logical syntax* of the 'logical forms' used in these reasoning patterns, (ii) the *logical semantics* in terms of which these logical forms can be interpreted, (iii) the *logical rules* which determine which sequences of logical forms constitute valid patterns of reasoning. The type of logic which we envisage as a component of M[NLU] will be called 'Functional Logic' (FL).

2.1. The syntax of FL

We assume that the syntax of FL is co-extensive with the set of underlying predications as defined by FG. This assumption, which follows from (H2), entails the claim that there is no difference between the underlying grammatical form and the logical form of a linguistic expression. It also means that the logical form of a linguistic expression should not only be logically adequate, but also linguistically adequate in the sense that it must play a direct role in the production and the interpretation of the linguistic expression. This imposes clear restrictions on what counts as a well-formed 'logical form' in FL.

2.2. The semantics of FL

For the semantics of FL we adopt a number of non-standard assumptions which, however, seem to be required for a logic which is to function as a sub-component of M[NLU]:

(a) FL expressions are to be interpreted in terms of a system of mental representations (called 'pictures') which have the following properties:[4]

(i) Pictures consist of perceptual representations ('images') and conceptual representations; the latter are coded in propositions of the format defined by FG.[5]

(ii) Pictures are subject-dependent; any picture is somebody's picture.

(iii) Pictures are dynamic structures: they may be created, modified, and discarded. X's picture at t_i (XPt_i) is not necessarily identical to X's picture at t_j (XPt_j).

(iv) Pictures are finite: they do not contain everything that can be known, but only what X knows at t_i.

(v) Pictures can be nested: X's picture XP may contain an 'image' of Y's picture YP.

(vi) Several pictures may be considered at the same time.
Pictures may be represented as follows:

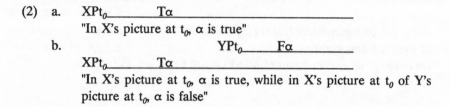

(2) a. XPt_0 _____ $T\alpha$ _____
   "In X's picture at t_0, α is true"

   b. _____ YPt_0 _____ $F\alpha$ _____
   XPt_0 _____ $T\alpha$ _____
   "In X's picture at t_0, α is true, while in X's picture at t_0 of Y's picture at t_0, α is false"

The overlap between X's picture and X's picture of Y's picture may be called the 'shared knowledge' of X and Y, according to X. Thus:

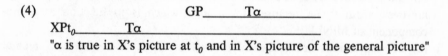

(3) _____ YPt_0 _____ $T\alpha$ _____
   XPt_0 _____ $T\alpha$ _____
   "In X's picture at t_0, α is true, and in X's picture of Y's picture at t_0, α is also true; $T\alpha$ is shared knowledge of X and Y, according to X"

(b) 'Truth' is limited to given pictures or picture constellations. 'α is true' = 'α is true in a picture P_i'. What is true in one picture may be false in another.
(c) 'Objective truth' is analysed as what is true in the 'general picture' GP as internalized by X. In other words, it concerns that which X thinks 'everybody' accepts as being true. Let α = 'the earth is round'. Then:

(4) _____ GP _____ $T\alpha$ _____
   XPt_0 _____ $T\alpha$ _____
   "α is true in X's picture at t_0 and in X's picture of the general picture"

What is true in X's picture of the general picture XP[GP] may in general be assumed to also be true in X's picture, as well as in X's picture of Y's picture, unless there is evidence to the contrary.
(d) Truth values for propositions are 'true' (T), 'false' (F) and 'uncertain' (?). For 'α is true' we may write '$T\alpha$'; for 'α is false' we may write '$F\alpha$'; for 'α is uncertain' we write '$?\alpha$'. Uncertainty may be subdivided according to 'degrees of probability', ranging between 1 and 0. We can write '$p(T\alpha) = n$' for 'it is n probable that α is true'.

3. The interpretation of conditionals

Conditional constructions can be generally represented as:

(5) $(\alpha)_{Cond}$, ß
      "If α, then ß"

In such a construction, the value of ß is considered as dependent on the truth of α. The 'value of ß' may be the truth value of ß, or the communicative relevance value of ß, in a sense to be made more precise below. α will be called the *protasis* (or *antecedent*), ß the *apodosis* (or *consequent*) of the conditional construction.

Grammatically, $(\alpha)_{Cond}$ is a Conditional satellite to ß. When the condition α relates to the truth value of ß, the Conditional satellite can be analysed as a propositional satellite; when it relates to the communicative relevance of ß, it can be analysed as an illocutionary satellite.[6] Conditional satellites may be expressed in different ways in different languages. The most common expression models are the following:

(6)   a.   (If) John stays (if), (then) Peter will leave
      b.   (If) John **should** stay (if), (then) Peter will leave
      c.   **Should** John stay, (then) Peter will leave
      d.   (If) John **would** stay (if), (then) Peter **would** leave

Thus, the protasis may be marked by a subordinating particle such as *if*, which may precede or follow the protasis (depending on the basic constituent ordering of the language), and/or the apodosis may be marked by a resumptive particle (*then*); the protasis may be marked by a special form or 'mood' of the predicate (*should stay* instead of *stay*); especially (only?) in irrealis conditionals, the apodosis predicate may also occur in a special mood.

As for constituent ordering, the protasis may in principle occur in four positions, which can be represented as follows:

(7)   P2, [P1...........X], P3
      a.   If John stays Peter will leave   (P1)
      b.   If John stays, then Peter will leave   (P2)
      c.   Peter will leave if John stays   (X)
      d.   Peter will leave, if John stays   (P3)

Thus, the protasis is placed inside the clause, either in P1 or in clause-final position; or it is placed outside the clause, in pre-clausal (P2) or post-clausal (P3) position. If it is placed outside the clause, it will be separated from the clause by an intonational contour.

The difference between P2 and P1 position is not very clear in English, but it comes out more clearly in a language like Dutch, where the finite verb is strongly fixed in clause-second position. This makes it clear that the protasis is in P1 in (8a), but in P2 in (8b):

(8) a. *Als   Jan   blijft gaat Piet   weg*
         if   John stays goes Peter away
         "If John stays Peter will leave"

     b. *Als   Jan   blijft, dan   gaat Piet   weg*
         if   John stays then goes Peter away
         "If John stays, then Peter will leave"

In (8a), the conditional protasis is in P1 position as evidenced by the postverbal position of the Subject *Piet*. In (8b), *dan* is in P1 position, and the conditional protasis takes the extraclausal P2 position.

Cross-linguistically, the protasis has a strong preference for the initial positions P1 and P2, independently of the basic constituent order of the language in question (Greenberg 1966: universal 14); when it is placed in P2 it takes the same position as 'Themes' such as:

(9) **As for Paris,** the Eiffel Tower is spectacular

In many languages, protases which occur in this position also take the same formal marking as Themes. This has led to the view that protases can be identified with 'Topics' or 'Themes' (see Haiman 1978; Haller and Watters 1984; Reesink 1987; Rijksbaron 1986). As an additional argument for the similarity between Themes and protases, Rijksbaron mentions the fact that both may occur outside the scope of illocutionary operators, as in:

(10) a. **As for Paris,** have you never been there?
     b. **If you feel so bad about this matter,** shouldn't you try and discuss it with your boss?

Haiman went as far as identifying the conditional protasis with a 'Topic', and argued that the common factor was that both presented 'given' information.

Akatsuka (1986) argues against this, makes a distinction between 'Given Topic' and 'Contrastive Topic', and claims that protases are 'Contrastive Topics'. We return to this point below.

We shall now interpret the conditional construction in general as a means through which the speaker S can create a 'hypothetical picture' which differs in certain crucial ways from his current picture.[7] Consider (6a). This construction will often be used when it is uncertain for S whether the protasis 'John stays' is true, in order to signal that in the hypothetical case that it should be true, something else will be true as well. This can be represented as follows:

(11) $\qquad\qquad\qquad\qquad$ HP$\underline{\quad T\alpha ==> T\beta\quad}$
$\quad$ SPt$_0\underline{\qquad\quad ?\alpha\qquad\qquad\qquad\qquad\qquad\qquad\qquad}$

"In S's current picture it is uncertain whether α is true or false, but in S's hypothetical picture in which α is true, β is true as well"

Note the following points concerning this interpretation of conditionals.

The protasis is a means for creating a hypothetical picture. It is an 'entry condition' to a picture in which the apodosis is held to be true. This picture-creating character explains the preference for the protasis to be placed in initial position, before the apodosis, and its similarity to Themes, both in position and formal marking. We do not have to go as far as to identify 'protasis' and 'Theme', however: this would be difficult in view of the fact that the protasis does not always or necessarily occur in P2 position. Rather than identifying 'protasis' and 'Theme', we should like to say that they are similar in having the common function of picture creation.

The traditional view of propositional logic is that conditionals can be interpreted in terms of the truth table for 'material implication':

(12)	α	β	$\alpha \text{-->} \beta$
	T	T	T
	T	F	F
	F	T	T
	F	F	T

This interpretation creates problems in relation to the most common usage of conditionals in natural languages. We can now see why this is so:

(i) It makes no sense to evaluate the truth value of the protasis independently of the hypothetical picture which it is used to create.

(ii) It makes no sense to evaluate the protasis as false within the hypothetical picture which it is used to create, for the truth of the protasis is specifically used to create that picture.

(iii) It makes no sense to create a hypothetical picture in which the protasis is true, if the protasis is also true in the current picture.

In other words: for the most common usage of a conditional construction, the protasis must be taken to be true in the hypothetical picture which it is used to create, and not true (i.e., uncertain or false) in the speaker's current picture.

It is not quite clear whether this characterization can be maintained for *all* (usages of) conditional constructions. Several examples have been mentioned in which a conditional construction can be used even though the speaker may well take the protasis to be true in his current picture. First of all, consider an example such as:

(13) X: I don't want to go to the movies.
     Y: Well, if you don't want to go to the movies, let us stay home and watch television.

In this case it is clear to Y that 'I don't want to go to the movies' is true in X's picture. Nevertheless, it can be assumed that by using the conditional, Y signals that he has not fully accepted this in his own picture: Y thus disclaims any responsibility for the truth of X's claim. On this interpretation, (13) is only an apparent counterexample to the idea that conditionals are not used appropriately when the speaker is convinced of the truth of the protasis (in his own picture). I return to this in 4.1.1.2.3 below.

Secondly, it was pointed out (Wakker p.c.; Van der Auwera p.c.) that 'creating a hypothetical picture' would seem less appropriate for general conditional statements of the form:

(14) If a lioness is hungry, she attacks

(15) If a person is generous, everybody likes him

For these cases Van der Auwera (1985) recognizes a distinct type, not concerned with 'uncertainty' on the part of the speaker, but with 'contingency': although it is not the case that lionesses are always hungry and persons are always generous, whenever they are, they are liable to show a certain kind of behaviour or receive a certain kind of esteem.

Thirdly, Van der Auwera (1985, p.c.) points to cases of 'thinking aloud' as in:

(16) I know that John is here. I also know that if John is here, his dog must be here too. So where is John's dog?

In this case, the conditional is not so much used for creating a hypothetical picture in a situation in which it is not clear whether the protasis is true, but rather to activate a general rule which provides a link in the reasoning process.

In view of such real and apparent counterexamples, I do not claim that my analysis in terms of hypothetical pictures which create a situation distinct from what the speaker takes to be the case in his current picture necessarily accounts for all usages of conditional constructions. I do claim that this analysis accounts for a large and important subset of such usages.

What is the use of creating hypothetical pictures in which α is true in a situation in which it is unknown whether α is true, or even known that α is false? This use is twofold:

(a) Hypothetical pictures may be used in patterns of hypothetical reasoning. Suppose that in our current picture α is uncertain, but that we accept that in an HP in which α is true, β is also true. We can then use HP in the following ways:

(i) If we find out (later on) that α is in fact true, we may conclude that β is also true.

(ii) If we find out that β is false, we may conclude that α is also false, since we accepted that β is true in any picture in which α is true.

(iii) If we find out that β is true, we may conclude that at least a necessary condition for the truth of α is fulfilled. We cannot conclude that α is true, but neither can we conclude that the truth value of β shows that α must be false.

(b) Hypothetical pictures may be used in considering alternatives to situations which are currently taken to be/have been the case. Suppose I am not rich; then, an HP opened up by 'if I were rich' may be used to consider an alternative to the present situation. Suppose that you have stayed for a drink and have (thereby) missed your train. Then, if it is accepted that (17) is true:

(17) If you had not stayed for a drink, you would not have missed your train

you may use this hypothetical picture next time when the same circumstances obtain to decide that you would better not stay for a drink.

4. Different types of conditionals

Within the framework of the general interpretation of conditionals presented in 3. several different types of conditional can be distinguished. These different types can be differentiated from each other in terms of different picture constellations. Depending on these different picture constellations, conditionals may have different communicative effects. In a number of cases, the difference in picture constellation will also lead to a different kind of expression of the conditional construction.

In describing different types of conditionals in terms of different picture constellations, we are able to account in a systematic way for the relations between form, meaning, and communicative usage of conditionals.

The different types of conditionals to be discussed below can be summarized in the following diagram:

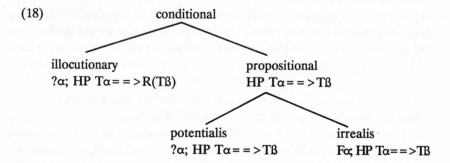

(18)   conditional

        illocutionary   propositional
        ?α; HP Tα= = >R(Tß)   HP Tα= = >Tß

                                potentialis   irrealis
                                ?α; HP Tα= = >Tß   Fα; HP Tα= = >Tß

Thus, we make a first major division between 'propositional conditionals' (4.1) and 'illocutionary conditionals' (4.2), depending on whether the protasis formulates a condition for the truth of the apodosis, or for the 'relevance' (R) of the information contained in the apodosis to the addressee. Within the class of propositional conditionals, a major distinction is made between potentialis and irrealis conditionals, depending on whether the protasis is antecedently considered uncertain (?α) or false (Fα). Within each of these types, further subdivisions will be made; and for some of the resulting sub-types, certain special 'rhetoric' usages will be identified.

4.1. Propositional conditionals

Propositional conditionals present the truth of one proposition, α, as a sufficient condition for the truth of a second proposition, ß (cf. Van der Auwera 1985). In other words, they claim that in a picture in which α is true, ß is also true.

4.1.1. Potentialis. Potentialis conditionals are used in the following picture constellation:

(19) $\qquad$ HP$\underline{\qquad T\alpha = = > T\beta \qquad}$

$\quad$ SPt$_0$$\underline{\qquad ?\alpha \qquad\qquad\qquad\qquad\qquad\qquad}$

S is uncertain about the truth of α at the moment of speaking, and creates an HP in which the truth of α entails the truth of ß. α may refer to an SoA in past, present, or future; but since we are most commonly uncertain about future SoAs, the potentialis will most often be found with reference to the future. If S has no presupposition concerning the probability of the truth of α, the potentialis will typically be expressed in the indicative:

(20) John may stay or he may not stay. But **if John stays, Peter will leave.**

4.1.1.1. Probability-monitored potentialis. The potentialis may be influenced by S's opinion on the probability that α is true or false. Compare:

(21) a. John will probably stay. And **if John does indeed stay, Peter will leave.**

$\quad$ b. John will probably not stay. But **if John should stay / should John stay, Peter will leave.**[8]

Note that the formulation of the protases in (21a-b) depends on the context, and cannot be switched around. 'Context' here means: S's current picture as established up to this point in the communication. Probability-monitored potentialis conditionals thus require a picture constellation of the following form:

(22) $\qquad$ HP$\underline{\qquad T\alpha = = > T\beta \qquad}$

$\quad$ SPt$_0$$\underline{\qquad ?\alpha; \; p(T\alpha) = n \qquad\qquad\qquad\qquad}$

in which n indicates the probability value that S attaches to α's being true. S's picture can thus be paraphrased as: 'I don't know whether α; I believe there is an n chance that α.'.

It appears that three potentially distinctive probability values must be recognized in this domain:

(23) α is (i) relatively probable
         (ii) neutral as to probability
         (iii) relatively improbable

In Classical Greek (Rijksbaron 1986) we find three clearly distinct forms of the protasis for these three cases: in the neutral case (ii) the protasis is formulated with the conjunction *ei* + indicative mood; in case (iii) we find *ei* + optative mood; and in case (i) we have *eán* + subjunctive mood, at least in 'interactive speech'.[9]

Swahili has a similar three-way distinction among potentialis conditionals (Saloné 1983): if α is considered relatively improbable, one uses one of the conjunctions *ikiwa* or *iwapo*, usually construed with a future verb; the conjunction *kama* is used in the neutral case; and if the condition is considered very likely to be fulfilled, one uses the imperfective or participial form of the verb with *-ki-*, which can also get temporal interpretations.

4.1.1.2. *Special uses of the potentialis.* Potentialis conditionals may be put to special usages, with special communicative effects. We shall try to explain these special usages in terms of picture theory.

4.1.1.2.1. *Potentialis and exclusive disjunction.* Consider a situation in which there are only two possibilities, as in:

(24) A baby is either a boy or a girl.

In such a situation the following entailments hold:

(25) a. It is a boy; therefore, it is not a girl
     b. It is not a boy; therefore, it is a girl
     c. It is a girl; therefore, it is not a boy
     d. It is not a girl; therefore, it is a boy

Note that these entailments hold by virtue of the fact that (24) is silently accepted as an exhaustive characterization of the possibilities. Now consider conditional statements of the following form:

(26) If it is a boy, then it is not a girl

In such a situation, more or less independently of the conditional, we know that if the protasis is true, the apodosis must be true, too; and when the protasis is false, the apodosis must be false as well. However, this is not because of any special properties of the conditional, but because of the background knowledge contained in (24).

We can thus represent a conditional of the form of (26) in the following way:[10]

(27) HP___Tα= = >T-ß___
SP___?α; either Tα or Tß_____

The fact that the relevant background knowledge may in this case be cast in the form of an exclusive disjunction may explain the curiously 'tautological' character of conditionals of type (26).

4.1.1.2.2. Biconditional implicatures. It has often been noted (e.g. Geis and Zwicky 1971; Karttunen 1971; Levinson 1983; Comrie 1986) that in certain usages the potentialis 'invites' a biconditional interpretation. For example, from (28a) it will often be concluded that (28b):

(28) a. If you cross that bridge, you will die
b. If I do not cross that bridge, I will not die

Such an inference is not logically entailed by the potentialis as such. It only follows logically if the conditional is formulated as a two-way biconditional:

(29) **If and only if** you cross that bridge, you will die

We agree with those who claim that this usage of the conditional does not reveal a genuine ambiguity, but is rather a matter of pragmatically determined 'invited inference' or 'implicature'. In terms of picture theory we can formulate the relevant conditions as follows:

(30) A conditional of the form 'if α, then ß' invites the inference 'if not α, then not ß' in a situation in which it is clear to both S and A that ß will not occur in the normal course of events.

This can be symbolized by means of the following picture constellation:[11]

(31)   HP____Tα= = >Tß____
                             AP_____Fß_____
        SP___?α; Fß _____

Thus, S assumes that A is (normally) not going to die (ß), and that A assumes the same. S then asserts that in a picture in which A crosses the bridge (α), he will die. The underlying assumption is that if A does not cross the bridge, the situation will remain the same as under normal standard assumptions, i.e. he will not die.

In a situation defined by this constellation, when ß is something which may be assumed to be non-preferred by A, the conditional will be interpreted as a warning or a threat. If ß is something preferable to A, the conditional will be interpreted as promising a reward to A.

4.1.1.2.3. Semi-factual conditionals. Potentialis conditionals are sometimes used in conditions in which at first sight it is clear that the protasis is true. These are sometimes called 'factual' or 'semi-factual' conditionals. Consider the following example (from Akatsuka 1986):

(32) Son (looking out of the window):
              It's raining, mommy.
     Mother: If it's raining, let's not go to the park.

As Comrie (1986) and Akatsuka (1986) correctly point out, however, even in a case such as (32) the conditional is not properly used if S is convinced that the protasis is true (unless S wishes to give the impression that he is not certain about the truth of the protasis). What is involved in (32) can be accounted for as follows within our present framework.

First of all, we make a distinction between 'recording' and 'accepting' the content of what another person says.[12] Thus, X's statement (33) may lead to a picture structure of the form (34a) or of the form (34b) on the part of Y:

(33) X: John is a fool (α)

(34) a.   XP____Ta_____
        YP_____
     b.   XP____Ta_____
        YP_____Ta_____

In (34a) Y has simply recorded the fact that John is a fool in the opinion of X. In (34b), however, Y has admitted the truth of X's statement to his own picture: Y has 'accepted' the claim made by X. From the point of view of X, X has 'informed' Y of his opinion with respect to α in (34a), but he has 'convinced' Y of his opinion in (34b). Sub-cases may be distinguished according to whether Y already had an opinion on α before X's statement.

Now consider a possible continuation on the part of Y:

(35) Y: Well, if John is a fool, why are you still in love with him?

I believe some consideration will show that (35) is compatible with (34a), but not with (34b). In other words, the general condition remains true that the protasis of (35) is uncertain in Y's picture. However, now that X has just told Y that the protasis is true, Y's response may be interpreted as a sign of 'stalling acceptance': Y is willing to entertain what may be the case if what X says is true, but clearly X has so far not been able to convince Y of the truth of his statement.

In the case in which α is a very strongly held opinion on the part of X, and/or in case X believes he is in a position of authority in relation to Y, Y's conditional response may create an effect of impertinence, as in:

(36) Teacher: Sugar dissolves in water.
      Johnny: Well, if sugar dissolves in water, how come I still get sticky fingers?

Inoue (1983) argues that Japanese has a special syntactic form (the 'cleft conditional'), which is specifically used in 'semi-factual' circumstances.

4.1.1.2.4. Ex absurdo conditionals. For the phenomenon of 'ex absurdo' conditionals, we take another example from Akatsuka (1986):

(37) X: I'm the Pope.
     Y: If you're the Pope, I'm the empress of China.

This kind of example has often been adduced as proof that natural language conditionals may be true even when the protasis is false. But this ignores the very special circumstances in which this kind of conditional is used, and the special effect which it creates. I submit that (37) may be associated with the following picture constellation, in which α = 'X is the Pope', and ß = 'Y is the empress of China':

(38)   HP___ Tα= = >Tß____
                                          GP_____Fß_____
                                          XP_____Tα_____
                 YP___?α; p(Tα)=approx Ø; Fß_____

Though Y cannot be positive that X's claim 'α' is false, he believes the probability of this claim to approximate zero. Y now wishes to express:

(39) If α is true, anything can be true

For that purpose, Y selects something which he believes anybody will consider to be untrue (e.g. ß = 'I'm the empress of China', which Y considers to be obviously false in the general picture GP), and thus uses (37Y) to signal his utter disbelief of what X has said.

The communicative status of this kind of conditional is so special that many languages have special idiomatic expressions for this purpose. Rather telling in the present context is the following English idiom:

(40) If that is true, I am a Dutchman

4.1.1.2.5. Sarcastic conditionals. For an example of a sarcastic usage of the potentialis I borrow an example from Comrie's (1986) discussion of this usage:

(41) (X and Y are in Amsterdam)
      X: We're still in Belgium, are we?
      Y: Yes, if Amsterdam is in Belgium, we're still in Belgium.

For Y, the proposition proffered by X ('we're still in Belgium') is so obviously untrue (and the question so stupid), that he does not feel like repudiating it in a serious way. Therefore, he presents it as following from something else ('Amsterdam is in Belgium') which he believes every normal person should know is false.

The picture constellation from which Y operates in this case has the following form (ß$_1$ = 'we're in Holland', ß$_2$ = 'we're in Belgium', α = 'Amsterdam is in Belgium'):

(42)   HP____ $T\alpha = = > T\beta_2$____
                              XP____ $?\beta_2$____
                              GP____ $T\beta_1; F\beta_2; F\alpha$____

YP____ $'?\alpha'; T\beta_1; F\beta_2$____

Thus, it is part of Y's picture of the general picture that 'we' are in Holland, that 'we' are not in Belgium, and that Amsterdam is not in Belgium. Y has recorded X's insecurity about the 'obvious' fact that they are in Holland. Instead of straightforwardly giving X a correct answer to his question, Y creates a picture in which the falsehood ß2 is entailed by the truth of another obvious falsehood, α. By presenting α in the protasis of a potentialis conditional, Y creates the impression that he is uncertain about the truth of α. In this way, Y is fooling X rather than communicating with him. The difference with the 'ex absurdo' usage as exemplified in (35) is that the apodosis in (39) is not obviously false in another context: it could well have been true.

   Again, this usage of potentialis conditionals is communicatively so special that it should not be taken as a model for the analysis of conditionals in general.

4.1.2. Irrealis conditionals. Irrealis or counterfactual conditionals are used in the following picture constellation:

(43)   HP____ $T\alpha = = > T\beta$____
        SP____ $F\alpha$____

Thus, in a situation in which S considers α to be false, he nevertheless creates a picture in which the truth of ß is entailed by the truth of α, through a conditional of the form:

(44) If α were/had been the case, then ß would be/would have been the case too

(45) a.   If John stayed, Peter would leave
      b.   If John had stayed, Peter would have left

Note that, although ß will usually be assumed to be false as well, this is not a necessary feature of the irrealis conditional; it is rather a matter of standard assumptions or invited inference (Karttunen 1971). Thus, the irrealis is not incompatible with the assertion of the apodosis:

(46) If Harry had known that Sheila survived, he would have gone home,
     which he did anyway

More usually, however, the irrealis is used to argue how ß might have come
about if conditions had been different than they were/are.

The irrealis is used when S is certain that α is false. Since we can usually
only be certain about what has already happened or is happening right now, the
irrealis is mostly confined to present and past, a fact through which it is usually
in quasi-complementary distribution with the potentialis. However, irrealis
conditionals with future reference are not wholly excluded. Suppose John and
Mary are discussing their stubborn son Peter, who has firmly decided to leave
university at the end of next term. Then it would be perfectly all right for John
to say:

(47) If only Peter did not leave university at the end of next term, ...

The irrealis then signals that the speaker is quite certain that this may be an
idle hope.

What is the point of creating pictures in which things are true which, in the
speaker's current picture, are manifestly false? There is a difference here
between the non-past irrealis in (45a) and the past irrealis of (45b). The latter
could be used to sketch an alternative to the course of events which actually
took place. It could be used, for example, to explain why S did not do anything
to prevent John from leaving. The suggestion in this case is: the consequences
of the alternative would have been worse than what actually happened. It could
also be that the irrealis conditional is presented as a better course of events
than what actually happened. In that case it can be used to formulate a
reproach to those responsible for John's leaving. In both cases, the irrealis is
used in discussions of potential alternatives to the course of events which
actually took place.

The non-past irrealis in (45a) can be used to sketch a course of events and
consider its consequences, without committing oneself to the truth of the
protasis. Consider:

(48) So you don't go to London. But if you went, this could be quite pro-
     fitable for the company.

Through the irrealis, S proffers a course of events which he thinks the addressee should seriously consider, without suggesting that he wishes to impose his opinion on him. Note that in the context of (48), it is not possible to use a potentialis conditional:

(49) So you don't go to London. *But if you go, this can be quite profitable for the company.

The potentialis in this context easily gives the impression that S does not attach much importance to the other's opinion.

Irrealis conditionals can be distinguished according to whether they relate to a past or a non-past event. From a different angle, they can be distinguished according to whether α could in principle be fulfilled or not. According to Saloné (1983) the difference between 'possible in principle' and 'utterly impossible' ('*adunaton*') is dominant in the choice between Swahili irrealis constructions marked by -*nge*- vs. -*ngali*-. Where such distinctions as these are relevant, they can be added to the picture constellation from which the conditional is produced.

Just as in the case of the potentialis, the irrealis may be used for special communicative effects. Consider the following example:

(50) You don't get the money. Even if I were a millionaire, you (still) wouldn't get it.

This irrealis is used in a situation in which, unlike what is normally the case, it is quite clear to S (and A) that ß (= *you won't get the money*) is in fact true. Note, however, that the construction is also formally marked off from the normal irrealis, in that it contains the extra elements *even* and (optionally) *still*. These elements stress the 'cumulative' character of this usage: S does not consider it sufficient to refuse the money here and now, but wishes to add that this is a matter of principle, not of availability: even in alternative circumstances, he would not give the money. Thus, the situation for A is even worse than it seems to be at first sight.

4.1.3. Summary of propositional conditionals. The different types of propositional conditionals distinguished above can be summarized as follows:

(51) potentialis: (i)   ?α; p(Tα) = neutral
                    (ii)   ?α; p(Tα) = high
                    (iii) ?α; p(Tα) = low
     time reference: future > present > past

(52) irrealis: (i)   Fα; possible(α)
                    (ii)   Fα; impossible(α)
     time reference: past > present > (future)

It will be evident that in practice there may be only a slight difference between the potentialis with low probability, and the irrealis about an event which is considered as possible in principle. Compare such cases as:

(53) a.   John is most probably not coming to the party. But if he comes, we're in big trouble.
      b.   John is not coming to the party. If he had come, we would have been in big trouble.

Wakker (1986) studied the choice between these two construction types in Classical Greek. See note 8.

4.2. Illocutionary conditionals

The conditionals considered so far all have in common that they relate two propositions in a way which can be paraphrased as follows:

(54) S submits that in a picture in which α is true, ß is also true.

We can thus say that the conditional makes the truth of ß depend on the truth of α. This only makes sense if the occurrence of ß can be thought of as in some way determined by the occurrence of α. We could thus also say that the conditional relates two SoAs, as in the following paraphrase:

(55) S submits that in a picture in which α occurs/is the case, ß will occur/be the case as well.

There is a whole class of natural language conditionals which cannot be analysed according to this pattern. Consider the following examples:

(56) a. If you're interested, John is a catholic
    b. If you're hungry, there's some sandwiches in the fridge

Such conditionals do not establish a relation between two SoAs or propositions; in (56a), for example, it is not suggested that John's being a catholic has anything to do with your interest (although in principle it *could* be so interpreted). Rather, these satellites present a condition for the 'relevance' to the addressee of what S has to say in the consequent (Austin 1961; Johnson-Laird 1986):

(57) If you're hungry, (it is relevant for you to know that) there's some sandwiches in the fridge

Because of this property, I shall term these constructions *illocutionary conditionals*.[13] Illocutionary conditionals specify a condition with respect to properties of the speech act currently performed by the speaker. They thus have a 'meta-communicative' character. Though 'relevance' seems to be the dominant dimension for illocutionary conditionals to relate to, it is not the only dimension. In principle, any feature pertaining to the pragmatic rights and duties of speaker and addressee, and to the appropriateness of (features of) the speech act performed, could be commented upon through an illocutionary conditional. Compare:

(58) a. **If you allow me to say so**, sir, ...
    b. Communisms, **if it still deserves this name**, is in a sorry state

For a Latin example, consider the famous verses (Catullus 51):

(59) *Ille*   *mi*   *par* *esse* *deo* *videtur*
    that.man me equal be   god seem
    Ille,   *si fas est,* *superare* *divos,*
    that.man if right be surpass the.divine
    Qui ...
    who
    "He, me thinks, is equal to a god,
    He, **if it is allowed to say so**, surpasses the divine,
    Who ..."

For more examples from Latin, see Van de Griend (1988, 1989).

4.2.1. Some special features of illocutionary conditionals. We saw in 3. above that conditional protases are usually placed in P1 position (inside the clause) or in P2 position (outside the clause). In the latter case, they take a position similar to Themes. Illocutionary conditionals, however, *necessarily* occur outside the clause, mostly in P2, sometimes in P3 (= Tail) position. Compare the following Dutch constructions:

(60) a. *Als je hem nodig hebt, is Jan in de keuken*
      if   you   him   needy   have   is   John   in the   kitchen
      "If you need him John is in the kitchen"

    b. *Als je hem nodig hebt, **dan** is Jan in de keuken*
      if   you   him   needy   have   then   is   John   in the   kitchen
      "If you need him John is in the kitchen"

    c. *Als je hem nodig hebt: Jan is in de keuken*
      if   you   him   needy   have   John   is   in the   kitchen
      "If you need him, John is in the kitchen"

The inversion in (60a) reveals that the protasis is inside the clause in P1 position. This construction can only be interpreted as a non-illocutionary, propositional conditional. In (60b), the conditional is outside the clause, in P2 position; the P1 position inside the clause is occupied by 'resumptive' *dan* "then". This construction is preferably interpreted as non-illocutionary, but it can marginally also be interpreted as illocutionary. Construction (60c) has the apodosis in the form of a full, unmodified main clause. This construction can only get the illocutionary interpretation.

Another features which points to the 'disconnected' status of illocutionary conditionals is that they may often occur in parenthesis, as in (58b) and (59) above.

As noted by Johnson-Laird (1986), the truth of the apodosis in the illocutionary conditional is in no way dependent on the truth of the protasis. The protasis and the apodosis are only connected *via* the notion of 'relevance' (or any other pragmatic dimension relating to the illocutionary act).

4.2.2. Interpretation of illocutionary conditionals in FG. Hengeveld (1988) suggested that the full structure underlying a clause in FG should be analysed in terms of the following 'layers':

(61) layer   variable   semantic category

    1. predicate (frame)   : f_i :   property/relation
    2. predication   : e_i :   state of affairs
    3. proposition   : X_i :   possible fact
    4. clause   : E_i :   speech act

Correspondingly, four levels of operators and four levels of satellites[14] can be distinguished:

(62) 1. predicate operators (π_1)   and satellites (σ_1)
      2. predication operators (π_2)   and satellites (σ_2)
      3. propositional operators (π_3)   and satellites (σ_3)
      4. illocutionary operators (π_4)   and satellites (σ_4)

Non-illocutionary protases can be interpreted as propositional satellites. They relate the condition to the propositional content of the apodosis. Illocutionary protases can now be interpreted as illocutionary satellites. They relate the condition to the (relevance of the) speech act. Thus, a construction such as (56b) can be represented as follows:

(63) (Pres e_i: [you are hungry] (e_i))$_{Cond}$,
      DECL E_i: [there's some sandwiches in the fridge] (E_i)

Thus, the protasis is not conditionally related to some SoA described in the apodosis, but to the event E_i which consists in doing the speech act. In this way, the conditional is naturally interpreted as referring to the relevance or appropriateness of performing the speech act, just as is the case in other illocutionary satellites which provide a reason or a purpose for performing the speech act (cf. Boër and Lycan 1980), as in:

(64) a.   Since you asked, John is a catholic
      b.   Just so I can tell my mother, what's this stuff we're smoking?

4.2.3. Interpretation in terms of picture theory. How can illocutionary conditionals be interpreted in terms of picture theory? We shall approach this question from the point of view of the paraphrase given in (57) above. We shall thus write:

(65) HP_____Tα= = >R(Tß)_____

"In a hypothetical picture in which α is true, it is relevant (R) for you
to know that ß is also true"

It seems that if we analyse illocutionary conditionals in this way, inserting these
hypothetical pictures into the picture structures used for propositional
conditionals above yields the correct picture structure for illocutionary
conditionals. (65) correctly expresses what S wishes A to add to his knowledge
base through using a conditional of this type.

One fact about illocutionary conditionals appears to be that they do not take
irrealis form. Consider:

(66) *If you were hungry: there would be sandwiches in the kitchen

The closest we could get to an irrealis would be in constructions of the form:[15]

(67) If you had been hungry: there were sandwiches in the kitchen!

This construction type (with an indicative apodosis!) fulfils the special function
of mentioning something the speaker 'forgot to say'. As a communicative event,
it is decidedly unhelpful.

How can the non-occurrence of illocutionary conditionals in the true irrealis
be explained? Let us first consider the present: if I know now that you are not
hungry, then it would hardly be relevant to tell you where to look for food if
you were. A fortiori, when I know that you were not hungry yesterday, there is
even less relevance to know that yesterday there were sandwiches in the
kitchen:

(68) *If you had been hungry: there would have been sandwiches in the
      kitchen

Phrased somewhat differently: the illocutionary conditional presents something
as relevant to the addressee, provided the protasis holds. It would be rather
pointless to use this construction if it were already certain to S that the protasis
does not hold.

5. Conclusion

In this paper I have argued for the following approach to the semantics of conditionals constructions:

(a) Linguistic expressions are produced from, and interpreted in terms of, mental representations called pictures.

(b) Different pictures may be simultaneously relevant for the production and interpretation of linguistic expressions.

(c) Conditional constructions are used to create hypothetical pictures in which the antecedent is taken to be true.

(d) Two types of conditional have to be distinguished in terms of what they *assert*: *propositional conditionals* (HP Tα= = >Tß), and *illocutionary conditionals* (HP Tα= = >R(Tß)).

(e) All other differences between propositional conditionals can be described in terms of 'background' pictures *from which they are asserted*. The main distinction here is between *potentialis conditionals* (SP ?α) and *irrealis conditionals* (SP Fα).

(f) Both potentialis and irrealis conditionals can be distinguished according to whether the apodosis SoA refers to a time interval preceding, overlapping, or following the moment of speaking. Due to the difference between (?α) and (Fα), the potentialis more commonly refers to the future, the irrealis more commonly to the non-future.

(g) Potentialis conditionals can be distinguished in terms of whether S believes that Tα is rather probable, rather improbable, or neither.

(h) Irrealis conditionals can be distinguished in terms of whether or not α is something which could, in principle, be/have been the case.

(i) Several special 'rhetorical' usages of conditionals can be accounted for in terms of more specific picture constellations, created around the common core of the background conditions required for the correct production and interpretation of potentialis and irrealis conditionals.

Notes

1.   I am grateful to Johan Van der Auwera, Margreet van de Griend, Gerry Wakker, Hans Weigand, and the editors of this volume for comments which have led to improvements of the paper.

2.   By 'logical form' I understand that representation of a linguistic expression which can be used in rules of entailment and in inference schemas which serve to specify the inferences which can be validly drawn from the content of the expression. Note that a linguistic expression does not 'have' a logical form. Rather, a logical form is assigned to an expression by virtue of a theory of logical reasoning.

3.   For the SoA-variable e_i, cf. Vet (1986); for the operator Gen, see Dik et al. (1989).

4.   The notion of 'picture' is close to Johnson-Laird's concept of 'mental model' (see Johnson-Laird 1983). It is also similar to such concepts as 'discourse model' or 'discourse representation structure' (Kamp 1984; Vet 1987).

5.   As a working hypothesis I assume that mental representations consist of distinct perceptual and non-perceptual items, and that the non-perceptual items are coded in the form of (abstract) verbal representations (in fact, FG representations). This is consonant with the dual coding hypothesis of Paivio (1971, 1986), and to what is called 'multimodal' mental representation in Glass and Holyoak (1986).

6.   For this distinction of satellite types, compare Dik et al. (this vol.).

7.   This is consonant with what might be called a 'pragmatic' or 'interactive' analysis of conditionals. Cf. Rijksbaron (1986) and the formulation from Ducrot (1972: 167) quoted there: "(la supposition) consiste à demander à l'auditeur d'accepter pour un temps une certaine proposition 'p' qui devient, provisoirement, le cadre du discours, et notamment de la proposition principale, 'q'." Our approach is also compatible with Johnson-Laird's (1986) analysis of conditionals in terms of 'mental models'. Consider some of Johnson-Laird's characterizations of conditionals: "the function of the antecedent is to establish a context, i.e. a state of affairs that should be taken for granted in considering the consequent." (1986: 64); "What underlies the meaning of conditionals [...] is the ability to envisage states of affairs that may or may not correspond to reality, that is, the ability to construct mental models of such states of affairs and to bear in mind their existential status." (1986: 65); "the natural way in which to think of such conditionals is that the consequent is evaluated with respect to a model of the state of affairs that is described by the antecedent taken in conjunction with general knowledge." (1986: 71).

8.   Saloné (1983) mentions in passing that unlikely protases in English may also be marked by prosodic means: *John will probably not stay; but if he does stay, Peter will leave.* Note also the occurrence of supportive *do*.

9.   Rijksbaron shows that the interpretation of conditionals is co-dependent on discourse type. For the factors influencing the choice between 'unlikely' potentialis and irrealis in Classical Greek, see Wakker (1986). As Wakker demonstrates, this choice is co-dependent on the features [±dynamic] and [±momentaneous] of the SoA described in the protasis, and on pragmatic or 'rhetorical' factors concerned with how S wishes to present his belief structure to A.

10. I leave out the temporal index on pictures when this is irrelevant to the point under discussion.

11. AP = the addressee's picture; SP[AP] = the picture which the speaker has of the picture of the addressee.

12. Remember Austin's (1962) distinction between the 'understanding' and the 'uptake' of a statement. Compare Wunderlich (1974: 332) for discussion of this distinction between 'understanding' and 'accepting' a proposition.

13. Illocutionary conditionals can be analysed as 'illocutionary satellites' in the sense of Dik (1989), Dik et al. (this vol.). Pinkster (1988) speaks of 'pseudoconditions'. For a study of these conditionals in Latin, see Van de Griend (1988, 1989).

14. For these four types of satellites, see Dik et al. (this vol.).

15. Van de Griend (p.c.); cf. Van de Griend (1988) from some exceptional Latin cases.

References

Akatsuka, Noriko
1986 "Conditionals are discourse-bound". In E.C.Traugott et al. (eds.), 333-351.

Austin, J.L.
1961 "Ifs and cans". In J.O.Urmson and G.J.Warnock (eds.), *Philosophical papers of J.L.Austin*. (Edition 1970.) Oxford: Oxford UP, 205-232.
1962 *How to do things with words*. Cambridge: MIT-Press.

Auwera, Johan van der
1985 *Language and logic: A speculative and condition-theoretic study*. Amsterdam: Benjamins.

Boër, Steven E. and William G.Lycan
1980 "A performadox in truth-conditional semantics". *Linguistics and Philosophy* 4: 71-100.

Comrie, Bernard
1986 "Conditionals: A typology". In E.C.Traugott et al. (eds.), 77-99.

Dik, Simon C.
1987 "Linguistically motivated knowledge representation". In M.Nagao (ed.), *Language and artificial intelligence*. Amsterdam: North-Holland, 145-170.
1988 "Towards a unified cognitive language". *Worlds behind words: Essays in honour of Prof.Dr. F.G. Droste*. Leuven: University of Leuven.
1989 *The theory of functional grammar, pt.1: The structure of the clause*. Dordrecht: Foris.

Dik, S.C., H.Dik, I.Genee, J.van den Hauwe, R.de Jong, H.J.van der Meulen, M.de Roeck and C.Zijlemakers
1989 "Specific and generic reference in FG". Paper, Institute for General Linguistics, University of Amsterdam.

Ducrot, Oswald
1972   *Dire et ne pas dire: Principes de sémantique linguistique.* Paris: Hermann.

Geis, Michael L. and Arnold M.Zwicky
1971   "On invited inferences". *Linguistic Inquiry* 2: 561-566.

Glass, Arnold Lewis and Keith James Holyoak
1986   *Cognition.* Second edition. New York: Random House.

Griend, Margreet E.van de
1988   *How to do things with si.* MA-Thesis, University of Amsterdam.
1989   "Pseudoconditionals in Latin". *Cahiers de l'Institut de Linguistique de Louvain* 15: 447-456.

Haiman, John
1978   "Conditionals are topics". *Language* 54: 564-589.

Haller, Beat and John Watters
1984   "Topic in Zulgo". *Studies in African Linguistics* 15: 27-46.

Hengeveld, P.C.
1988   *Layers and operators.* Working Papers in Functional Grammar 27. (Revised version reprinted in: *Journal of Linguistics* 25: 127-157. 1989)

Inoue, Kyoko
1983   "An analysis of a cleft conditional in Japanese: Where the grammar meets rhetoric". *Journal of Pragmatics* 7: 251-262.

Johnson-Laird, Philip N.
1983   *Mental models.* Cambridge: Cambridge UP.
1986   "Conditionals and mental models". In E.C.Traugott et al. (eds.), 55-75.

Kamp, Hans
1984   "A theory of truth and semantic representation". In J.Groenendijk, T.M.V.Janssen and M.Stohof (eds.), *Truth, interpretation, and information.* Dordrecht: Foris, 1-41.

Karttunen, Lauri
1971   "Counterfactual conditionals". *Linguistic Inquiry* 2: 566-569.

Levinson, Stephen C.
1983   *Pragmatics.* Cambridge: Cambridge UP.

Paivio, A.
1971   *Imagery and verbal processes.* New York: Holt, Rinehart and Winston.
1986   *Mental representations: A dual coding approach.* New York: Oxford UP.

Pinkster, Harm
1988 *Lateinische Syntax und Semantik*. Tübingen: Francke Verlag.

Reesink, Ger P.
1987 *Structures and their functions in Usan, a Papuan language of Papua New Guinea*. Amsterdam: Benjamins.

Rijksbaron, Albert
1986 *The pragmatics and semantics of conditional and temporal clauses: Some evidence from Dutch and Classical Greek*. Working Papers in Functional Grammar 13.

Saloné, Sukari
1983 "The pragmatics of reality and unreality conditional sentences in Swahili". *Journal of Pragmatics* 7: 311-324.

Traugott, Elizabeth Closs, Alice ter Meulen, Judy Snitzer Reilly and Charles A.Ferguson (eds.)
1986 *On conditionals*. Cambridge: Cambridge UP.

Vet, C.
1986 *A pragmatic approach to tense in functional grammar*. Working Papers in Functional Grammar 16.
1987 "Temporele relaties in teksten". *TTT* 7: 149-166.

Wakker, G.C.
1986 "Potential and contrary-to-fact conditionals in Classical Greek". *Glotta* 64: 222-246.

Wunderlich, Dieter
1974 *Grundlagen der Linguistik*. Reinbek: Rowohlt.

Linguistic Representation and Conceptual Knowledge Representation

Jan Nuyts

Belgian National Fund for Scientific Research
University of Antwerp

O. Introduction

Recently, Simon Dik (1987a, b, c, 1988a, b, this vol.) has argued that human conceptual knowledge might be cognitively represented in a linguistic format, and particularly in the form of predications as postulated in Functional Grammar (FG). In this paper I will object to this claim, suggesting that conceptual knowledge would rather be non-linguistic. This discussion has obvious consequences for the organization of grammar: while Dik's position implies that current FG is roughly sufficient as a model of the linguistic knowledge of language users, the alternative implies that it will require important 'in depth' expansions with systems relating predications and conceptual knowledge representations. Though I cannot go into these procedural systems here, I will make some speculative suggestions about the direction the development of a conceptual knowledge representation system might take, with special attention to the role of the principle of layering as was introduced in the FG predications by Hengeveld (1987, 1988).

1. Dik's cognitive theory

According to Dik (1988a, this vol.), a language user must possess at least the following cognitive capacities:
(i) A linguistic capacity: the ability to produce and understand linguistic expressions.
(ii) An epistemological capacity: the ability to develop, maintain, and utilize a structured body of knowledge.
(iii) A logical capacity: the ability to reason with knowledge.
(iv) A social capacity: the ability to decide what to say when and where to

whom in order to achieve the communicative intentions.

(v) A perceptual capacity: the ability to perceive the world and to integrate this information into the knowledge base.

So far, Dik's attention has been focussed on capacities (i-iii). For these, he has developed the following hypotheses.

Each of these systems requires some kind of symbolic representation, a 'language': linguistic utterances are generally assumed to be based on more abstract underlying representations (L_{ur}), conceptual knowledge must be coded in some kind of symbolic system (L_{ck}), and the reasoning processes depend on a logical calculus which requires some logical syntax (L_{log}). Of course, one might suppose that these three 'languages' are different. But it is much more attractive to suppose that

(1)   There is one general cognitive representation language L_{cog}, such that
$$L_{cog} = L_{ur} = L_{ck} = L_{log}$$

(Dik 1988a). Let's call this the 'cognitive simplicity postulate' (CSP). If FG-predications are taken to be plausible hypotheses concerning L_{ur}, then, one can conclude that

(2) L_{cog} = predications

Thus, the representation of the language user's knowledge of the state of affairs (SoA) involved in utterance (3a) would be identical to the FG-predication underlying this utterance, (3b).

(3)   a.   Mary gives an apple to John
       b. $give_v$ $(d1x_1: Mary_{pN} (x_1))_{Ag}$ $(i1x_2: apple_N (x_2))_{Go}$
             $(d1x_3: John_{pN} (x_3))_{Rec}$

Hypothesis (2) implies that L_{cog} is linguistic (and even language-specific) in nature, which is in conflict with the more widespread view (especially in artificial intelligence and cognitive psychology - cf. 4.) that conceptual representations have a non-linguistic format. Dik's arguments in favor of his claim include the following.

(a) By accepting (2) there is no need for a very intricate interface which in the alternative view would be required to relate the levels of linguistic and non-linguistic representation (Dik 1988a).

(b) Since humans already possess a representational system with endless possibilities, viz. natural language, why should they not make use of this system for conceptualization? Why should they develop 'shadow-expressions' in some other representational language? (Dik 1987c, 1988a.)

(c) Those claiming that conceptualization is non-linguistic seem not to be able to avoid using lexical labels for identifying concepts when illustrating their models. Where are the non-linguistic representations, then? (Dik 1987c, 1988a.)

(d) If conceptualization is linguistic, knowledge differs with the particular language the individual knows, while the claim as to the non-linguistic nature of conceptualization usually implies that conceptualization is much more universal. But if the latter were the case, why is it that languages are so different? Why should they cover rather than reveal the conceptual structures? (Dik 1987c.)

(e) If conceptualization is language dependent, speakers of different languages can hardly ever be said to have the same knowledge. But this corresponds to the fact that knowledge is strongly culture-bound. And it explains the fact that translatability is hardly ever complete. (Dik 1987c, 1988a.)

Next to conceptual representations, Dik also postulates the existence of 'perceptual representations' or 'images', being the result of perceptual processes due to capacity (v) above (Dik 1987b, 1988b, this vol.). They are introduced in the framework of the 'semantic component' of the Functional Logic (FL) embodying capacity (iii) above. Expressions input to FL (i.e. knowledge in the form of predications) are to be interpreted in terms of a system of mental representations, called 'pictures', which consist of a mixture of conceptual representations (having predicational format again) and perceptual representations (having a non-linguistic format). The exact format of these pictures, and ipso facto of the images, remains open, however.

2. Basic representations in FG

While I have no quarrel with the potential plausibility of predications as representations at some (intermediate) stage in language processing (I take it that FG is a potentially plausible hypothesis concerning (parts of) the systems for language production involved in capacity (i) above - cf. Nuyts 1988: 487ff), there are various reasons to doubt the appropriateness of hypothesis (2). Let's start by considering some linguistic facts from the perspective of FG.

In recent FG, the phenomenon of layering in utterances is beginning to receive due attention (cf. Hengeveld 1988 and many contributions in this vol.).[1] In principle, each layer can bear operators and satellites which somehow qualify the SoA or its expression. Crucial for the present is the fact that at each level, operators and satellites can represent identical qualifications (e.g. tense, modality, aspect), the difference being that operators occur if the qualification gets expression by grammatical means, and satellites if the qualification gets lexical expression. A possible hypothesis is that this difference is determined by the degree of specificity of the qualification and/or of its communicative saliency. As a general principle, one could assume that for each qualification, all values are expressible by lexical means, while only some rough distinctions are grammaticalized in a language (although the degree of grammaticalization is language-specific, of course).

Consider time deixis. The tense operator only allows expression of some rough temporal categories (in English, e.g., past, present, future, relative to the moment of speaking or relative to some moment in the past or in the future). If the speaker wants to give any detail about the temporal situation of an event, he will have to use lexical means. It is very unlikely that there will be any language allowing a grammatical coding of, say, 'in 1585', or 'on the Monday before we first met'.[2] A speaker can also express the categories involved in grammatical tense marking by means of a satellite, and the decision to do so seems determined by communicative considerations (focalizing the temporal element is much easier, or even possible only if it is expressed lexically).

Now, FG adheres to a 'lexical constancy principle' (LCP), saying that

(4)   after determining the predication in the fund of the grammar no
       changes are allowed in the lexical setup of an utterance

(a consequence of the 'no transformations principle' - Dik 1978: 10ff). Hence, it is appropriate to have the division between satellites and operators at the level of the predication. Still, one might wish to have some deeper level in the grammar at which each qualification can be treated as the coherent conceptual phenomenon it appears to be, irrespective of its varying expression forms. This level should be linked to the level of predications by means of decision procedures sensitive to the specificity and communicative saliency of the qualification. (A more complex argumentation on the basis of the interaction of polarity and modality in 'negative raising' can be found in Nuyts 1988: 672ff, 1990.[3])

Not only the level of the layers, but also the 'basic' level of the 'core' predication expressing SoAs provides arguments against (2). A consequence of the claim as to the predicational nature of conceptual knowledge (one which Dik 1987a explicitly accepts) is that, even among speakers of a single language, what appears to be one SoA can be represented in different ways. For example, knowledge of the fact that a person named Johnson has 35 people working for him at least can be represented in terms of the predications (which are given here in a strongly simplified form) corresponding to (5a-d) (examples taken from Dik 1987a),

(5) a. Johnson has 35 employees
     have (Johnson) (35 employees)
    b. Johnson employs 35 people
     employ (Johnson) (35 employees)
    c. There are 35 people working for Johnson
     (there) (work (35 people) (for Johnson))
    d. Johnson gives work to 35 people
     give (Johnson) (work) (to 35 people)

and four individuals can each hold a different one of these. One can say that they do have the same knowledge indirectly, since the language user can derive each of these predications from each of the other ones by means of the FL. This proposal is strongly counterintuitive, however, and even from a strict FG-perspective it is theoretically questionable.

Intuitively, (5a-d) do seem to represent one and the same SoA, the differences between the variants being a matter of alternative presentation of this SoA due to contextual factors (see also 4.1). The relationship between (5a-d) is akin to the relationship between (5b) and (6), and FG does acknowledge the latter to have one underlying predication and only differ in terms of pragmatic function assignment.

(6) 35 people are employed by Johnson

Why should this not be the case for (5a-d) too?

This point is more clearly seen in (7).

(7) a. Mary gives an apple to John
     $give_v$ (d1x_1: Mary$_{pN}$ (x_1))$_{Ag}$ (i1x_2: apple$_N$ (x_2))$_{Go}$
     (d1x_3: John$_{pN}$ (x_3))$_{Rec}$
    b. ?(To) John is given an apple by Mary
     (?)To John an apple is given by Mary
     (?)An apple is given to John by Mary

c.   John gets an apple from Mary
     get_V $(d1x_1: John_{pN} (x_1))_{Ben}$ $(i1x_2: apple_N (x_2))_{Go}$
     $(d1x_3: Mary_{pN} (x_3))_{So(?)}$
d.   ??From Mary an apple is gotten by John
     ??An apple is gotten from Mary by John
     ??An apple is gotten by John from Mary

(7a) and (7c) have different predicational representations in FG, and, hence, would be different pieces of knowledge, while (7a) and (7b), or (7c) and (7d), are distinguished in the expression component, and thus would represent the same piece of knowledge. But the fact that passive variants (7b) (certainly the one closest in word order to (7c)) of (7a) sound somewhat unusual, and that passive variants (7d) of (7c) are practically excluded, can be explained by the fact that (7a) and (7c) already show a relationship very similar to active-passive variation. Both (7b) and (7c) are ways to avoid giving the Agent/Source in the SoA (viz. 'Mary') primary perspective (if necessary it can be left implicit in both cases), and apparently, speakers prefer the lexically coded possibility (7c) over the grammatical operation in (7b). The fact that (7b) remains acceptable while (7d) is nearly impossible, is no doubt due to the fact that it still makes sense to passivize a normal active construction like (7a), while it would be rather paradoxical to further passivize an already passive-like construction like (7c). What would it mean, functionally, to have double passivization?

Another, similar case is (8) (examples from Foley and Van Valin 1984: 57).

(8)   a.   Peter stole the valuable book from Sam
      b.   Peter stole Sam the valuable book
      c.   Peter robbed Sam of the valuable book
      d.   *Peter robbed the valuable book from Sam

(8b) is not synonymous with (8a). Hence, (8a) cannot undergo normal 'dative shift', a generally acknowledged means to de-focalize or de-perspectivize the Recipient in the SoA. Yet, (8c) precisely gives the effect which dative shift of (8a) might have given. (8d) is out because it would involve another dative shift, or rather an 'undoing of the shifting' involved in using (8c) instead of (8a). If no dative-shift is required, the speaker will choose the less marked variant (8a). Hence, the same functional effect frequently achieved by means of alternative function assignment and expression rules in one predication, is achieved by using different predications in (8a) and (8c). (Similar examples from Latin can be found in Bolkestein and Risselada 1987.)

Basically the same observation can be made with special constructions such as clefts, pseudo-clefts, existentials, 'right-dislocations', etc. These are all generally accepted to be marked variants of more neutral utterances, expressing the same basic SoA in different ways due to marked informational (pragmatic-functional) conditions. But they have different predicational representations in FG (cf. e.g. Dik 1980: 210ff; Hannay 1985), and hence, according to (2), would represent different conceptualizations.

This leads at least to the following objections:

(i) If four different individuals each can know one of the predicational alternatives in (5), it seems unavoidable to accept that one individual can know all four of them, too. The fact that these representations might be derivable from each other by means of reasoning rules is no argument in se, since results of reasoning processes can be stored in themselves. Thus, Dik's proposal implies an enormous redundancy in human information storage, which from a cognitive viewpoint is a very unattractive claim.

(ii) It is undesirable to accept the high degree of situation-specificity of conceptual knowledge representation introduced by this proposal. Certainly, people do acquire information (knowledge) in specific situations, but in order to make it available for use in as many different situations as possible, it is necessary to store it in a situation-unbound way. Otherwise, transfer of the information to situations different from those in which it was acquired would be difficult. Dik (1987c: 149) himself mentions among the "good reasons [...] for assuming that knowledge representation structures are more abstract than the actual linguistic expressions of any one language", the fact that "some linguistic expressions are synonymous in the sense of embodying the same knowledge, presented in different ways". He refers to active-passive variants, in which "the differences of presentation may be contextually motivated, but they are not essential to the knowledge of what happened". Apparently, precisely the same is the case in the examples above.

(iii) It is unattractive to handle the relationship between variants like those in (5) in a logic, on a par with real syllogistic reasoning in which different SoAs are combined in order to draw conclusions about other SoAs. This means overburdening a system with two entirely different matters. At the same time it is illogical to treat distinctions such as the active-passive alternation in the grammar properly, and to treat basically similar distinctions such as those between the utterances in (4) or between (7/8a) and (7/8c) as a matter of variability baked into the knowledge representations.

From an FG-perspective, what seems to be required is a representational level more basic than the predicational, allowing the specification of one common structure for the alternative expressions of modifiers, for the variants in (5), (7), (8), etc. This level will have to be linked to the predicational level by contextualization strategies which determine not only word order and intonation, but also the choice of lexical items and construction types.[4] The structures at this more basic level constitute the L_{cog} in (2), and FL would apply only to them.

One might suggest that this deeper level is still predicational, containing only pragmatically neutral predications. But it is hard to see which of the variants in (5), e.g., could be chosen as the neutral one on a non-arbitrary basis. Moreover, this proposal would mean allowing at a deeper level in the grammar what is forbidden at more superficial levels according to the LCP. For, changing from the 'neutral' predication at the deepest level to pragmatically marked types of predications will frequently involve considerable changes in the lexical material.

In fact, various other arguments also bring the very idea of conceptualizations being lexical in nature into question.

3. Questions for lexical conceptualizations

3.1. Lexical form and meaning

Various behavioral phenomena indicate that, cognitively, information and lexical expression of information are different things. Consider the simple everyday phenomenon of having word-finding problems, or, in the domain of language pathology, amnesia. Apparently, speakers can know what to say, but fail to find appropriate lexicalizations. Basically the same has been observed in (part of the) experimental research into memory for the verbal form of utterances (Bransford and Franks 1972; Johnson-Laird 1974; cf. also Hesp this vol.). Language users soon forget the exact verbal structure of utterances, and only remember the meaning, enriched with inferential information based on general knowledge of the world. It is not clear why these things should happen if conceptualizations are lexical.

More recent experiments have shown better recognition or remembrance of the verbal form of utterances produced or heard in experimental conditions (e.g. Bates et al. 1978; Hjelmquist 1984, 1987). But these results do not challenge the earlier findings, on the contrary. First of all, recognition of meaning still proved to be much better than recognition of the verbal form in which it was caught. Secondly, the recognition of verbal aspects of utterances can, contrary to Hjelmquist's suggestion, easily be explained on the basis of a principle of 'reconstructability' (Brewer and Hay 1984). A speaker's utterances in context are not accidental expressions of their meaning: the situational conditions lead him to very specific choices in order to get a functionally appropriate formulation. Hence, most utterances are not exchangeable in their context. Thus, when tested on his recognition or remembrance of verbal patterns which he has uttered or heard before, it is not unlikely that a speaker is able to quite accurately reconstruct which utterances have been used and which not, because he has information stored concerning the meaning and the specific situational conditions.

This explains the differences between these recent findings and the older results in which no memory for verbal form was found. The latter were due to experimental conditions in which utterances were used without a natural conversational context, which therefore excluded reconstructability, while the results showing some gist for verbal form stem from experiments in which there was a realistic conversational context, indeed. Another observation fitting in nicely with the reconstructability hypothesis is that memory for verbal form was much better for the subject's own utterances than for utterances made by the conversation partner (Jarvella and Collas 1974; Hjelmquist and Gidlund 1985). Each individual has his/her own linguistic style, and a speaker can judge better what he himself would say in some context than what someone else would say in the same context.

Another case in point is translation. Translating is transposing an expression in one language into an expression in another language, preserving the meaning as precisely as possible. How should this be accounted for without accepting a to-be-preserved and hence language-independent meaning next to the lexical expressions in the languages involved? Moreover, accepting a more abstract meaning representation as the mediator for translation between verbal structures in languages seems hardly less attractive than the procedure which would have to be followed according to Dik's proposal, contrary to what he (1987a, 1987c) suggests.

In Dik's proposal translation would only be possible through a 'translation dictionary'. E.g., translating the lexical item *pinball machine* into Dutch would only be possible through a dictionary entry saying '*pinball machine* = *flipperkast*'. But suppose some language which does not have a lexical item for this object. Translation would only be possible by means of the 'meaning definition' (present in the FG-lexicon, and, of course, again predicational, and thus language-specific) linked to the English word (e.g. something in the style of Webster's definition: "an amusement device in which a ball propelled by a plunger scores points as it rolls down a slanting surface among pins and targets"), of which each individual word would have to be translated into the target language (of course supposing that there is a translation entry for each of these words) (see Van der Korst 1987). It seems no less efficient to suppose that the translator grasps an abstract concept of the object 'pinball machine', and has to look for a related concept for which the target language does have a lexical item, or, alternatively, has to circumscribe the concept through specifying its embedding in a larger conceptual context in terms of the target language.

The fact that translation may be difficult (cf. 1. (e)) does not affect this proposal. It is no doubt true that knowledge is culture bound (this is not at all in conflict with the claim that conceptualization is non-verbal, contrary to what is suggested in 1. (d) - if the object 'pinball machine' is not known in some culture, people do not have a concept for it), and that language plays a crucial role in transmitting it. The way language, being an important means for acquiring and transmitting knowledge, allows us to structure information undoubtedly influences the way we conceptualize the world, just as the way we conceptualize the world no doubt influences linguistic structure (cf. e.g. Miller and Johnson-Laird 1976 for illustrations of how general perceptual categories are reflected in linguistic structure). Translation problems may be due, then, to differences in the way languages allow the structuring of the same basic information, but also, mainly, to the difficulties facing a translator in communicating the way speakers of a specific language conceptualize the world to speakers of another language.

The fact that languages seem to cover conceptualizations and do structure information differently is not an argument either. Argument (d) in 1. could be used against any proposal accepting representations more abstract than surface structure. If predications were basic, why do languages not reveal them directly? Obviously, the answer is that languages must allow one piece of information to be expressed in pragmatically different ways (cf. 2.). And if predications were basic, why do different languages use such different grammatical devices for expressing them? Here, the answer is that every language makes its own choice from the means for information structuring made available by the transmission channel it uses (the articulatory, acoustic and auditive), and this choice is due to a historically developed convention within the linguistic community. But, obviously, these answers are equally valid for non-lexical basic representations. Of course, it is misleading in itself to claim that linguistic utterances 'cover' non-verbal conceptualizations. Their purpose is to allow a speaker to communicate the conceptual information as exactly as possible (which is not an easy thing to do, as any scientist knows - again, it is not clear why that would be if conceptualization were verbal). Only, this happens (or has to happen) according to structural principles different from those of the conceptual representations.

Actually, if conceptualization is language specific, this would seem to imply that bilinguals or multilinguals conceptualize the world two or more times. This is cognitively not a very attractive claim.

The main point of the above observations can also be stated theoretically. According to traditional (Saussurean) definitions, language is a system of forms and meanings which are conventionally linked together, the former being arbitrary symbolizations of the latter. From a functional perspective, the formal symbols are used by humans to communicate, i.e. to transmit information (meanings) in order to act upon other humans. Formulating meanings and recovering meanings, that is what communication is all about. This seems trivial, but it is hard to see how the claim that conceptualizations are linguistic can be reconciled with it. Lexical items being formal and arbitrary labels referring to meanings (a view which is recognized in FG, since terms, and recently also predications (Vet 1986), do contain referential variables), where are these meanings (the referents of the terms and predications)? Unless one wants to return to an objectivist semantics, i.e. a semantics in which meaning is caught in terms of reference to the external world (a semantics which Dik (cf. e.g. 1988b) clearly rejects, too) it seems hard to avoid accepting non-verbal conceptual systems representing the meaning of verbal expressions.

In fact, Dik (1987c: 164) himself introduces a notion of concepts to which lexical labels are attached:

(9) a. $x_{320} = (d1x_{320}:$ John Parker$_{pN}$ $(x_{320}))$
     b. $x_{203} = (d1$ next $x_{203}:$ month$_N$ $(x_{203}):$ August$_{pN}$ $(x_{203}))$

Moreover, Dik (1988b, this vol.) postulates that predications have to be interpreted in terms of pictures, which (at least partially) appear to be non-verbal in nature (we can suppose that concepts such as x_{320} and x_{203} belong to this non-verbal part of the pictures, the 'images'). It is strange, however, that he considers this interpretation process to be a matter of reasoning with knowledge, and not of genuine utterance interpretation. Dik's proposal implies that conceptual knowledge is stored as non-interpreted (non-understood, so to speak) form, which can be interpreted if required.[5]

Correlated with this, it is also misleading to speak of conceptual representation in terms of a 'language', as is done in (1). A language would be defined as a formal system used for communication of meanings, and hence having a semantics. But conceptualization is obviously not a communication system. It is improper to consider it to be a syntax having a semantics, it must rather be understood as a 'pure semantics', whatever that will turn out to be (cf. Johnson-Laird 1983: 419). Otherwise we end up with a (potentially infinite) regression, in which the conceptual language has to be interpreted in terms of another 'language' which again has to be interpreted ... (etc.). The latter may be common practice in many (especially formal semantic) theories, but it is cognitively very implausible.

3.2. Language and other aspects of behavior

Let's view the matter from the wider perspective of human cognition and action in general. Obviously, language is only one of the sources for human perception, next to other auditory, but also visual, tactile, olfactory, etc. sources, which all lead to knowledge of the world.[6] And language is only one of the means humans have for communication, and more generally for interaction with the environment, and the many other behaviors are based on conceptualizations all the same. Should we suppose, then, that for each type of perceptual and behavioral 'channel' there is a different type of conceptual representation specific to the channel's characteristics? Or, alternatively, that there is one central type of conceptual representation integrating information from all perceptual sources, and serving as the common basis for all types of behaviors? The former view is unattractive: it implies that a lot of information might have to be stored many times in terms of the different conceptualization types, it requires an enormous amount of cross-interfacing between them if human knowledge is still to be seen as an integrated system (considering a human being as an internally segregated system would be rather counterintuitive), and it leads to an overly complex reasoning system which has to be able to work in terms of the different representation types. It is much more attractive to accept the latter view, i.e. the CSP (cf. (1)) also used by Dik in his argumentation.

Yet, note that Dik, his own argumentation notwithstanding, abandons the CSP by proposing that predicational representations and 'images', whatever their nature, exist side by side, since this implies that there are two cognitive representation systems anyway.[7] If we do stick to the CSP and accept only one type of core representation, however, the claim that it is verbal raises a number of questions, also from this more general perspective. A child starts perceiving and behaving (also communicatively) before it starts developing language, and, as is widely accepted in developmental psychology, language acquisition strongly depends upon the development of general conceptual capacities, and upon more primitive, non-verbal communication systems existing prior to language (a survey of the literature in Gillis 1984). How are we to understand the nature of pre-linguistic conceptualization in a child, then? And why should a representation type due to a perceptual and behavioral system which develops relatively late acquire the status of central representational system for conceptualization, while representations due to earlier perceptual and behavioral systems do not?[8] One could as well, or maybe even better, claim that visually based representations acquire this status. After all, they are crucial from the beginning of human development, and remain so throughout human life. Though such as suggestion would have its problems, too: it is hard to see how concept x_{203} in (9b) above, or a conceptualization of whatever other non-physical element, could be visual. Finally, how are we to grapple with the knowledge that people born deaf and/or mute, who hardly ever acquire natural language, still have cognitive capacities which seem qualitatively undistinguishable from the cognitive capacities of normal individuals (e.g. Lenneberg 1967)?

It seems more reasonable to assume that conceptualization is a matter of developing a representational system which is not specifically determined by and thus not biased toward one specific mode of perception and behavior such as the linguistic or visual one, but which steers a midway between the different channels (i.e. allows to store information from the different channels in a uniform way). (The above at once provides an answer to argument (b) in 1.)

Of course, between this system and the purely physical level of perception and behavior there have to be levels of representation more specific to the different channels. One can assume that the principles of these representations are constantly accessible by the central system. And one can also assume a perfect parallelism between language and the other channels in this respect. For each channel one could assume a 'lexicon' of basic 'labels' which correspond to concepts or conceptual conglomerates of the central system, and which can be used in perceiving and behaving through the specific channel according to the 'rules' or 'procedures' for combining them, or for decoding their combination. Thus, the concept of garlic might have linked to it a verbal lexical, but also a 'visual-lexical', an 'olfactory-lexical', etc. label. If someone is asked how garlic smells, he can mentally 'imagine' this smell by invoking its 'olfactory-lexical' label. Humans have not developed the olfactory channel into a means for actively interacting or communicating with their environment (though production of smell does play an important role in human interaction at an unconscious level, e.g. in mating behavior - cf. Argyle and Trower 1979). That is, they do have a limited 'receptive grammar' for smell, but hardly a 'productive grammar'. Thus, in absence of a piece of garlic, the one asked might try to imagine an object with a comparable smell (onion for example) and provide the information requested by verbally referring to this object.

The situation is quantitatively, but not qualitatively different for vision. Humans not only have an extensive capacity for visual perception, but also for visual behavior. They can productively create quite complicated visual images mentally, and they can also exteriorize them in drawings, paintings, etc. Cf. also the fact that some written communication systems, e.g. the Egyptian, strongly rely(d) on visual representation. Hence, not only the receptive, but also the productive 'grammar' of the visual channel is rather well-developed. (An interesting parallelism between the different channels (including the linguistic) is that the receptive capacity seems always to be stronger than the productive capacity.)

This proposal allows us to account for the empirical evidence 'pictorialists' have always used for their claim that imagery is pictorial in nature (cf. Block (ed.) 1981), without having to claim that conceptualization is pictorial indeed. It also allows us to account for the difference between individuals' intuitions, frequently mentioned in the imagery debate: some people suggest they frequently take recourse to 'pictorial' representations in mental activity, while others claim they often make use of language-like representations (cf. also Chafe 1977b). One can suppose that the conceptual system of rather visually oriented individuals is inclined to draw upon the visual channel if necessary, while the conceptual system of the more verbally oriented individuals will rather draw upon the linguistic channel.

Note that the interface problem, which Dik uses in his argumentation ((a) in 1.), exists whatever theory one adopts, since there have to be connections between types of representations occurring in cognitive processing anyway. If conceptualizations were verbal, there would still have to be interfaces with other levels of representation (visual, olfactory, etc.). In Dik's 'pictures', there has to be an interface between the predications and the images. Hence, Dik's proposal only moves the interface-problem from grammar to other domains of inquiry. For the linguist this may be a practical situation, but within a larger cognitive framework it is not likely to reduce the problems at all.

The foregoing argumentation obviously does not exclude humans storing more complex channel-specific representations, if necessary. In an experiment Johnson-Laird (1983: 162ff) has found that people better remember a verbal representation in case of indeterminate discourse, i.e. discourse for which they cannot form a clear interpretation (a 'mental model'). Yet, nothing in the experiment shows that this representation is definitively stored as a conceptualization (the experiment only tested memory during a short time span). Rather (and remaining within the spirit of Johnson-Laird's proposals), one could assume that the language user keeps this representation in memory for a while, still trying to interpret it, and ultimately either forcing an interpretation in terms of a mental model (which frequently happens, as Johnson-Laird states - cf. also Bredart 1987), or, if this is not possible, gradually forgetting it. The same mechanism might be postulated for the other channels as well.

Another case of storing channel specific representations occurs when memorizing a text, a picture, etc. Yet, it is not a priori clear whether in such case a person stores, e.g., the text itself, or rather the meaning of the text plus a path through lexicon and grammar allowing a reconstruction of the verbal form of the text. However, in the former case predicational representations cannot do the job either: the language user has to memorize the surface structure of the utterances. Moreover, it will be clear that this type of storing is rather exceptional. Which is reflected in the fact that it is much more difficult than simply understanding and storing the meaning of a text.

4. Prospects for a model of conceptualization

If representations more abstract than predications (something which in Dik's model would constitute the 'images'[9]) have to be introduced as conceptual representations, and, hence, as basic representations in the grammar, what should they look like? At present, no full-fledged answer is possible. There are plenty of proposals available in the literature (different types of logical representations (e.g. Winograd 1972), of semantic networks (e.g. Quillian 1968; Schank 1975), Johnson-Laird's (1983) mental models, etc.). But they are either undeveloped (e.g. Johnson-Laird's mental models) or disputable (e.g. one can question whether Schank's 'primitive relations' really are primitive - cf. also Johnson-Laird 1977; a general critique of models of conceptual representation in Johnson-Laird 1983: 205ff). One difficulty is that proposals are mainly based on intuitive choices, without clear arguments for the plausibility of the representations introduced. This is due to the fact that at present it is hard to pin down which characteristics the system should have in order to account for the many complex aspects of human behavior and perception. As indicated in 3.2, one needs insight into the requirements posed by the different channels of perception and behavior and their interactions. But of these, language is no doubt the best explored, and even then our knowledge is far from stable. (The fact that most proposals have been conceived from the perspective of natural language only is also potentially biasing - cf. Chafe 1977a.) Developing a serious hypothesis about the format of conceptual representation is thus going to be a very long term project.

Hence, the fact that current discussions of conceptualizations tend to use lexical labels to refer to concepts (cf. (c) in 1.) can hardly be used against them. As long as it is unclear how they should be conceived, some arbitrary notational convention is needed for the purpose of scientific communication. One can use numbers, as Dik does in (8), but since scientific communication is normally linguistic, one can use linguistic means as well. The fact that we are still innocent about what conceptualizations might look like is not an argument either. (Dik's model is faced with the same problem as far as the 'images' are concerned.) More and more physicists accept that there must be a fifth dimension (and some claim even more) next to the four dimensions of space and time on which modern physics is built, even though so far nobody has been able to indicate how this fifth dimension is realized physically. If the argumentation for non-verbal conceptualizations is sound, we simply have to accept the idea, and develop strategies to find out about them.

One thing is clear from the outset: conceptualization will not turn out to be a simple thing.[10] Most probably, it should be conceived as a complex system of representations of 'basic' information about the world, which can have or receive different kinds of most probably hierarchically organized 'meta-level qualifications' from the speaker.

4.1. The representation of states of affairs

The 'basic' level is constituted by the states of affairs (SoA) in reality about which the language user has knowledge. This has to be a vast system, including knowledge of things in the object-world (a taxonomy of animals, how my kitchen is organized, etc.) and the social world (what is a president, which social norms exist in the different social communities to which I belong, etc.), of persons and who they are, what they know, etc. (including knowledge of what I myself (think I) am), of past experiences, etc. This involves both 'knowledge that' (that a robin is a bird, that xyz is my boss, etc.) and 'knowledge how' (how to play chess, how to socially behave toward a president, etc.). Moreover, there will have to be different levels of generality in knowledge (one has knowledge about individual restaurant-experiences, but also, and (partially) as a generalization about them, knowledge about what happens and how one behaves in a restaurant in general). Hence, conceptual knowledge is multidimensional, and how this can be modelled at a macro-level, respecting the many different relations between parts of this knowledge, is an open question (cf. e.g. Schank 1980 for some suggestions).

At the micro-level of organization, conceptualizations have to consist of mutually related concepts. Most probably we have to assume the existence of quite complex clusters of interrelated concepts - in any case more complex than the information which is normally represented in one natural language utterance. The experimental investigations cited in 3.1 have shown that understanding utterances involves embedding the information in a larger context of inferentially related information. And forming an utterance can be seen as abstracting a piece of information from a larger 'chunk' (Chafe 1977a, 1977b) (a discourse can be seen as a systematic deployment of all the relevant information from a coherent chunk of conceptual knowledge). This might be taken as a suggestion that a semantic network really is the most appropriate way to represent conceptual knowledge (despite its disadvantages, cf. Johnson-Laird 1983: 211ff). If so, one can assume that the organizational principles of this network (the types of relations occurring) are universal, while which concepts are present, and how they are interrelated, is variable, and, hence, specific to cultures, social groups, education, etc. No two individuals have identical conceptual networks. Thus, it is no problem to account for the fact that houses are quite different things in different cultures. Although an 'average' western European, an 'average' Nepalese and an 'average' Eskimo all have a concept of a house, the conceptual information linked to it and defining it will be quite different, irrespective of the languages spoken.

With respect to the concepts, there is no need for 'semantic decomposition': concepts do not have to be primitive, not further analyzable elements. People have concepts of whatever is a discrete phenomenon to them, while in reality these phenomena can be complex, composed of more fundamental elements. E.g., many people will have a concept of '(biological) evolution', although this is a very complex phenomenon. In the conceptual world of some (e.g. biologists), this may be reflected in the fact that 'evolution' will be a 'very high generalization' concept which, at lower levels of generalization, is linked to much more detailed chunks of information. But in most laymen's conceptualizations, evolution will be a rather 'low generalization' concept having hardly any more specific information linked to it.

Since the conceptual relations are supposedly universal, however, one might look for a set of primitive relations. The problem is to determine what relations are 'primitive'. One could start out with a minimal assumption. There can be little doubt about the primitiveness of the relations of 'being' (B), 'having' (H) and 'doing' (D). Probably this set is too limited, and there is no reason not to expand it if further analyses force one to. But it already suffices to represent a number of other relations which in the literature have been claimed to be primitive. E.g., causation might be represented as in (10).

(10)
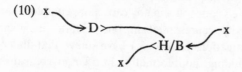

('x' represents concepts, >D>, >H>, and >B> indicate the type of (oriented) relationship holding between them.) 'Cause' is then a 'higher generalization' concept over cluster (10).

By means of this set, one can also provide basic representations for the sets of utterances discussed in 2. (7), e.g., involves the transfer of an object. Schank (1975) considers this a primitive relation, yet (11) seems to provide an even more basic representation (in which 'T' stands for the temporal situation of a conceptual relationship or cluster).

(11)
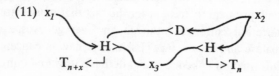

Verbal lexicon:
$x_1 = (d1x_1: John_{pN} (x_1))$
$x_2 = (d1x_2: Mary_{pN} (x_2))$
$x_3 = (i1x_3: apple_N (x_3))$

Of course, the D-relation in this network can have different properties. If there is no further conceptual specification, the 'neutral' predicates *give/ get* can be chosen. But the D-arrow could also have a B-relation with a concept of 'throw', e.g., which would be a 'higher generalization' concept having linked to it a 'lower generalization' conceptual cluster specifying what is involved in throwing. In that case, the speaker might choose *throw* as a predicate. Or the conceptualization in (11) might be embedded in a wider conceptualization also involving the knowledge that this happened in an official context, which might lead the speaker to the predicate *hand over/receive*. This clearly shows how a relatively simple utterance can require a rather complex conceptual representation.

The same can be said for the examples in (5). A conceptual representation would also include indirect information provided in these utterances, e.g. that Johnson is the boss of a business, that he pays people to do work for him, etc. In this respect, there can (but does not have to) be a difference between (5a-b) and (5c-d). Though they all provide the same direct information, the former only seem possible if the further information just mentioned does apply, while the latter are less committing with respect to this indirect information. Hence, a speaker can choose the latter as 'synonymous' with the former in a context in which this indirect information is or will become clear to the hearer. He can choose the former if he wants to provide this indirect information at once.

The above analysis suggests that there is no direct correspondence between the distinctions concept/relation at the conceptual level and noun/verb at the linguistic level: the relationship is complex. Neither does there have to be a one-to-one relationship between concepts and lexical items (as Dik's example (9b) already suggests). Though there certainly will be a tendency to introduce a verbal lexical label for every concept that is sufficiently salient and general, people can have concepts for which they have no single lexical label, and which they can only express verbally by means of circumscriptions. Thus, you will certainly not have a name for every single chair you have at home, and in their immediate neighborhood you can refer to them by means of deictic elements like *that chair* (combined with finger pointing), but otherwise you can only use circumscriptions like *the chair between the table and the window*. All of this goes to show that conceptualization is certainly not a 'shadow-representation' (cf. (b) in 1.) of linguistic representation.

4.2. Meta-level qualifications of SoAs

Next to this 'basic' level of representation of SoAs, conceptualization also has to involve various sorts of meta-qualifications. This corresponds to the principle of layering accepted at the predicational level in current FG, but then at a more basic level.[11] Again, there is no reason to believe that representations of qualifications at the conceptual level are a simple 'shadow' of qualifying expressions at the linguistic level, as was already indicated in 2. Although we may expect that all major distinctions at the conceptual level will somehow find expression at the linguistic level, and that this expression will respect the (hierarchical) relationships holding between qualifications at the conceptual level, the structuring principles at each level may be quite different.

Let's take Hengeveld's (1987, 1988) proposal for a layered structure of the predication as a starting point. How does this fit into a system distinguishing between conceptual and predicational representations? In the first place, Hengeveld's motivation for structuring the layers at the predicational level (which in our system is an intermediate level in the constitution of an utterance) is not obvious. In his characterization of the two main layers of a clause (each of which contains two further layers), the inner layer stands for the utterance as a structure referring to (designating) an SoA (the narrated event), while the outer layer stands for the utterance as a structure serving a communicative intention of the speaker (the speech event). This distinction is further motivated with the distinction between the representational and the interpersonal dimensions of language (for which he refers to Bühler (1934) and Halliday (1970), respectively).

But, first, in terms of a general analysis of the functionality of linguistic behavior the distinction between a representational and an interpersonal dimension is not evident (Nuyts 1988: 155ff, 1989a). The notion 'interpersonal' can be interpreted in at least two ways. From one perspective, language is a medium for interpersonal (in the sense of 'interactive', 'communicative') behavior (communication is the 'role function' of language), and utterances have a number of properties ('organic functions') which allow them to serve this purpose. Representation of information is one of them. Hence, in this perspective the representational dimension is one of a number of dimensions of language which constitute its use as a medium for interpersonal interaction. The representational is an aspect of the interpersonal, and therefore they cannot be juxtaposed.

From another perspective, viz. that of the 'organic functions' of language (what language does in communication), the conflation of Bühler's 'Ausdruck' and 'Appell' functions into one 'interpersonal' function in Halliday's system is very disputable. Without going into details here (cf. Nuyts 1988: 182ff, 1989a), the main point is that the speaker and the hearer are two distinct positions in communication, which from the perspective of the speaker have a distinct influence on the constitution of utterances. Hence, at this level the interpersonal (in Halliday's sense) is not a distinct dimension at all. Rather, one has to differentiate between an intentional and a social dimension, next to the 'referential' or 'informative' dimension.

Second, Hengeveld's suggestion that specific strata in the structure of an utterance would directly relate to specific functional dimensions of the type just mentioned is akin to Halliday's conception of grammar, but is again disputable (cf. Nuyts 1988: 278ff). It is more likely that there is a complex relation between function and form (cf. also Dik 1986), in which the (conceptually) different functional dimensions can interfere in determining individual structural phenomena at the different levels in a grammar (including the predicational level). The latter view is explicitly accepted in the expression component in FG (and FPG), so it would seem illogical to introduce a conflicting principle in the predicational component of the grammar. This observation corresponds to the fact that it is hard to conceive what it means to say that an utterance consists of a narrated event and a speech event as distinguishable things. There is only one event, the 'speech event', which involves aspects of narration (at least sometimes: in questions and orders it is hard to use this notion).

Of course, in view of a differentiation between the conceptual and the linguistic level of representation it is appropriate to make a distinction between matters which relate to the conceptual SoA and its relation to other aspects of conceptualization, and matters which relate to the constitution of an utterance in which the SoA is expressed, in terms of where and how they ought to play a role in the grammar. To the latter category one can count all elements related to the illocutionary potential of an utterance (Hengeveld's ILL and its mitigating and reinforcing operators). Since illocutions are markers of an action potential, they are only introduced at the moment when the process of constituting an utterance is being started. They are not aspects of the conceptual knowledge representations, although the sources for their assignment (including mitigated or reinforced variants) obviously do have to be present in conceptualization. Actions are caused and determined by specific constellations in the speaker's knowledge of the SoA (e.g. conflict between pieces of information or lacking information can lead to a question, a divergence of an SoA in reality from the speaker's ideal conception of that SoA can lead to a request or an order, etc.), by his intentions evolving from the specifics of the SoA (the intention to complete knowledge of an SoA can lead to a question, the intention to change an SoA to a request or an order, etc.), and by his social relationship with the hearer (e.g. the choice between a certain illocution (e.g. an order) or a mitigated variant of it (e.g. a request)).[12]

All other qualifications in Hengeveld's proposal can be assumed to be relevant in conceptualization, since they all concern the information contained in the conceptual SoA. This also goes for what in Hengeveld's system could be called 'proposition qualifiers' (operators and satellites): in line with the above argumentation, it is unclear why they should be a matter of the speech event more or less like illocutionary matters and as opposed to lower level qualifications which would be a matter of the SoA referred to, as in Hengeveld's system. Evidentiality concerns the source of the speaker's information, and there is no need to relate this to the utterance per se rather than to the SoA referred to. Similarly for subjective modality. Hengeveld (1987: 16) postulates that the difference between 'subjective' and 'objective' modality is a matter of different types of modal qualifications concerning different aspects of an utterance. The latter would be a matter of the speaker's evaluation of an SoA in terms of his general knowledge; the former would be a matter of expressing a degree of commitment of the speaker as to the truth of the content of the proposition put forward. Yet, one would assume that the degree of commitment of a speaker as to the truth of the content of an utterance *is* a matter of evaluating the chances of occurrence of the SoA expressed in the utterance, on the basis of his general knowledge. As argued in Nuyts (1988: 711ff, 1990), rather than being modal qualifications at different levels, the difference between Hengeveld's 'subjective' and 'objective' modality is a matter of a difference in the speaker's evidence (sources) for formulating one and the same modal qualification of an SoA. In the former the source is the speaker's purely subjective evaluation, in the latter it is a more widespread 'public' opinion.[13]

As to the types of conceptual qualifications, one can largely adopt the individual categories occurring in Hengeveld's proposal, although specific alterations (as in the case of subjective vs. objective modality discussed above) and additions may be required. E.g., one could add a qualification indicating whether the SoA belongs to the real world or to a deviant possible world (realis/irrealis), and one indicating the speaker's attitude toward the SoA (emotional involvement in terms of liking or disliking, required to account e.g. for satellites such as 'damned', or for the choice between ameliorative vs. pejorative terms or predicates).

Concerning the hierarchical ordering of the qualifications, we may have to drop the division in 'macro-layers' proposed by Hengeveld. As argued above, Hengeveld's main division seems hard to motivate; and upon closer examination one has to accept hierarchical relations between qualifications which in Hengeveld's system are situated at one 'macro-layer' as well (see below - cf. also Harder this vol.). Hence, there seem to be reasons to introduce (at least at the conceptual level - see below) a much more gradual system in which each qualification occupies its own 'layer' or level (as in Foley and Van Valin 1984).[14] The succession may be more or less according to the hierarchy of individual qualifications in Hengeveld's proposal, and the rationale behind it seems to be that a qualification more inherent to the SoA is on a lower level than a qualification imposed upon the SoA by the speaker.[15] E.g., a temporal location is a more inherent property of an SoA than a qualification in terms epistemic modality. In view of this, the 'attitude' qualifier will certainly constitute one of the outermost layers. The 'reality/irreality' qualification can be expected to be somewhere between temporal qualification and epistemic modality.

In some respects Hengeveld's hierarchy seems to require changes. E.g., deontic modality is certainly not at the same level as epistemic modality. While epistemic modality can only have temporal qualification within its domain, and not vice versa, deontic modality and temporal qualification can extend over each other, as appears in (12).

(12) a.   John was probably going yesterday
      b.   John was obliged to go yesterday
      c.   John was probably obliged to go yesterday

(12a) can only be read with the temporal qualification within the domain of the epistemic modality. (12b/c), however, are ambiguous as to the relative domain of the temporal and deontic qualifications. In (12c), the deontic modality can only be read as being within the domain of the epistemic modality, but not vice versa. Cf. also (13).

(13) *John was obliged probably to go yesterday

We may also have to allow a greater flexibility in the hierarchical position and scope of (some of the) qualifiers than is accorded in Hengeveld's system. As to hierarchical position, a first example was given in (12b). Apparently, it is not possible to postulate a fixed position of temporal qualification and deontic modality relative to each other. Another example is negation, which in Hengeveld's proposal is already introduced at two levels (predicate negation, and polarity as a predication operator). Rather than being two different qualifiers, this can be considered one qualification operating at two different levels. Cf. also (14).

(14) John didn't go to the movies yesterday

(14) can be read as 'not < John went to the movies yesterday >' or as 'yesterday < John did not go to the movies >' (next to other readings, e.g. with the negative only covering the temporal qualification - see below).

As to the extension of scope, each qualification may cover chunks of conceptual knowledge of variable size: one relator, a set of two related concepts, or some larger complex of concepts. (They can certainly extend over the information provided in a series of subsequent natural language utterances; but they can also extend over information provided in a single term only. Hence, the different qualifications which can occur in an utterance can also occur in a term, albeit in a different formal expression (cf. Rijkhoff's this vol. attempt to relate qualifications at the term level and at the predication level). Cf. Nuyts (1989b) on these matters of extension of scope.) They can also cover each other. Thus, a temporal location of a SoA can be qualified in terms of its probability, without necessarily implying that the SoA itself is also qualified in terms of this probability. E.g., (12c) is ambiguous as to whether the epistemic modality only covers the temporal qualification, or the SoA and the temporal qualification, or even the SoA and the temporal and deontic qualifications. Or it can also be read with the epistemic modality only having the deontic modality in its scope. Similar problems exist in (14). Obviously, the precise relationship between extension of scope and hierarchical position is a matter which deserves further investigation.

A factor which may play a role in the very complex picture emerging from the above examples is that, next to levels of qualification, it is also possible to have levels of embedding of conceptualization (i.e. having 'mental models' within 'mental models'). E.g., in (15)

(15) Probably John thinks that I am crazy

John thinks that I am crazy is a SoA to the speaker, in itself involving a qualification by John of a SoA, which is qualified by the speaker for epistemic modality.

Finally, if all these qualifications are present in conceptualization, one may wonder whether it is still necessary to maintain a detailed system such as Hengeveld's at the predicational level. Maybe it is sufficient to distinguish a relatively small set of categories of operators and satellites there, each of which is 'used' by a number of different conceptual qualifications according to principles which ought to be further investigated. E.g., tense as an operator at the predicational level can be used to express temporal situation, but also irreality (cf. the use of the preterit for that purpose). Or mood can be used to express matters related to evidentiality (cf. the use of the subjunctive in certain types of quotatives in some languages, including German) or to modality (cf. the use of the indicative or subjunctive in Spanish - Hengeveld 1987), next to matters related to illocution. Maybe it is also not necessary to explicitly handle matters of scope at the predicational level: cf. the difficulties that would arise if one attempted to handle the different readings of the scope relationships in (12c) in terms of layers in the FG-predications. A treatment in these terms at the conceptual level of representation would be much easier - cf. Nuyts (1990). At the predicational level, it could be sufficient to specify an operator on the predicate or to add a satellite to the predication, and to clearly mark the Focus of the utterance (very often a qualification only appears to have the Focus in its scope - cf. Bossuyt 1982, Dik et al. this vol.), or just to leave the rest to the interpretation of the hearer if there are enough contextual clues to disambiguate possible alternative scope assignments.

It seems that only the tip of the veil has been lifted in matters layering (and conceptualization). How qualifications in conceptual and predicational representation will ultimately have to look like is an entirely open question.

5. Conclusion

I have argued that Dik's suggestion that conceptualization is predicational faces a number of difficulties. Further, I have tried to make some suggestions for the direction an alternative proposal might take. Obviously, developing a full-fledged model is not going to be an easy job. But that is not a reason not to go ahead with it.[16]

Notes

1. This fits into a more widespread tendency, not only in linguistics (Foley and Van Valin 1984), but also in cognitive psychology (Johnson-Laird 1983; Clark 1987). Layering (meta-level qualification of states of affairs) has also been proposed in Functional Procedural Grammar (FPG) (De Schutter and Nuyts 1983; Nuyts 1988: 636ff, 1989b). See also 4. The (sometimes considerable) differences between these proposals are immaterial to the present discussion.

2. This principle also works for term-modification: English, e.g., only allows a grammatical marking for 'one' (singular) and 'more than one' (plural). Some languages also have a marking for 'two', or for 'few'. But no language has a grammatical category for every numeral it has.

3. This analysis also provides some difficulties for Hengeveld's (1987) conception of modality, and for some of his proposals concerning layering - cf. Nuyts (1988: 711ff, 1990).

4. Once again, this is an argument for replacing the pragmatic functions in FG, not only to a position before the syntactic functions, but also to a position before the predication, as in FPG. Cf. Nuyts (1988: 487ff). See also Bolkestein and Risselada (1987).

5. Dik's proposal that the pictures against which representations input to FL are interpreted include conceptual representations, also leads to the rather paradoxical suggestion that 'non-

'interpreted' conceptual representations can play a role in interpreting conceptual representations.

6. Dik distinguishes between conceptual and perceptual knowledge, but it is hard to see why such a distinction should be made. Obviously, conceptualization is based on perception, as is widely accepted in cognitive psychology (cf. Miller and Johnson-Laird 1976; Block (ed.) 1981: 9ff). One could only speak of perceptual representations as intermediate representations formed in the course of processing all kinds of inputs and leading to conceptual representations.

7. In itself, this is not an exceptional proposal. Some 'pictorialists' (e.g. Kosslyn 1978) also claim that mental representation consists of a mixture of propositional (i.e. descriptional) and pictorial representations. I will not go into the 'imagery' debate here (an overview in Block (ed.) 1981).

8. These considerations are formulated from a Piagetian rather than a Wygotskian perspective. But even in Wygotski's (1974) view, in which language (inner speech) plays a crucial role in developing general conceptual capacities (which certainly is plausible, and is not really in conflict with Piaget's views), conceptualizations end up being non-verbal.

9. Dik apparently does not intend his images to be visual - this is clear from his reference to, e.g., Johnson-Laird's (1983) mental models as a possible filling in for them. Actually, Johnson-Laird's general theory corresponds to the one presented here rather than to Dik's: in his view language understanding is a matter of forming a mental model indeed; and reasoning is done in terms of these abstract conceptualizations, and not in terms of some propositional logic (as Dik's FL would be).

10. For reasons of space the following can only be a cursory overview of some elementary ideas, intended to show the complexity of the problems one will have to face. A more elaborate discussion in Nuyts (1988: 558ff).

11. For more information on meta-qualification in FPG, see also Nuyts (1988: 636ff).

12. The suggestion to draw a distinction between illocution and qualifications obviously does not imply that there is no interaction between these categories, both conceptually (e.g. a modal qualification of a piece of conceptual information as 'uncertain' can lead to a request for clarification) and linguistically. More on the position of illocution in conceptualization and utterance formation in Nuyts (1989b). Note also that even the marking of the illocution of an utterance is determined by (conceptually) different functional dimensions.

13. Actually, many of the phenomena which are currently being ascribed to the illocutionary layer in FG do not seem to me to have anything to do with illocutionary matters. Dik's (this vol.) 'illocutionary conditionals' certainly do constitute a clearly different type as compared to his 'propositional conditionals'. Yet, the difference is that in the latter the fact stated in the protasis specifies a condition for the *occurrence* of the fact stated in the apodosis, while in the former the fact stated in the protasis is a condition for the *relevance* of the fact stated in the apodosis. There is not a relationship of relevance between a fact and a speech act,

but between a fact and a fact. Similar considerations can be made for many of the 'illocutionary satellites' specified by Dik et al. (this vol.).

14.   Of course, this means that many of the observations made by Dik et al. (this vol.) in favor of their layering system will have to be reconsidered in the present proposal. For reasons of time and space I cannot go into this here. But, for one thing, it is no problem to suppose that in the hierarchy of qualifications there are 'break off' points for the possibility to invoke certain types of processes in the grammar. For another thing, it is not so certain that all the criteria used by Dik et al. do support the strict layering system they propose. E.g., consider the argumentation on the basis of negation. The difference in negation of utterances with predicate satellites and predication satellites would be that in the former case only the relation between the nucleus and the predicate satellite would be negated, while in the latter case the predication can be negated. But consider (a), which contains a Beneficiary, i.e. a predicate satellite.

(a)   John didn't buy cookies for his aunt

This can be read in different ways, depending on how one pronounces the utterance. But in one of the 'natural' readings, the nuclear predication is negated, as with predication satellites. Or consider the argument that 'representational satellites' form an informational unit with the core predication while 'interpersonal satellites' do not, on the basis of the observation that the former can be questioned with a yes/no question together with the core predication while the latter cannot. An explanation might be that the 'interpersonal satellites' for which this is illustrated all involve an element of uncertainty about whether the SoA applies (or is relevant), while a question is precisely the result of uncertainty about whether the SoA applies (or is relevant). The question aims to resolve the uncertainty. Hence, questions and modal, evidential, conditional, etc. satellites are simply incompatible, independently of how they are hierarchically organized.

15.   Note that there is some similarity between this definition of the motivation for the hierarchical order of qualifications and Hengeveld's definition of it (the lower layers have more to do with the SoA itself, the higher layers have more to do with the relationship between the individual and the SoA). The difference is that the present definition does not rely on the notion 'speech event'.

16.   As long as the exact format of conceptualization is undetermined, it is also difficult to pin down the exact format of the mechanisms that have to be postulated in the grammar for linking conceptualizations with predications. Yet, for some suggestions (in the framework of FPG), see De Schutter and Nuyts (1983) and Nuyts (1988: 622ff), (1989b).

References

Argyle, M. and P.Trower
    1979   *Person to person: Ways of communicating.* London: Harper and Row.

Bates, E., M.Masling and W.Kintsch
    1978 "Recognition memory for aspects of dialogue". *Journal of Experimental Psychology: Human Learning and Memory* 4: 187-197.

Block, N. (ed.)
    1981 *Imagery*. Cambridge: MIT-Press.

Bolkestein, M. and R.Risselada
    1987 "The pragmatic motivation of syntactic and semantic perspective". In J.Verschueren and M.Bertuccelli-Papi (eds.), 497-512.

Bossuyt, A.
    1982 *Aspekten van de geschiedenis van de negatieve zin in het Nederlands*. PhD-thesis, Free University of Brussels.

Bransford, J. and J.Franks
    1972 "The abstraction of linguistic ideas". *Cognition* 1: 211-249.

Bredart, S.
    1987 "Two ways of coping with indeterminate spatial discourse". *Psychologica Belgica* 27.143-151.

Brewer, W. and A.Hay
    1984 "Reconstructive recall of linguistic style". *Journal of Verbal Learning and Verbal Behavior* 23: 237-249.

Bühler, K.
    1934 *Sprachtheorie*. Jena: Fischer.

Chafe, W.
    1977a "Creativity in verbalization and its implications for the nature of stored knowledge". In R.Freedle (ed.), *Discourse production and comprehension*. Norwood: Ablex, 41-55.
    1977b "The recall and verbalization of past experience". In R.Cole (ed.), *Current issues in linguistic theory*. Bloomington: Indiana UP, 215-246.

Clark, H.H.
    1987 "Four dimensions of language use". In J.Verschueren and M.Bertuccelli-Papi (eds.), 9-25.

Dik, S.
    1978 *Functional grammar*. Amsterdam: North Holland.
    1980 *Studies in functional grammar*. New York: Academic Press.
    1986 "On the notion 'functional explanation'". *Belgian Journal of Linguistics* 1: 11-52.
    1987a "Functional grammar and its potential computer applications". In W.Meijs (ed.), *Corpus linguistics and beyond*. Amsterdam: Rodopi, 253-268.
    1987b "Generating answers from a linguistically coded knowledge base". In G.Kempen (ed.),

Natural language generation. Dordrecht: Nijhoff, 301-314.

1987c "Linguistically motivated knowledge representation". In M.Nagao (ed.), *Language and artificial intelligence*. Amsterdam: North Holland, 145-170.

1988a "Towards a unified cognitive language". *Worlds behind words*. Leuven: K.U.L. To appear.

1988b "Concerning the logical component of a natural language generator". In M.Zock and G.Sabah (eds.), *Advances in natural language generation, vol.1*. London: Pinter, 73-91.

1989 *The theory of functional grammar, pt.1*. Dordrecht: Foris.

Foley, W. and R.Van Valin

1984 *Functional syntax and universal grammar*. Cambridge: Cambridge UP.

Gillis, S.

1984 *De verwerving van talige referentie*. PhD-thesis, University of Antwerp.

Halliday, M.A.K.

1970 "Functional diversity in language". *Foundations of Language* 6: 322-361.

Hannay, M.

1985 *English existentials in functional grammar*. Dordrecht: Foris.

Hengeveld, K.

1987 *The Spanish mood system*. Working Papers in Functional Grammar 22. (Revised version reprinted as: "Illocution, mood and modality in a functional grammar of Spanish". *Journal of Semantics* 6: 227-269. 1989.)

1988 *Layers and operators*. Working Papers in Functional Grammar 27. (Revised version reprinted as: "Layers and operators in functional grammar". *Journal of Linguistics* 25: 127-157. 1989.)

Hjelmquist, E.

1984 "Memory for conversations". *Discourse Processes* 7: 321-336.

1987 "Where is the meaning of verbal discourse?" In J.Verschueren and M.Bertuccelli-Papi (eds.), 667-680.

Hjelmquist, E. and A.Gidlund

1985 "Free recall of conversations". *Text* 5: 169-185.

Jarvella, R. and J.Collas

1974 "Memory for intentions of sentences". *Memory and Cognition* 2: 185-188.

Johnson-Laird, P.

1974 "Experimental psycholinguistics". *Annual Review of Psychology* 25: 135-160.

1977 "Psycholinguistics without linguistics". In N.Sutherland (ed.), *Tutorial essays in psychology I*. Hillsdale: Erlbaum, 75-135.

1983 *Mental models*. Cambridge: Cambridge UP.

Korst, B.Van der
1987 *Twelve sentences: A translation procedure in terms of FG*. Working Papers in Functional Grammar 19.

Kosslyn, S.
1978 "Imagery and internal representation". In E.Rosch and B.Lloyd (eds.), *Cognition and categorization*. Hillsdale: Erlbaum, 217-257.

Lenneberg, E.
1967 *Biological foundations of language*. New York: Wiley.

Miller, G. and P.Johnson-Laird
1976 *Language and perception*. Cambridge: Cambridge UP.

Nuyts, J.
1988 *Aspekten van een kognitief-pragmatische taaltheorie*. PhD-thesis, University of Antwerp. (Shortened English version to appear as: *Aspects of a cognitive-pragmatic language theory*. Amsterdam: J.Benjamins.)
1989a "On the functionality of language". *Papers in Pragmatics* 3. To appear.
1989b *Functional procedural grammar: An overview*. Working Papers in Functional Grammar 31.
1990 "Negative raising reconsidered". *Journal of Pragmatics* 14. To appear.

Quillian, M.
1968 "Semantic memory". In M.Minsky (ed.), *Semantic information processing*. Cambridge: MIT-Press, 227-270.

Schank, R.
1975 *Conceptual information processing*. Amsterdam: North Holland.
1980 "Language and memory". *Cognitive Science* 4: 243-284.

Schutter, G.De and J.Nuyts
1983 "Towards an integrated model of a functional grammar". In S.Dik (ed.), *Advances in functional grammar*. Dordrecht: Foris, 387-404.

Verschueren, J. and M.Bertuccelli-Papi (eds.)
1987 *The pragmatic perspective*. Amsterdam: J.Benjamins.

Vet, C.
1986 *A pragmatic approach to tense in functional grammar*. Working Papers in Functional Grammar 16

Winograd, T.
1972 *Understanding natural language*. New York: Academic Press.

Wygotski, L.
1974 *Denken und Sprechen*. Frankfurt: Fischer.

The Functional Grammar Computational Natural Language User and Psychological Adequacy

Cees Hesp
Free University at Amsterdam

0. Introduction[1]

Recently Dik (1986a, b, c, d, 1987a, b) has formulated proposals to build a process model of the natural language user (NLU) based on the principles of Functional Grammar (FG). This model is called the Functional Grammar - Computational Natural Language User (FG-CNLU). One of the aims of the enterprise is to simulate the "actual, natural performance of (Human) NLUs in normal communicative circumstances," and to do so in a "psychologically adequate and realistic way" (Dik 1987b: 4). A second objective is the "(re)unification of grammar, logic and cognition" (Dik 1986c: 18).

In this paper we will show that, from a language comprehension point of view, the measures taken to achieve the second requirement are responsible for not achieving the first. We will argue that, in order to approximate to the first objective, FG-CNLU needs to acknowledge more differences in levels and types of representation than presented in Dik's current proposals.

We will first briefly describe Dik's model, again from a language comprehension point of view. We will then follow up on some of the predictions that can be based on the model to assess the extent to which its first aim has been met - or can be met given the present assumptions of the model. In making this assessment, it seems reasonable to apply Dik's (1986b: 1) working definition of psychological adequacy as a measure stick: "A theory (of language use) is psychologically adequate when it is compatible with what is known about the psychological mechanisms involved in natural language processing".

1. An outline of FG-CNLU

FG-CNLU's language comprehension apparatus as presented in Dik (1987b) consists roughly of two parts: a language module and a conceptual system. The language module derives 'fully specified underlying predications' (FSUPs) from its spoken or written linguistic input, and is further subdivided into a 'phonetic' and a 'syntactic' processor for each of the input modalities. The conceptual system consists largely of a knowledge base or memory, an inference engine called Functional Logic (FL), and an evaluator. FL is used to deduce pieces of information from the knowledge already stored in memory. The evaluator stores representations of the input in the knowledge base, if they have sufficient retention value. Unification of grammar, logic and cognition is achieved by assuming that the same representational format is used throughout the system.

The knowledge representations (KRs) in memory and the input and output of FL are hypothesized to have largely the same format as the output of the language module, namely that of underlying predications (UPs). The difference between FSUPs (the output of the language module) and UPs (the knowledge representations of the cognitive system) is that UPs do not usually contain illocutionary operators (viz. declarative (DEC), interrogative (INT) or imperative (IMP) - Dik 1987a: 21). These labels are used to determine what should be done with the information contained in the utterance. INT, for instance, is taken to mean that the hearer should consult his knowledge base and provide an answer if possible (Dik 1986c: 8). Similar interpretations are intended for DEC and IMP. From the examples of KRs that Dik gives we may also gather that the labels denoting the syntactic and pragmatic functions of terms are not stored in memory.[2] The UPs or KRs in memory can thus be said to have the general format as given in (1).

(1)   tense predicate$_{N/V/A}$ (term x_1)$_{SemFunc}$ (term x_n)$_{SemFunc}$

The above scheme expresses that an UP consists of a 'tensed' predicate and a n-number of terms or arguments.[3] The predicate belongs to the grammatical category of N(oun), V(erb) or A(djective). The terms each have a semantic function - such as Agent, Goal, Recipient, etc. (see Dik 1978).

Since the underlying representations of FG contain lexical items of the object language described, it will be clear that the FG-CNLU model makes a strong linguistic claim about the nature of conceptual knowledge. To be able to maintain such a view, Dik (1986a: 16) holds that *all* knowledge is either conceptual (i.e. represented in predications) or perceptual (i.e. represented in 'pictures') or a combination of both. In 2. and 3. we will consider whether there is evidence for the various predictions that could be based on these claims.

2. Some predictions from the model

2.1. Predictions based on the storage of UPs in memory

The model suggests that the conceptual knowledge of humans is not just linguistic in nature but that it is the actual predication that underlies a particular sentence that is stored in memory (when it has sufficient retention value). Consequently, people should be reasonably good at remembering those aspects of sentences that are coded in the memory representation (i.e. the UP). And, since UPs form the only output of the language processor, people should not remember what is not specified therein.[4]

2.1.1. What people should remember. If UPs are stored in memory, then according to (1), people should be able to remember:
(a) what the tense was;
(b) what the predicate was;
(c) whether the predicate was a N(oun), a V(erb) or an A(djective);
(d) what the terms were;
(e) what the semantic functions of the terms were.
Moreover, they should be able to remember:
(f) what information was conveyed in one utterance, and what in others, since each utterance receives one representation.
To falsify these predictions one would have to show that people do not remember these aspects of utterances well and/or that they confuse them with similar expressions.

The memory experiments of the late sixties and early seventies provided just such falsification by showing that memory for sentences is not normally verbatim in this sense (e.g. Fillenbaum 1966; Sachs 1967; Wanner 1974; etc.). With respect to predictions (a)-(e), consider for instance the following pairs of sentences (from Johnson-Laird and Stevenson 1970; Johnson-Laird et al. 1974; Schweller et al. 1976; and Johnson et al. 1973 respectively).

(2) a. John **liked** the painting and he **bought** it from the duchess
     b. The painting **pleased** John and the duchess **sold** it to him

(3) a. The **owner** of the magic staff **dispatched** the ship
     b. The **dispatcher** of the ship **owned** the magic staff

(4) a. The cute little girl **told** her mother she **wanted** a drink

    b.   The cute little girl **asked** her mother **for** a drink

(5)   a.   He slipped on a wet spot and **dropped** the delicate glass pitcher on the floor
       b.   He slipped on a wet spot and **broke** the delicate glass pitcher **when it fell** on the floor

In each of these experiments subjects were shown lists of sentences and were asked to answer questions about them. The object of the latter was to ensure that the sentences were understood sufficiently. The types of sentences that subjects were shown are given in (2a)-(5a). Later these subjects were given a surprise recognition test, i.e. they were given a new set of sentences in which some of the 'old' sentences were mixed with 'new' ones. They were then asked to indicate which sentences they had seen before. Sentences that were mistakenly identified as 'old' sentences are (2b)-(5b).

As one can judge from the confusion over the examples, none of the aspects coded in UPs are remembered well, except for the tense of predicates.[5] Consider e.g. (3a-b). In (3a) *The owner etc.* is the Agent term of the verbal predicate *dispatch*, whereas *the dispatcher etc.* in (3b) has zero semantic function in the verbal predicate *own*. Thus, neither the main predicate nor the semantic functions of its terms are remembered well. In (4b)-(5b), moreover, even roots of words appear that were not present in the original sentences (4a-b).

As concerns prediction (f), Bransford and Franks (1971) conducted an experiment in which subjects were shown sentences in which either one, two, or three of the four propositions listed under (6) appeared.

(6)   a.   The rock rolled down the mountain
       b.   The rock crushed the hut
       c.   The hut is at the river
       d.   The hut is tiny

Thus, subjects were presented with sentences like *The hut is tiny* (one proposition), *The tiny hut is at the river* (two propositions), or *The rock crushed the tiny hut at the river* (three propositions). Later they were given a surprise recognition test in which they were asked to indicate which sentences they had seen before. In addition, they were asked to indicate how sure they were of their judgments. The set of sentences used in the recognition test again consisted of some 'old' sentences and some 'new' sentences. The sentences that subjects were most sure about were of the type given in (7). These sentences contained all four propositions, but had not, in fact, been presented before.

(7)   The rock that rolled down the mountain crushed the tiny hut at the river

Experiments such as the above clearly indicate that, except for tense, the aspects coded in the UP are not (normally) remembered well, and that people do not strictly separate information expressed in one sentence from that expressed in others. In other words, there is no simple one-to-one relationship between the wording of the original input and the resulting memory representation. Such observations have led many to conclude that only the 'gist' of a sentence is (normally) remembered (e.g. Fillenbaum 1966).

What has also become clear from such experiments is that what people do remember of any given input is to a large extent determined by the context during input (e.g. the task they face) on the one hand (Bobrow and Bower 1969; Craik and Lockhart 1972; etc.), and by the context during recall on the other (Anderson and Pitchert 1978; Spiro 1980; etc.).

2.1.2. What people should not remember. If only the information contained in UPs is stored in memory, then there should be many aspects of utterances that do not produce memory traces. Since such aspects are not specified elsewhere in the system either, the model predicts that people should never be able to remember them. The system does not specify, for instance, whether the utterance of which the UP is the internal representation was heard or read, nor does it register certain physical attributes of the input. Experiments have shown, however, that at least for lists of unrelated words people are quite good at remembering the input modality (e.g. Hintzman et al. 1972; Bray and Batchelder 1972). In the study by Bray and Batchelder, moreover, people could even remember the modality when they could not remember the item itself. What this indicates is that input modality is not stored with the 'sentence representation' itself (e.g. in a label attached to it), but separately and independently (Kintsch 1977). The same holds for certain physical attributes of utterances - such as the shape and size of printed characters - of which Brooks (1968) has shown that people are quite good at remembering them, at least over short periods of time.

Since people are able to remember aspects of utterances that are not coded in the UP, which is the only output of the language module in the FG-CNLU model, we can only conclude that such purely linguistic or grammatical representations cannot be the only output of the language module.

2.2. Predictions based on UPs as the arguments of thought processes

A different approach to the problem of establishing what the relation is between the wording of input sentences and the resulting cognitive representations that people store in memory and argue with has been taken by Kintsch and Monk (1972) and King and Greeno (1974). They reasoned that if thought is characterized as the manipulation of cognitive representations, and if the grammatical representations of sentences are at the same time the cognitive representations, then it should take longer to reason with information expressed in syntactically complex sentences than with the 'same' information expressed in simple sentences. In their experiments, subjects were given instructions to perform a particular task, for which they had to make certain inferences. These instructions were couched in simple sentences for one group and in complex ones for another. Subjects of both groups were asked to give a signal as soon as they had read the instructions and understood what they were required to do. They were then asked to carry out the instructions. The result of both experiments was that, although the 'complex' group took longer to comprehend the instructions, actual performance of the task was equally fast and accurate for both groups.

This can only be explained, of course, by assuming that the representations with which subjects reasoned were (highly) similar for both groups, and thus that lexico-syntactic differences had disappeared. These experiments show, again, that there is no simple one-to-one relationship between the wording of the input sentence and the resulting cognitive representation.

The results from the memory experiments as well as those obtained in the reasoning experiments argue against the view taken in the FG-CNLU model in which the output of the language module is fed directly into the conceptual system, where it is stored in memory and further reasoned with. We conclude, therefore, that conceptual knowledge does not consist of the actual UPs of utterances, and that FG-CNLU does not attain psychological adequacy in this respect.

3. Is conceptual knowledge linguistic in a more abstract sense?

Since all available evidence refutes the idea that the actual predications are stored in memory and reasoned with, one might entertain the idea that conceptual knowledge is linguistic in a more abstract sense (if the actual words are not stored in memory then, perhaps, input sentences are first translated into other words before they are stored in memory). The problems posed by the memory experiments, however, are then likely to receive rather ad hoc solutions. To account for confusion between (8a-b) (from Barclay 1973), for instance, one might suggest that, since *taller* and *shorter* are each other's converses, deduction of the one from the other may lead to confusion as to what the original was (Dik p.c.).

(8)   a.   John is **taller** than Peter
      b.   Peter is **shorter** than John

Many types of memory confusions, however, cannot be explained by this deduction account. The information in (5b), for instance, cannot be deduced from (5a) - it can only be inferred by means of abduction, of which FL is incapable. (In abduction, one could hypothesize that there is a general rule that says that if delicate glass objects are dropped, they break.)

Or, to account for confusion between (4a-b), one might suggest that *ask (for)* is provided with a meaning definition 'tell someone you want something' (Dik p.c.). Such a definition, which would allow substitution of the one for the other, clearly leaves out many of the finer differences in meaning. To see why 'tell someone you want something' would be inadequate as a meaning definition one would only have to muse that there must be some (culturally defined) reason why in most situations it is more appropriate to ask someone something than to tell someone you want something.

Or, to account for confusion between (3a-b), one might suggest that UPs might be broken down into more basic predications before they are stored in memory. Thus, the common representation of (3a) and (3b) might be 'x own ship & x dispatch ship' (Dik p.c.). One would still have to show, however, which basic predications are actually stored in memory. A priori, there does not seem much reason why *x dispatch ship* should be more basic than, for instance, *x send off ship*.

Moreover, as we will see below, there are many other arguments against a linguistic view of conceptual knowledge, and also against the strict distinction between 'verbal' and 'perceptual' knowledge that is necessary in order to maintain such a view.

3.1. Declarative and procedural knowledge

A first argument against a linguistic view of conceptual knowledge is that, generally speaking, a distinction can be made between declarative and procedural knowledge (e.g Ryle 1949; Winograd 1975). Declarative knowledge is knowledge of facts, and procedural knowledge is knowledge of how to do things. If one claims that *all* conceptual knowledge is verbal in nature (Dik 1986a: 16), then both declarative and procedural conceptual knowledge are such. Procedural knowledge, however, cannot be verbalized. If one's procedural knowledge were represented linguistically - and if, as in the model, no constraints are posited as to what information is available to what processes - then there would be no reason for this to be so. Moreover, if one assumes that *all* knowledge is either verbal or perceptual or a combination of both (Dik ibid.), then one should be able to verbalize or to imagine one's non-conceptual procedural knowledge. (Examples of non-conceptual procedural knowledge are motor knowledge and the knowledge represented by the rules that constitute the language processor.) However, one cannot give an exact report (in words and/or in pictures) of one's actions while riding a bike, nor can one give a report of what happens during language comprehension.

Also, if thought is the manipulation of facts by means of procedures - as is the common assumption in cognitive science - and if both facts and procedures are linguistic in nature, then the congenitally deaf should not only be handicapped but also severely mentally retarded. They should lack both the means to represent facts and the means to manipulate them. There is evidence, however, that they classify and categorize, in other words think, in much the same way that their speaking peers do (Furth 1966). By the same token, pre-linguistic children should never be able to learn languages, since without language they would not have the required apparatus to learn anything. They too should lack the means to represent and to manipulate facts. Since the congenitally deaf do think, and since pre-linguistic children are able to learn languages, one can only conclude that language is not a prerequisite for thought (cf. Lenneberg 1967; Fodor 1975; Glucksberg and Danks 1975; Clark and Clark 1977; etc.).

3.2. Bilinguals

A second argument is that, if one assumes that conceptual knowledge is linguistic in nature, one is also committed to the view that bilinguals should have two separate conceptual systems, each with their own knowledge base. Moreover, each of the conceptual systems would need its own interface with the perceptual apparatus.

The first hypothesis has been tested by Kolers (1966), using a list learning task. In such a task, subjects are asked to memorize lists of unrelated words, which they have to recall later. A well-known fact concerning such tasks is that the repetition of a word increases the likelihood of its being remembered. Kolers found that for English-French bilinguals a translated repetition (e.g. *ten - dix*) acted just like a verbatim repetition. Since these subjects took no longer to recall the lists of words (than monolinguals on similar monolinguistic tasks) - which one would expect if two separate memories had to be queried - or to memorize them, this provides evidence that the information was stored in a single uniform way in a single memory.

The second hypothesis has been tested by Preston and Lambert (1969), using a version of the 'Stroop' colour word test (Stroop 1935). In this test subjects are presented colour words that are printed in coloured ink (e.g. the word *red* in blue ink). They are then asked to name the colour of the ink as quickly as possible. For monolinguals this is quite difficult because the tendency to read the word interferes with naming the colour. Preston and Lambert reasoned that bilinguals should be able to do better on this test if they could 'turn off' one of their linguistic conceptual systems. (The rationale of this condition lies in the fact that bilinguals are not normally hindered by thoughts in language B while, for instance, reading language A. The two languages, thus, are not 'switched on' at all times.) For the English-French bilinguals they tested, Preston and Lambert argued that, if one were able to switch off one of the conceptual systems, it should be possible to ignore the word *red* and answer the question in French with *bleu*. The subjects, however, performed no better on this task than monolinguals. This was taken as evidence that one is not able to switch off a conceptual system - even when it would have been useful. Since on the other hand it is possible to switch off a language, this was interpreted as indicating that in bilinguals the two languages converge upon a common conceptual core, and therefore, that there is just one conceptual system for both languages.

This conclusion may be considered a little strong since it is difficult to see how one should differentiate between the linguistic and the conceptual systems in this task. Nevertheless, this experiment does indicate that if bilinguals do have two conceptual systems, they are at least not completely separated.

3.3. Conceptual and perceptual knowledge

Another difficulty for a linguistic view of conceptual knowledge is that one is then forced to make a strict distinction between 'verbal' and 'perceptual' knowledge. As we have seen in paragraph 2.1.2, however, linguistic utterances have perceptual aspects too, the memory traces of which can be considered natural byproducts of the language processor (Kintsch 1977). Moreover, many, if not most, concepts have both 'verbal' and 'perceptual' aspects, and there are many phenomena that are more easily explained by assuming a common code of representation for perceptual and verbal input. Consider sentences (9a-b) (from Bransford et al. 1971).

(9) a. The woman stood on a chair and the mouse sat beneath **her**
    b. The woman stood on a chair and the mouse sat beneath **it**

These sentences were used in a memory experiment of the same paradigm as those described in paragraph 2.1.1. Again, subjects mistakenly reported having seen (9b) before, when it should have been (9a). When *beneath* was changed to *beside* to yield (10a-b), however, subjects were not confused as to what the original was.

(10) a. The woman stood on a chair and the mouse sat beside **her**
     b. The woman stood on a chair and the mouse sat beside **it**

Obviously, (9a-b) could be represented by the same perceptual picture, which would account for the confusion, whereas (10a-b) would have to be represented in different pictures (Dik p.c.). As obvious, however, is the fact that linguistic input is then not stored in linguistic form. Instead of having to formulate under which circumstances linguistic input is translated into perceptual pictures, it is easier to assume that both types of input are represented in the same code. One would then adhere to the good scientific practice of preferring the simplest explanation that can account for any body of data - in other words, why assume two codes if one can do the job. A second example may illustrate this.

E. Loftus has done a number of studies on eye-witness reports. Loftus and Palmer (1974), for instance, showed subjects a film of a multicar accident, and afterwards had subjects answer a number of questions about the film. One group of subjects was asked, for instance, what their estimate was of the speed of the cars when they *hit* each other, while another group was asked what their estimate was of the speed of the cars when they *crashed* into each other. The speed of the cars was estimated significantly higher by the 'crashed group' than by the 'hit group'. A considerable time later subjects returned for another round of questions. This time they were asked, for instance, whether they had seen *the glass flying around* in the film (in the film there had not been any). Again, the 'crashed group' answered this question significantly more often with 'yes' than the 'hit group'.

To account for this, Loftus and Palmer assumed the following. Subjects first built up a memory representation of the events in the film. When asked later to estimate the speed of the cars, the wording of the question clearly influenced the answers that subjects gave. Apparently, the abstract idea or schema (cf. Bartlett 1932; Rumelhart and Ortony 1977) or frame (Minsky 1975) or mental model (Johnson-Laird 1983) that people have of 'crash(ing)' and which they apply in order to account for their experience involves a 'high-speed' component. The answers given at the later session indicate, moreover, that the original memory representations of the second group had been changed to incorporate the idea of crashing, which in turn led them to 'remember' flying glass - apparently, another component of the crash schema. The use of the definite article *the* in the later question, suggesting a known and identifiable referent, not only made subjects believe that there probably had been glass flying around - which would explain why some of the 'hit group' also answered 'yes' to this question - but also fits well with the general *crash* schema-account of the film. Memory representations that incorporate both perceptual and verbal aspects (e.g. schemas, frames or mental models) can, therefore, relatively easily account for the influences that one source of information may have on the other by assuming that the same type of more abstract representation results from them. Additional processing-levels for translating one form of knowledge into another can be left out in this manner.

3.4. Linguistic relativity

As a final point in case against a linguistic view of conceptual knowledge, let us consider the differences that it needs to posit in the cognitive make-up of speakers of different languages - this is called linguistic relativity.

The theory of linguistic relativity holds, in weaker and stronger forms, that languages influences thought. A strong version, sometimes called the Sapir-Whorf hypothesis after two of its advocates (Sapir 1921; Whorf 1956), holds that languages are free to cut up our experiences of the world into categories as they see fit, and that the words we learn to name these categories determine the way we think and perceive.

Most experimental studies designed to test this hypothesis have focused on the naming and perception of colours. Berlin and Kay (1969), for instance, were interested to find out whether the different segmentations of the colour spectrum by different cultures actually means that people perceive colours differently. They presented speakers of twenty diverse languages with 329 coloured chips, which the subjects then had to name. Berlin and Kay then distilled the basic colour terms for each language by establishing from what 'atoms' compound descriptions were built up. After this, they asked their subjects to indicate on the spectrum which basic term covered what area, and to mark the best exemplar of each term. The best exemplars were called 'focal colours'. When they compared the results of the different languages, they found two things. First, the number of basic colour terms that languages have is highly restricted, ranging from two to eleven. Second, and more importantly, the divisions into focal colours are respected across languages. That is, what is considered a focal colour by speakers of one language is never subdivided by others. E.g., if one language has four basic colour terms and another language six, then the four focal colours chosen by speakers of the first language will correspond to four of the six focals chosen by speakers of the latter. These results thus provide evidence against the view that there are no intrinsic (universal) properties of, or constraints on, perception. Also, it suggests that language reflects rather than causes the distinctions that we make. As Minsky (1986: 79) puts it, "Words should be our servants, not our masters".

Further evidence for this view was provided by Heider and Olivier (1972), Heider (1972) and Rosch (1973) in a series of studies on the Dani, a Stone Age tribe living in New Guinea, who have only two colour words (corresponding to bright/warm and dark/cool). In the Heider and Olivier study, English and Dani subjects performed equally well in a recognition memory experiment, in which they had to indicate which one of the colours on a chip had been shown before. The Sapir-Whorf hypothesis, in contrast, predicts that English subjects should perform much better because their language offers greater opportunity for distinctly naming the colours, and thus for keeping them apart in memory. Moreover, both groups tended to confuse and keep apart the same colours, which indicates that the memory representations must have been highly similar for both groups. Secondly, Heider showed that the Dani and the English are both better at recognizing (i.e. correctly identifying) previously presented colours that are focal to the English than at colours that are non-focal (e.g. a focal red is recognized better than a non-focal red), even though the Dani do not have distinctive names for the items in the pair, and even though they do not have a word that names the pair as a whole. Thirdly, Rosch showed that the Dani, when required to learn names for English colours, did better when the test material consisted of (English) focal colours than when it consisted of non-focal or intermediate colours.

From all these studies, one may conclude that there is something universal about the perception and processing of focal colours. Data obtained from speakers of one language (the English) could be used to predict the behaviour of others (the Dani) in memory and learning experiments. All in all, then, this can hardly be a case of linguistic determinism (cf. Foss and Hakes 1978).

The above findings are difficult to reconcile with claims to the extent that conceptual knowledge is verbal in nature - even if this claim were limited to declarative knowledge. For even if one maintains that there is a difference between the perception of colours and the perception of language, which seems a quite reasonable assumption, there still is little evidence that the knowledge that results from each is represented in different formats. There is all the less evidence that 'conceptual' knowledge is *linguistic* in nature. We may conclude, therefore, that the FG-CNLU model will not attain psychological adequacy as long as its representational format is the same linguistic format for language module and conceptual system alike. To all intents and purposes, it would be incompatible with what is known about language processing and cognition.

4. Improvements

In the previous paragraphs we have seen that the FG-CNLU model does not attain psychological adequacy on a number of major points. We have also seen that the inadequacies all hinge on one crucial assumption, namely on the nature of the representational format. The recipe for attaining psychological adequacy in this respect is therefore quite simple - and it does not even harm FG as a descriptive tool. If we want to maintain that FG-type predications are a reasonable candidate for characterizing the output of the language (comprehension) module, we only have to assume that the conceptual code has a different format. Thus, a difference must be posited between the linguistic or grammatical level of representation and the conceptual level of representation. One could assume, for instance, that the output of the language module is but a temporary structure, which is further processed by the conceptual system or the 'semantic processor' as it is sometimes called.[6] One could also assume that the output of the conceptual system is then stored in memory. Admittedly, the nature of the conceptual code is still very much in the open.

In this view the role of grammar in language comprehension would be truly functional: like the proverbial ladder it is discarded when it has served its purpose.

5. Conclusion

In this paper we have reviewed the psychological adequacy of the FG-CNLU model from a language comprehension point of view. We have shown that a number of its major assumptions are incompatible with what is currently known about the psychological mechanisms involved, and thus that the model does not attain psychological adequacy. In the course of this investigation we have shown that there are reasons to postulate different levels of representation for the language processor and for the conceptual system. If the FG-CNLU model were to adopt such a distinction it would be psychologically adequate in this respect.

Notes

1.   Research for this paper was conducted in the framework of my MA thesis at the Free University of Amsterdam. I would like to thank J. Lachlan Mackenzie for his encouraging comments.

2.   Here, too, we will assume that these labels are somehow utilized by the hearer, otherwise the speaker would assign syntactic and pragmatic functions to terms to no avail.

3.   In the model, episodic knowledge is dated either in a relative sense (as indicated by the tense operator), or in an absolute sense (when a date can be fixed to it) (Dik 1987b: 21). Other predicate operators such as mood and aspect have been left out of the discussion. The present papers on the FG-CNLU model do not indicate whether or not they are stored in memory.

4.   The present papers on the FG-CNLU model do not indicate that 'perceptual representations' of the linguistic input, which are necessary to identify the input in the first place, are stored in (some) memory.

5.   This exception does not really follow from the experiments discussed here since the tense of sentences was not varied in them.

6.   As Johnson-Laird (1988: 324) points out, there may be no need for the parser to deliver an explicit grammatical representation of a sentence (such as a FSUP) to the semantic processor, because the parser could directly control the process of combining elements of meaning - "If there are signposts all the way, a destination can be reached without a map".

References

Anderson, R.C. and J.W.Pitchert
  1978 "Recall of previously unrecallable informationfollowing a shift in perspective". *Journal of Verbal Learning and Verbal Behavior* 17: 1-12.

Barclay, J.R.
  1973 "The role of comprehension in remembering sentences". *Cognitive Psychology* 4: 229-254.

Bartlett, F.C.
  1932 *Remembering: a study in experimental and social psychology*. Cambridge: Cambridge UP.

Berlin, B.R. and P.Kay
  1969 *Basic colour terms: Their universality and evolution*. Berkeley: University of California Press.

Bobrow, D.G. and G.H.Bower
  1969 "Comprehension and recall of sentences". *Journal of Experimental Psychology* 80: 455-461.

Bransford, J.D. and J.R.Franks
  1971 "The abstraction of linguistic ideas". *Cognitive Psychology* 2: 331-350.

Bransford, J.D., J.R.Barclay and J.J.Franks
  1972 "Sentence memory: A constructive versus interpretive approach". *Cognitive Psychology* 3: 193-201.

Bray, N.W. and W.H.Batchelder
  1972 "Effects of instruction and retention interval for presentation mode". *Journal of Verbal Learning and Verbal Behavior* 11: 367-374.

Brooks, L.
  1968 "Spatial and verbal compounds of the act of recall". *Canadian Journal of Psychology* 22: 349-368.

Clark, H.H. and E.V.Clark
  1977 *Psychology and language*. New York: Harcourt Brace Jovanovich.

Craik, F.I.M. and R.S.Lockhart
  1972 "Levels of processing: A framework for memory research". *Journal of Verbal Learning and Verbal Behavior* 11: 671-684.

Dik, S.C.
   1978   *Functional grammar.* Amsterdam: North Holland.
   1986a *Linguistically motivated knowledge representations.* Working Papers in Functional Grammar 9. (Reprinted in: M.Nagao (ed.), *Language and artificial intelligence.* Amsterdam: North Holland, 145-170. 1987.)
   1986b "Functional grammar and its potential computer applications". In S.Dik 1986d. (Reprinted in: W.Meijs (ed.), *Corpus linguistics and beyond.* Amsterdam: Rodopi, 253-268. 1987.)
   1986c "Generating answers from a linguistically coded knowledge base". In S.Dik 1986d. (Reprinted in: G.Kempen (ed.), *Natural language generation.* Dordrecht: Nijhoff, 301-314. 1987.)
   1986d *Two papers on the computational application of functional grammar.* Working papers in Functional Grammar 18.
   1987a "Concerning the logical component of a natural language generator". Unpublished paper, University of Amsterdam.
   1987b "Functional Grammar Computational Natural Language User; a research program". Report, University of Amsterdam.

Fillenbaum, S.
   1966   "Memory for gist: Some relevant variables". *Language & Speech* 9: 217-229.

Fodor, J.A.
   1975   *The language of thought.* New York: Thomas Y.Crowell.

Foss, D.J. and D.T.Hakes
   1978   *Psycholinguistics.* Englewood Cliffs: Prentice Hall.

Furth, H.
   1966   *Thinking without language.* New York: Free Press.

Glucksberg, S. and J.H.Danks
   1975   *Experimental psycholinguistics: an introduction.* Hillsdale: Lawrence Erlbaum.

Heider, E.R.
   1972   "Universals in colour naming and memory". *Journal of Experimental Psychology* 92: 337-354.

Heider, E.R. and D.C.Olivier
   1972   "The structure of the colourspace in naming and memory for two languages". *Cognitive Psychology* 3: 337-354.

Hintzman, D.L., R.A.Block and N.R.Inskeep
   1972   "Memory for mode of input". *Journal of Verbal Learning and Verbal Behavior* 11: 741-749.

Johnson, M.K., J.D.Bransford and S.Solomon
1973 "Memory for tacit implications of sentences". *Journal of Experimental Psychology* 98: 203-205.

Johnson-Laird, P.N.
1983 *Mental models*. Cambridge: Cambridge UP.
1988 *The computer and the mind*. London: Fontana.

Johnson-Laird, P.N. and R.Stevenson
1970 "Memory for syntax". *Nature* 227: 412.

Johnson-Laird, P.N., C.Robins and L.Velicogna
1974 "Memory for words". *Nature* 251: 704-705.

King, D.R.W. and J.G.Greeno
1974 "Invariance of inference times when information was presented in different linguistic forms". *Memory and Cognition* 2: 233-235.

Kintsch, W.
1977 *Memory and cognition*. (2nd edn). New York: Wiley.

Kintsch, W. and D.Monk
1972 "Storage of complex information in memory: Some implications of the speed with which inferences can be made". *Journal of Experimental Psychology* 94: 25-32.

Kolers, P.A.
1966 "Interlingual facilitation of short-term memory". *Journal of Verbal Learning and Verbal Behavior* 5: 314-319.

Lenneberg, E.H.
1967 *Biological foundations of language*. New York: Wiley.

Loftus, E.F. and S.Palmer
1974 "Reconstruction of automobile destruction: An example of the interaction between language and memory". *Journal of Verbal Learning and Verbal Behavior* 13: 585-589.

Minsky, M.
1975 "A framework for representing knowledge". In P.Winston (ed.), *The psychology of computer vision*. New York: McGraw Hill, 211-277.
1986 *The society of mind*. New York: Simon and Schuster.

Preston, M.S. and W.E.Lambert
1969 "Interlingual interference in a bilingual version of the Stroop colour word task". *Journal of Verbal Learning and Verbal Behavior* 8: 295-301.

Rosch, E.R.
   1973   "On the internal structure of perceptual and semantic categories". In T.Moore (ed.),
          Cognitive development and the acquisition of language. New York: Academic Press, 111-
          144.

Rumelhart, D.E. and A.Ortony
   1977   "The representation of knowledge in memory". In R.C.Anderson, R.J.Spiro and
          W.E.Montaque (eds.), *Schooling and the acquisition of knowledge*. Hillsdale: L.Erlbaum,
          99-135.

Ryle, G.
   1949   *The concept of mind*. London: Hutchinson.

Sachs, J.S.
   1967   "Recognition memory for syntactic and semantic aspects of connected discourse".
          Perception and Psychophysics 2: 437-442.

Sapir, E.
   1921   *Language: An introduction to the study of speech*. New York: Harcourt, Brace and World.

Schweller, K.G., W.F.Brewer and D.A.Dahl
   1976   "Memory for illocutionary forces and perlocutionary effects of utterances". *Journal of
          Verbal Learning and Verbal Behavior* 15: 325-337.

Spiro, R.J.
   1980   "Accomodative reconstruction in prose recall". *Journal of Verbal Learning and Verbal
          Behavior* 19: 84-95.

Stroop, J.R.
   1935   "Studies of interference in serial verbal reactions". *Journal of Experimental Psychology*
          18: 643-662.

Wanner, E.
   1974   *On remembering, forgetting and understanding sentences: A study of the deep structure
          hypothesis*. The Hague: Mouton.

Whorf, B.L.
   1956   *Language, thought and reality*. Cambridge: MIT-Press.

Winograd, T.
   1975   "Frame representations and the declarative-procedural controversy". In D.G.Bobrow and
          A.M.Collins (eds.), *Representation and understanding: Studies in cognitive science*. New
          York: Academic Press, 185-210.

Context and Language

Erland Hjelmquist
University of Göteborg

0. Introduction[1]

Human language has developed into a tool which takes care of two crucial needs, the first being to channel ongoing face-to-face interaction with its immediate interpretational and interactional demands, and the second being to mediate the preservation of information over long time periods.

The idea behind many linguistic and cognitive theories is that what happens on-line, and in the 'shallow' perceptual and interpretative processes, can be language specific and allow for the preservation of 'stimulus-close' character-istics, but that the long-term preservation of knowledge is much less language dependent. The long-term result is thought to be in the form of an abstract conceptual representation. The point of view taken here is that there can be no qualitative difference between 'short-term' and 'long-term' aspects of a human being's contact with the world. Since our perceptions are not copies of the world, they must have a conceptual character. Even if one wants to include 'temporal strings', taking care of the time dimension of human experiences, and 'images' among the representational formats (Anderson 1983), they are still representations and thus abstracted from reality.

The point of departure in this chapter is different from Dik's (1987, this vol.). Dik's theory incorporates language specific content words in the mental representations, i.e. something which according to him is more concrete than concepts, although it still is an abstraction. I will try to show how this view differs from Hjelmquist (1984, 1987, 1989), although some of the empirical consequences are similar. The discussion will be framed partly in a historical perspective, partly in the perspective of recent experimental studies. On the one hand it will be argued that Dik's position shares some problems with other, more traditional conceptual views of human cognition. On the other hand Dik's program certainly does address crucial problems concerning the issue of mental representation, and to the extent that it puts into question the notion of an abstract conceptual code, remote from the particular wording of an expression, it is laudable. Yet, on the basis of recent memory research it will be argued that meaning is a contextual phenomenon. Meaning is to be regarded as a relational concept in which linguistic expression and context (including the speaker-listeners' mental states) are the two anchoring points. Therefore, even if one considers it in the wider framework of the preceding utterances and takes into account intonation and stress contours (cf. Dik 1987: 152), the information contained in a linguistic expression cannot in itself determine what will be taken as the meaning of that particular utterance in a specific communicative situation.

1. The roots of the problem of representation

It is important to consider the historical roots of the present scientific debate, which might be sought in the phenomenon of written language. The idea to represent language in alphabetical writing has been a (if not *the*) major human enterprise (Gelb 1963). Now, according to Gregory (1981: 359) the idea of perception as representation has first been launched by Theophrastus in the second and third century BC, and his suggestion is that it is precisely due to the conception of language in a written, *alphabetical* form. Furthermore, Gregory (1981: 54) suggests that Plato's notion of 'fixed ideal forms' may have its roots in the technology of writing. If so, this would be very instructive, for fixed ideal forms (in the form of primitives of some kind) are what most modern representational theories are about. In Dik's (1987) theory, content words are specified by selection restrictions such as 'human', 'male', etc., which are part of the predicate frame. The selection restrictions remind of "elements which symbolize the most fundamental conceptual distinctions that human beings make" (Dik 1987: 147). Thus, even Dik's theory uses some kind of primitives, despite the fact that this is what he wants to avoid. This issue will be discussed further below.

Probably the strongest arguments concerning the importance of writing for the fixation of 'meaning' in an alphabetical text, separate from the sender's communicative intentions, can be found in Olson (1977).

Thus, according to several researchers the idea of a linguistic structure as a meaning carrying vehicle that can be analyzed 'from the outside', so to speak, is something which arose after the introduction of alphabetical writing. If this is true, i.e. if the concept of representational structure has its roots in the human artifact of writing, then the object of investigation, viz. the representation of knowledge, is created by the tools of investigation, viz. language and metalanguage. Of course, this is no more exciting than the fact that mind investigates mind. But it is worth pointing out, since the 'representational problem' is generally taken for granted.

2. Language, thought, and memory

From its origins onwards language has been a means of direct face-to-face communication between people in which messages are conveyed and received on an on-line basis and in rapid succession. Hence, at the very dawn of homo sapiens sapiens the representational system must have aimed at capturing language in its spoken form, and there must be a core of representational principles exclusively related to this face-to-face communication which exists up to present.

A question raised by Dik (1987) and numerous other ancient and modern philosophers and researchers is, whether, to what extent, and how these representations of language on the one hand, and thought (knowledge) on the other, are interrelated. Dik suggests a very close relation. It is probably not controversial to claim that they *are* interrelated, but one does not want to end up with a Whorfian view on these matters. The arguments against any strong version of the Whorfian hypothesis are too well known to be repeated here. However, one could point to one problem which fits the context of this paper, viz. how development of new lexical items, reflecting new concepts, would be possible if our thinking is governed by the linguistic characteristics of particular languages. A Whorfian view seems to presuppose that linguistic change leads the way for conceptual change, which, if taken strictly, seems absurd.

What kind of relationship between external linguistic information and long-term knowledge representation is to be expected, then? The usual hypothesis has been that the human mind does not allow the storage of more than a limited amount of the original 'perceptual' (but according to the view proposed here abstract) information. What is preserved over a long time is usually called 'meaning', 'gist', 'content', etc., and this is what according to Olson (1977) later became codified in alphabetical writing. Often the representational format is defined by some logical or quasi logical calculus, relying on a truth conditional analysis of propositions. This general approach to language and language processing is widely accepted in cognitive psychology. The psychologists' claims are not ill founded. On the contrary, they rest on a very solid corpus of experimental studies on perception and memory of language (Johnson-Laird 1983). The main results of thirty years of research can easily be summarized:

they suggest that linguistically conveyed information is of an abstract, language independent nature. From this point of view a theory such as the one proposed by Dik is problematic, since it implies and makes a virtue of language dependent representation.

Human memory is limited, but still impressive. Recent memory research suggests that rather than forgetting what we have learned ('long-term memory'), memory problems may be due to a failure to get access to the relevant knowledge on specific occasions (Nilsson et al. 1987). But do we remember what has been said during a particular communicative event? As already mentioned, according to cognitive psychologists and psycholinguists the answer is that we do remember the meaning but not the wording. Synonymous expressions cannot be distinguished anymore some time after the communicative event, but the gist is preserved. This argumentation has received further support from researchers such as Goody and Watt (1972), Lord (1960), and Olson (1977).

Olson (1977) has provided strong and convincing arguments for the claim that certain crucial metaconcepts in the domain of language and communication have developed recently in history. The main argument is that originally, in traditional illiterate cultures, linguistic communication was about content, not form. Language was not thought of as a vehicle for communication, as an object with certain characteristics. Language was transparent. Attention was paid not to wording but to speakers' intentions. The same argument can be applied to children's development in literate societies (Olson 1984): it appears that a metavocabulary is responsible for the development of the conception of language as an object with certain characteristics.[2] This argumentation is supported by empirical evidence. Cross-cultural research shows that traditional illiterate societies sometimes lack lexical expressions for such concepts as 'word', 'sentence', 'intent', etc., and, accordingly, it is difficult if not impossible to entertain a conversation about 'wording' versus 'meaning' and related issues with people without this sort of metalanguage (Lord 1960). Goody and Watt (1972) made similar observations on the basis of field work in Ghana. Over the years people from the traditional society there changed the wording of a myth. Yet they did not pay attention to changes in what we would regard as content (e.g. with regard to the number of sons of the state founder) as long as the functions of the myth were the same. Goody and Watt suggest that as long as the myth was compatible with specific and important features of the *current* society, changes in the way the myth was told were not noticed by the speakers.

Olson's and Goody and Watt's views provide a strong case for the experimental psychologists' and psycholinguists' view that wording is unimportant in the long run with respect to what is conceptualized and remembered, and they pose problems for theories such as Dik's (1987), in which "actual content words of the language" (ibid.: 148) are considered crucial elements in knowledge representation. On the surface there is a strong resemblance between Dik's proposal and what was suggested in Hjelmquist (1984, 1987), viz. that contrary to the canonical cognitive psychologist view particular wordings in verbal messages should have memorial consequences. Dik's theory is also compatible with memory for particular wording. However, it is problematic to assume that linguistic entities have meaning in themselves, even in the context of predicate frames. This assumption seems to reflect the written language bias and the belief that language can be studied 'in vacuo' (Rommetveit 1974). This is so despite the fact that Dik emphasizes that language is used to achieve certain communicative goals in specific communicative situations. Dik's (1987) framework seems to imply that linguistic constructions have some independent status and contain meanings. The above discussion concerning the development of a metalanguage and the conceptual differentiation related to the development of writing technology has already indicated that basing a theory of mental representations on a particular (written) language code is arbitrary. Though literate people certainly have a mental concept corresponding to 'word', the lexical item itself is not the basis of a particular concept.

3. A paradox

Olson's (1977) and Goody and Watt's (1972) findings and arguments are extremely interesting and in some respects convincing. Yet, there is a paradox in the theory and the empirical findings. Why is it not important to notice "the very words" (Olson and Hildyard 1983: 42) in linguistic communication? Why does everything boil down to a conceptual representation which can be expressed, within limits, by some arbitrary wording? Why are there so many words? A first suggestion could be that different wording actually does matter for meaning in the sense that it can give rise to different conceptualizations in the short run, but that somehow these conceptualizations rapidly change and converge in some more basic representation of the meaning. Another answer could be that human beings need the possibility to vastly vary wording since wording must always be tailored to a particular communicative situation. E.g., sometimes it is proper to refer to an animal as 'the lion to the right' and sometimes as 'the big lion', depending on the referential structure (Olson 1970). The meaning would be the same in both instances, and the end result, conceptualization in long-term memory, would in each case be a particular lion. The communicative situation is thus supposed to be important only for the choice of wording, not for the way the communication is understood or remembered. I.e. meaning is not affected. This might seem plausible for types of referential communication such as the one about the lion, but it is much more problematic as a model for human communication in general.

One could suppose that communication among the ancestors of homo sapiens sapiens was largely devoted to referring to concrete things in the world surrounding them, including themselves and their interlocutors. Homo sapiens sapiens however can refer to much more than what is concretely at hand. The possibility to talk about imagined states of affairs, past and future, is a hallmark of linguistic communication of the species. There certainly are referential restrictions in these cases too, but they are in the mind, in a mental model or discourse model (Johnson-Laird 1983). That is, in such cases certain ways of talking about something (claiming, proposing, denying, describing, etc.) are more suitable than others, just as certain ways of verbally referring to a concrete referent in a specific situation are more likely than others. The point is that the distinction between the particular verbal expression and the 'meaning' it conveys cannot be made in the same simple way as when the referent is a concrete phenomenon. Still, the paradox remains in the sense that most empirical data seem to contradict this reasoning by suggesting that in general there is very low preservation of a particular wording, and that this is aggravated by a lack of metavocabulary about language.

Probably, the problem is due not to the reasoning but to the data. Elsewhere (Hjelmquist 1984, 1987) it has been argued that at least in psychology the majority of empirical studies which have investigated the retention of verbal information have done so from an implicit written language bias (Linell 1982). They have not investigated prototypical types of language use in situation (face-to-face conversation, discussion, etc.). It seems that the non-communicative test situations have invoked certain attention and memory processes which favor certain aspects of the verbal information. As we shall see, it is not the experimental setting per se which has caused these results, but the particular instructions and procedures used.

In fact, some research provides us with a different picture. Nuyts (this vol.) draws attention to empirical findings which show that under certain conditions a particular wording can be remembered over quite substantial time intervals (Bates et al. 1978; Bates et al. 1980; Hjelmquist 1984). These results come from studies which have tried to use purposeful communicative situations rather than the confined settings used in traditional experiments on recognition and recall of verbal information. These data could be interpreted to go against the hypothesis of an abstract conceptual representation of verbally conveyed information. People seem to remember linguistic information which does not have any place in the 'standard' theories of mental representation. In line with the reasoning above Bates et al. (1978) and Hjelmquist (1981) have explained this by arguing that in purposeful communication it is problematic to apply the distinction between wording and meaning as it is used in the prevailing theories on memory and language.

This does not imply that no distinction between wording and meaning can be made. The interpretation of an utterance is of course an interpretation of something, which might be called wording or form, or even surface structure. The hypothesis is that in purposeful verbal communication conceptualization is much more closely tied to wording than one could expect on the basis of previous empirical studies (see Hjelmquist 1989 for an overview). It remains an abstraction, of course, but the abstraction is based on the contextualized meaning, which is supposed to have memorial consequences (see Nuyts this vol.). Therefore it is difficult to attain the same conceptualization when paraphrasing an expression or introducing synonymous expressions. Another way of stating this is to say that meaning is relational, i.e. that it is something which is constituted when a particular wording is used in a particular context (which also includes the speaker-listeners' mental states). This is what one might call the 'contextualized meaning' hypothesis of representation. This view differs from Dik's (1987), however, since it does not suppose that the representation includes language specific lexical items. In fact, while Dik stresses the importance of staying as close as possible to the surface level of linguistic expressions, his approach to a classical problem such as synonymy is very traditional, as can be seen from his treatment of active-passive constructions (Dik 1987: 149). The passive version of an active expression is supposed to embody the same knowledge as the active one does. This is not self-evident, and the view advocated here is that the representation of the two expressions should show the difference in what is asserted, in line with Clark (1974: 1394). In this respect Dik does not go far enough in acknowledging the role of surface structure.

4. The reconstruction problem

Nuyts (this vol.) suggests that the results in Hjelmquist (1984) and similar studies can be explained as effects of reconstructive processes. This is a crucial issue. The question is whether these reconstructive processes are veridical or nonveridical. Researchers have obtained results which seem to show extensive nonveridical reconstructive and/or biasing processes at work during recall and recognition tasks, i.e. processes which are not based on memory of the specific event, but on knowledge of different kinds (general, style specific, personal, etc.) (Brewer and Hay 1984; Stevenson 1988). The most striking results are perhaps those by Stevenson, who showed that what Bates et al. (1978) and Bates et al. (1980) interpreted as memory results seems to reflect biasing processes.

Yet, the possibility of nonveridical reconstructional processes must somehow be restricted, for otherwise we would end up in absurdity. If it were the case that context at recall or imagined context generally and substantially biases recall, it is difficult to see how this would be compatible with functionality and people's adjustment to the environment.

The issue of nonveridical reconstruction and biases has been tested empirically by using different kinds of control conditions, and on this basis it has been possible to rule out explanations in terms of nonveridical reconstruction, reflecting biased judgments, except in Stevenson (1988) and Brewer and Hay (1984). Hence, some empirical data are in favor of the possibility for nonveridical reconstruction in certain conditions, but they have been obtained only with respect to very particular linguistic phenomena, viz. referring statements and literary style. The issue is not 'no reconstruction vs. reconstruction', but rather: under what circumstances do people produce specific and veridical reconstructions?

5. Features of a frame of reference for the study of language and representation

While the finding that the particular wording of verbal communication can be remembered over quite some time may seem compatible with Dik's framework, it is suggested that it can better be understood in terms of a different system of concepts. Of interest in this context is one important theoretical notion introduced in psychology, viz. 'level of processing'. Craik and Lockhart (1972) have suggested that the representations which result from perceptual processes are dependent on the way they are used by the individual. In brief, their results showed that the more information was treated in terms of meaning or semantic content, the better it was remembered. On the surface this might seem to be perfectly in accord with the 'canonical' view of how people process linguistic information. The point is, however, that it is not predetermined which aspects of the information will be treated on a 'meaning' or 'semantic' level. In the framework of Hjelmquist (1984, 1987) this corresponds to the suggestion that meaning is a relational phenomenon.

Also interesting in this context are recent results presented by Mäntylä (1986). It was shown that under certain conditions it is possible for people to reach very high levels of recall of a very large number of words, even when presented only once and tested after a time lapse of a week. The experiments involved a new feature which seems to allow for an explanation of the results, viz. the element of self-generation of defining characteristics of the word to be remembered. The test-persons were presented with a long list of words without knowing that later they would be involved in a memory test. For each word each test-person was instructed to generate three aspects which he/she thought was characteristic of it. E.g., for the word 'banana' one could generate features such as 'yellow', 'fruit', or 'bent'. At the time of testing the test-person was presented with the three features he/she had generated for each word. With this procedure (which basically builds in the possibility for veridical reconstruction) remembrance was very good for more than one hundred words even after a week. Thus, the memory processes based on the three features were very efficient. It is also important that the experimental situation really qualified as purposeful communication: one person asks questions, and the other person gives his/her answers entirely according to his/her own opinions. So, in a way this is a highly contextualized situation in which the interlocutor him/herself tries to find the best answer to the question, which later also proves to be a very good aid to activate the original word. From this perspective it is clear that it would be wrong to suggest that Functional Grammar is a general theory of linguistic communication, since the model does not take care of attentional and goal directed activities which can be oriented towards different levels and aspects of linguistic information and thereby also influence what will be remembered. In other words, the relational character of meaning (including the meaning of lexical items) should be a prominent feature in any theory of linguistic communication.

6. Conclusion

Language has developed to meet the demands of face-to-face interaction in specific contexts, as well as to be a mediator for the preservation of information over a long period of time.

No representation of information can be nonconceptual in any radical way, since the mind does not contain copies of unique events in the world. All representations have to be abstract in this sense. Dik's (1987) theory, which includes content words, could be claimed to fulfill this abstraction criterion if lexical items are accepted as abstractions. Dik considers content words to be specifiable in terms of selection restrictions. The selection restrictions reoccur for different predicates, and in this sense they are more elementary than the predicates themselves. Thus Dik suggests an abstract representation to the extent that lexical items can be considered abstractions and to the extent that in a particular predicate frame selection restrictions can be regarded as more elementary than the predicate. Whether this should be regarded as qualitatively different from the more standard versions of knowledge representation remains an open question.

Dik's plea to pay due attention to the importance of the level of content words is compatible with the assumption that the particular wording of utterances is important in oral communication. And it is in accordance with recent empirical results showing better memory for wording in oral discourse than has been registered in experiments using language out of context. This awareness of the basic importance of wording and 'surface structure' in a theory of communication is shared here. But the theoretical approach, which was already suggested in Hjelmquist (1987) and was further explicated here is different. The suggestion is that the representations resulting from a verbal exchange can have consequences in memory if they are important for the meaning of what was said. But what is important for meaning is not something which can be determined once and for all by a linguistic analysis of written language in vacuo, but should be regarded as relational, with the verbal expression and the context being the two relata. It seems that Dik's (1987) theory, although it is intended to be a theory about spoken communication, is still influenced by the written language bias which is pervasive in linguistics.

Historical and cross-cultural studies on illiterate people's conception of language go hand in hand with empirical studies in psychology to show a typical pattern of 'memory for content' rather than for form (wording). Illiterate people, who lack a metalanguage of communication, focus on meaning in oral communication and do not use a distinction between meaning and particular wording. The same has been shown for preschool children in literate societies, who have not yet learned to read and write. All these facts create a paradox, for they seem to conflict with the observation that face-to-face communication is highly context bound and that the verbal expressions used are more or less consciously chosen to suit the contextual demands. As discussed, more recent theoretical developments and empirical results which show substantial memory for wording under certain circumstances suggest a resolution of the paradox. One crucial issue in the explanation is the influence of reconstruction on these memory results: one should expect that there are reconstruction processes at work in normal and veridical functions of memory.

The 'correct' theory of mental representation and the role of language in it is not yet formulated and perhaps never will be. But if there is to be one, it should treat meaning as a relational concept, pay due attention to context dependence (situational and historical) and the role of attention processes, and involve a concept of an active, reconstructive memory.

Notes

1.   This study was supported by a grant from the Swedish Council for Research in the Humanities and Social Sciences.

2.   However, a different view was proposed in Hedelin and Hjelmquist (1988).

References

Anderson, J.R.
    1983   *The architecture of cognition*. Cambridge: Harvard UP.

Bates, E., M.Masling and W.Kintsch
    1978   "Recognition memory for aspects of dialogue". *Journal of Experimental Psychology: Human Learning and Memory* 4: 187-197.

Bates, E., W.Kintsch, C.R.Fletcher and V.Guiliani
    1980   "The role of pronominalization and ellipsis in texts: Some memory experiments". *Journal of Experimental Psychology: Human Learning and Memory* 6: 676-691.

Brewer, W.F. and A.E.Hay
    1984   "Reconstructive recall of linguistic style". *Journal of Verbal Learning and Verbal Behavior* 23: 237-249.

Clark, H.H.
    1974   "Semantics and comprehension". In T.A.Sebeok (ed.), *Current trends in linguistics*. The Hague: Mouton, vol. 12, 1291-1428.

Craik, F.I.M. and R.S.Lockhart
    1972   "Levels of processing: A framework for memory research". *Journal of Verbal Learning and Verbal Behavior* 11: 671-684.

Dik, S.C.
1987　　"Linguistically motivated knowledge representation". In M.Nagao (ed.), *Language and artificial intelligence*. Amsterdam: North-Holland, 145-170.

Gelb, I.J.
1963　　*A study of writing*. Chicago: The University of Chicago Press.

Goody, J. and I.Watt
1972　　"The consequences of literacy". In P.P.Giglioli (ed.), *Language and social context*. Harmondsworth: Penguin, 311-357.

Gregory, R.L.
1981　　*Mind in science*. Harmondsworth: Penguin Books.

Hedelin, L. and E.Hjelmquist
1988　　"Preschool children's mastery of the form/content distinction in spoken language". In K.Ekberg and P.E.Mjaavatn (eds.), *Growing into a modern world*. Trondheim: Norwegian Center for Child Research, The University of Trondheim, 639-645.

Hjelmquist, E.
1981　　"A note of adult's conception of language and communication". *Osnabrücker Beiträge zur Sprachteorie* 20: 62-74.
1984　　"Memory for conversations". *Discourse Processes* 7: 321-336.
1987　　"Where is the meaning of verbal discourse?" In J.Verschueren and M.Bertuccelli-Papi (eds.), *The pragmatic perspective*. Amsterdam: Benjamins, 667-680.
1989　　"Recognition memory for utterances in conversation". *Scandinavian Journal of Psychology* 30: 168-176.

Johnson-Laird, P.N.
1983　　*Mental models*. Cambridge: Cambridge UP.

Linell, P.
1982　　*The written language bias in linguistics*. Lonköping: University of Linköping, Department of Communication Studies.

Lord, A.B.
1960　　*The singer of tales*. Cambridge: Harvard UP.

Mäntylä, T.
1986　　"Optimizing cue effectiveness: Recall of 500 and 600 incidentally learned words". *Journal of Experimental Psychology: Learning, Memory and Cognition* 12: 66-71.

Nilsson, L.-G., T.Mäntylä and K.Sandberg
1987　　"A functionalistic approach to memory: Theory and data". *Scandinavian Journal of Psychology* 28: 173-188.

Olson, D.R.
   1970   "Language and thought: Aspects of a cognitive theory of semantics". *Psychological Review* 77: 257-273.
   1977   "From utterance to text: The bias of language in speech and writing". *Harvard Educational Review* 47: 257-281.
   1984   "'See! Jumping!' Some oral language antecedents of literacy". In H.Goelman, A.Oberg and F.Smith (eds.), *Awakening to literacy*. Exeter: Heinemann, 185-192.

Olson, D.R. and A.Hildyard
   1983   Writing and literal meaning. In M.Martlew (ed.), *The psychology of written language: Developmental and educational perspectives*. New York: Wiley, 41-65.

Rommetveit, R.
   1974   *On message structure*. New York: Wiley.

Stevenson, R.J.
   1988   "Memory for referential statements in texts". *Journal of Experimental Psychology: Learning, Memory and Cognition* 14: 612-617.

Subject Index

ablative 50, 52
accusative 50f
accusativus cum infinitivo 74f, 82, 89f, 95
active-passive 46, 49, 95, 195, 226, 267f, 319
actuality 10, 176, 186
addressee 1, 7
adequacy
  psychological 295f, 300, 307f
  typological 201, 224
adjectival predicate 116
adjective 174
adjunct 29, 40, 63
  see also satellite
adposition 198f, 207f
adverb 6, 8, 13
  evaluative 78, 91, 93
  illocutionary 5
  modal 14, 78, 90, 119
  ordering of   see order of adverbs
  temporal 136f
adverbial 19, 20, 25f, 75, 78, 93, 173, 194, 196, 218, 221
Agent 48
agreement 7
anaphora 4, 108, 178
antecedent 7
  see also protasis
anterior 157f
antipassive 195
apodosis 237, 242, 249, 254
argument 43f, 48, 108, 194f, 201f,

209
predicational 116
propositional 116
argument type 112, 116, 118
article 143f, 160
  see also determiner - (in)definiteness
ascriptive construction 116
aspect 10f, 26, 166, 168f, 176, 185, 194, 266
  collective 172, 181, 186
  continuative 12
  directional 194
  durative 118, 168
  egressive 168
  imperfective 167f, 185
  individual 171f, 186
  nominal 168f, 180, 186
  perfective 167f, 185
  phasal 10, 159
  progressive 157f, 168
  qualificational 9
  quantificational 10, 175
attitude 2, 10, 25, 28, 35, 72, 284
  see also propositional attitude - speaker attitude
attitude qualifier 284
Attitudinal satellite 12f, 18f, 29, 35f, 38, 62, 75, 78, 92
  content-oriented 35f
  event-oriented 35f
  participant-oriented 35f

auxiliary 9, 153, 157f, 160, 177
  modal 9, 177

Beneficiary 30, 32, 38f, 42f, 49, 51, 62, 289
biconditional implicature 245
bilingual 302f

cardinal number 170f, 173f, 181f
case marker 198f
causal clause 42, 73, 78f, 81, 88f, 96
causation 280
causative 218
Cause argument 83
Cause satellite 33f, 50, 65f, 73, 88f
  Inner 30, 32f
Circumstance 19, 33, 35, 62
class affix 173, 182
classifying construction 116
clause 4, 25, 60f, 193f, 199f, 204, 206f, 210, 213f, 224f
clause linkage 217f
clause satellite 12f, 21, 65, 79
cleft construction 226, 269
cognition 295f, 307
cognitive development 288, 302, 316
cognitive psychology 270f, 287f, 297f, 315f, 322
cognitive representation 234, 264f, 274, 300
colour words 303, 306f
common noun 160
communication 139, 140
communicative relevance 237, 242
communicative saliency 266
communicative setting 13, 314, 317f
communicative strategy 10, 12

Company satellite 30, 32
complement 14f, 17f, 19, 20, 71f, 77f, 226
  finite 73f
  infinitival 73f, 226
complementizer 16, 109, 220, 226
complex sentences 213, 219, 222, 224, 300
complexity 3, 18, 60f
comprehension
  see language comprehension
concept 167, 170, 272f, 275, 279f, 285, 288, 317
conceptual knowledge
  see knowledge, conceptual
conceptual representation 235, 272f, 278, 280f, 283, 286f, 313, 317, 319
conceptualization 124, 265, 269f, 274f, 278f, 283, 286f, 289, 318
Concession 19
Condition satellite 12f, 34f, 38f, 41, 62, 237
conditional clause 78, 218, 233, 237f, 288f
  ex absurdo 247f
  illocutionary 242, 252f, 288
  propositional 242, 251f, 256f, 288
  sarcastic 248f
  see also (ir)realis - (semi-)factual - potentialis
conjunction 19
consecutio temporum 41f
consecutive clause 42
constituent ordering
  see order of constituents
content 1, 316
  of speech 87f
  of thought 87f, 97

exclamative 12
exclusive disjunction 244f
existence 5f, 176f, 184
existential construction 113f, 119, 186, 269
exocentric 209
expression 139f, 147f, 151, 157
expression rules 142, 145, 148f
expression syntax 148
extra-clausal constituent 77f, 94, 254
extraposition 226
eye-witness report 304f

fact 2, 72, 83, 90f, 126, 288f, 302
factivity 82f, 85f, 89f, 93f, 95, 97
factuality 126f, 131f, 245
felicity 5f, 13
focalization 78, 266, 268
Focus 40f, 57f, 66, 92f, 95, 212, 287
  contrastive 41
  scope of 40f, 78
Force 48, 62
form and meaning 96, 273
frame semantics 305
frequency 10, 173
Frequency satellite 33, 35, 61f
function
  ideational   see representational
  interpersonal 1f, 6, 27, 39f, 106, 200, 203, 282f, 289
  representational 1f, 3, 140, 282f
  textual 1
  see also pragmatic function - semantic function - syntactic function
Functional Grammar 193, 199f, 221f, 224f, 227f, 233f, 281f
Functional Logic 233f, 265, 287, 296

functionalism 224

gender 145
generic operator 97, 234
gerund 84, 95
given information 239
Goal 46f, 48, 51
grammatical category 26
grammatical competence 233
grammatical element 166, 171, 173, 180, 182, 266
grammatical form 235
grammatical operation 268
grammaticalization 129

head-marking 207f, 211, 213, 222f, 225
head noun 166, 170, 172, 185, 199
hierarchical clause structure
  see layering of the clause
historical change 149
hypothetical picture 239f, 256f

ideational level 1f, 140
identification 93, 160, 177f
illocution 20, 25, 74, 81, 135, 283, 288
  basic 6, 10, 13, 28, 73, 76f, 85, 88, 94f
illocutionary force 1f, 10, 54, 64, 79, 96, 126f, 132, 134f, 194, 217
  mitigation of 10, 132f, 135, 283
  modification of 10, 28, 38, 54, 64, 127, 201, 283
  reinforcing 10f, 283
illocutionary frame 3, 6f, 12, 73, 106,

136, 200f

illocution operator 9f, 20, 41f, 72f, 78, 81, 85, 96, 126f, 129, 133, 135f, 177, 194, 196, 198, 201, 210, 212, 216f, 296

illocution(ary) satellite 12f, 20f, 28, 38f, 41, 43, 54f, 59f, 62f, 78f, 81, 85, 90, 92, 237, 255, 259, 289

immediate constituent structure 193f

imperative 7, 20, 73f, 75f, 81f, 85, 92, 95f, 177, 296

implication 239

implicative verb 91

implicature 245

incorporation 47f, 66

indefiniteness 165, 178, 165f

indicative 177, 244

indirect reflexive predicate formation rule 49

indirect reflexive pronoun 88f

indirect speech 16, 77f, 83, 85, 218

individual 5, 106f, 175, 181

individual style 271

inference 257, 281, 300

infinitival complement 73f

inflection 166

inflectional morpheme 180

information 269f, 272

information storage 269

informational status 213

ingressive 10, 16f, 174

instructional semantics 139, 145, 153f

Instrument satellite 30, 32, 42f, 48, 58, 66, 174, 203

instrumental argument 203

interactive particle 97

interclausal relations hierarchy 219

interjection 77

interpersonal level 1f, 6, 27, 39f, 106,

200, 203, 282f, 289

interrogative 42, 73, 77, 93, 126f, 131f, 136, 296

yes/no 7

question-word 7, 40

see also question

Interval satellite 42

intonation 1, 36, 41

inversion 205

irrealis 10, 157, 176, 178, 186, 237, 242, 249f, 284, 286

iterative aspect 173, 180

juncture 213f, 216f, 220f, 226

jussive 218

knowledge 234, 263, 267, 269, 278, 284, 296, 315, 320

conceptual 234, 263f, 266, 269, 272f, 278f, 283, 285, 288, 296f, 300f, 304f, 307, 313

declarative 302

episodic 308

inferential 281, 296

linguistic 263, 265, 296, 300f, 304f

non-linguistic 265, 296, 300f, 304f, 316

non-perceptual 234

perceptual 234, 272, 274, 288, 296, 301, 303f, 315

procedural 302

shared 236

knowledge base 296

knowledge representation 263f, 296, 304, 307, 314f, 321

verbal 269f, 272, 282f, 287f, 300f, 304f, 307, 316f

interpersonal 39f, 43, 289
non-restrictive 21, 63
order see order of satellites
position of 14, 52f, 185
predicate   see predicate satellite
predication   see predication satel-
    lite
predicational 18f
proposition   see proposition satel-
    lite
propositional 18f, 20
representational 39f, 43f, 289
restrictive 21, 60, 63f
term see term satellite
scope of 53f, 59, 63, 96, 285f
typology of 25f, 258f
satellite absorption 50
schema 305
scope 8, 11, 40f, 53, 55, 59f, 63, 78,
    96, 127, 148f, 152, 155, 157f, 165f,
    174, 177-, 182, 184, 198, 212, 238,
    285f
    see also Focus - negation - operator
    - satellite
selection restriction 314, 322
semantic function 19, 44, 186, 197,
    203, 225, 296f
semantic function hierarchy 43
semantic macrorole 197
semantic network 277f
semantic primitive 277, 279f, 314
semantic role
    see semantic function
semantic structure 199f, 202
semantic representation 201, 222,
    224, 227
semantics 139f, 153, 224f
semelfactive aspect 173
semi-factive 17, 19

semi-factual conditionals 245, 247
sentence mood
    see (basic) illocution - mood -
    modality
sentence type 73, 75f, 126f, 135
    see also (basic) illocution
sentential complement 71f
    see also complement, embedded
construction
setting 64, 194
    cognitive 32, 34f, 64
    communicative 13, 314, 317f
    spatial 10f, 32, 35, 65
    temporal 8, 10f, 32f, 35, 64, 194,
    284f
shape 169f, 172
singular 173f, 181, 186
source 10
Source satellite 31f, 37f, 45, 50, 52,
    62
space 5, 31, 167, 170, 173, 175, 177
space/time region 8f, 12, 107, 124f,
    178, 183, 200
spatial characteristics 169, 172
spatial entity 171, 174
spatial orientation 32
speaker 1, 7, 9f, 14
    attitude of 1, 25, 27f, 314, 319
    intentions of 1
specificity 178
speech act 2f, 5f, 10f, 20, 25, 27f, 37f,
    64, 96, 106f, 126, 128, 133f, 136,
    140, 255, 289
    see also illocution
speech act verb 7f, 20, 74f
speech event 135, 282f
speech moment 128, 130f, 176f, 266
speech participant 314, 319
Speed satellite 31f, 42, 48, 174

183
relative 156
see also space/time region
Topic 40, 238f
Contrastive 239
Given 239
topic marker 212
topicality 92,95
topicalization 196
translatability 265, 271f
truth 5f, 7, 9f, 20, 55, 72, 84, 107,
112, 116, 126, 130, 236f, 239f, 246f,
284
suspended 130f, 135
truth value 75, 236f, 239
indeterminate 7
typological adequacy
see adequacy

warning 96
wish
fulfillable 14
word order
see order of constituents
wording
see memory
written language 314, 317f, 322

uncertain 236, 239f, 243, 289
universal 180, 186, 279
utterance 1f, 13, 27, 78, 107, 118,
124, 126, 299

V/2 constraint 204, 206f, 226
valency reduction 49f
variable 3f, 19, 166
verb see predicate
verbal knowledge
see knowledge
verbal memory
see memory
verbal noun 84
virtual states of affairs 81f, 83f, 91,
93f, 97
voice 66
see also active-passive

Index of Names

Index of languages

348 INDEX OF LANGUAGES

Oromo 181, 186
  Boraana dialect 181
  Orma dialect 181
  Waata dialect 181

Quechua 10

Russian 67, 207, 209

Sakao 186
Spanish 7, 105, 286
Swahili 44, 244, 251

Tagalog 44, 117
Tamil 177
Tonkawa 216
Turkish 105f, 111, 185, 196, 219f
Tzotzil 211, 213

Vietnamese 115f

Warlpiri 193
West Greenlandic 177

Yanomama 186

In the PRAGMATICS AND BEYOND NEW SERIES the following titles have been published and will be published during 1990:

1. WALTER, Bettyruth: *The Jury Summation as Speech Genre: An Ethnographic Study of What it Means to Those who Use it.* Amsterdam/Philadelphia, 1988.
2. BARTON, Ellen: *Nonsentential Constituents: A Theory of Grammatical Structure and Pragmatic Interpretation.* Amsterdam/Philadelphia, 1990.
3. OLEKSY, Wieslaw (ed.): *Contrastive Pragmatics.* Amsterdam/Philadelphia, 1989.
4. RAFFLER-ENGEL, Walburga von (ed.): *Doctor-Patient Interaction.* Amsterdam/Philadelphia, 1989.
5. THELIN, Nils B. (ed.): *Verbal Aspect in Discourse: Contributions to the Semantics of Time and Temporal Perspectives in Slavic and Non-Slavic Languages.* Amsterdam/Philadelphia, 1990. n.y.p.
6. VERSCHUEREN, Jef (ed.): *Selected Papers from the 1987 International Pragmatics Conference. Vol. I: Pragmatics at Issue. Vol. II: Levels of Linguistic Adaptation. Vol. III: Intercultural and International Communication (ed. with Jan Blommaert).* Amsterdam/Philadelphia, 1990. n.y.p.
7. LINDENFELD, Jacqueline: *Speech and Sociability at French Urban Market Places.* Amsterdam/Philadelphia, 1990. n.y.p.
8. YOUNG, Lynne: *Language as Behaviour, Language as Code: A Study of Academic English.* Amsterdam/Philadelphia, n.y.p.
9. LUKE, Kang-Kwong: *Utterance Particles in Cantonese Conversation.* Amsterdam/Philadelphia, n.y.p.
10. MURRAY, Denise E.: *Conversation for Action. The computer terminal as medium of communication.* Amsterdam/Philadelphia, n.y.p.
11. LUONG, Hy V.: *Discursive Practices and Linguistic Meanings. The Vietnamese system of person reference.* Amsterdam/Philadelphia, n.y.p.
12. ABRAHAM, Werner (ed.): *Discourse Particles. Descriptive and theoretical investigations on the logical, syntactic and pragmatic properties of discourse particles in German.* Amsterdam/Philadelphia, n.y.p.
13. NUYTS, Jan, A. Machtelt BOLKESTEIN and Co VET (eds): *Layers and Levels of Representation in Language Theory: a functional view.* Amsterdam/Philadelphia, 1990.